PENGUIN BOOKS
PLEASURE

Dr. Alexander Lowen is the creator of bioenergetics, a revolutionary form of psychotherapy
designed to reactivate the body through a regi-
men of exercise. The foremost exponent of this
method of incorporating direct work on the body
into the psychoanalytic process, he practices
psychiatry in New York and Connecticut and is
the executive director of the Institute of Bioenergetic Analysis. Dr. Lowen is married and lives in
New Canaan, Connecticut, with his wife and
son. His *Depression and the Body: The Biological Basis of Faith and Reality* and *Bioenergetics*
are also published by Penguin Books.

Alexander Lowen, M.D.

Pleasure

A Creaive Approach to Life

Penguin Books

Penguin Books Ltd, Harmondsworth,
Middlesex, England
Penguin Books, 625 Madison Avenue,
New York, New York 10022, U.S.A.
Penguin Books Australia Ltd, Ringwood,
Victoria, Australia
Penguin Books Canada Limited, 2801 John Street,
Markham, Ontario, Canada L3R 1B4
Penguin Books (N.Z.) Ltd, 182–190 Wairau Road,
Auckland 10, New Zealand

First published in the United States of America by
Coward-McCann, Inc., 1970
Published in Penguin Books 1975
Reprinted 1976, 1977
Copyright © Alexander Lowen, 1970
All rights reserved

Printed in the United States of America by
Offset Paperback Mfrs., Inc., Dallas, Pennsylvania
Set in Baskerville

TO MY SON, FRED,
      AND
TO RICKY, JO-JO, EMIR, AND FEYA,
WHO KNOW HOW TO ENJOY LIFE

CONTENTS

Preface

1. THE PSYCHOLOGY OF PLEASURE : 19

    The Morality of Fun
    The Dream of Happiness
    The Nature of Pleasure
    The Creative Process

2. THE PLEASURE OF BEING FULLY ALIVE : 35

    Breathing, Movement, and Feeling
    How to Breathe More Deeply
    Releasing Muscular Tension
    Feeling and Self-Awareness

3. THE BIOLOGY OF PLEASURE : 63

    Excitation and Lumination
    The Pleasure-Pain Spectrum
    The Nervous Regulation of Response
    The Fear of Pleasure

4. POWER VERSUS PLEASURE : 81

The Mass Individual
True Individuality
The Illusion of Power

5. THE EGO: SELF-EXPRESSION VERSUS
EGOTISM : 103

Self-Expression
The Role of the Ego in Pleasure
The Role of the Ego in Pain
Egotism

6. TRUTH, BEAUTY, AND GRACE : 125

Truth and Deception
Thinking and Feeling
Subjectivity and Objectivity
Beauty and Grace

7. SELF-AWARENESS AND SELF-ASSERTION : 147

Knowing and No-ing
Self-Possession and "No"
The Critical Faculty

8. THE EMOTIONAL RESPONSES : 167

Love
Affection and Hostility
Anger and Fear

9. GUILT, SHAME, AND DEPRESSION : 187

Guilt
Shame and Humiliation
Depression and Illusion

10. THE ROOTS OF PLEASURE : 207

Spontaneous Rhythms
Rhythms of Natural Functions

Rhythms of Movement
The Rhythm of Love

11. A CREATIVE APPROACH TO LIFE : 227

What is Creativity?
Creativity and Self-Awareness
The Loss of Integrity
Self-Realization

PREFACE

> But ye, unfallen sons of heavenly duty,
> Rejoice ye in the rich and living beauty:
> The ceaseless flux which living works and flows
> Envelope ye in bonds of love and grace;
> And what in shifting seeming wavering shows,
> Hold fast to it in thought's secure embrace.
>
> The Lord's words in Goethe's *Faust* *

Pleasure is not within the province of man to command or control. It is, in Goethe's opinion, God's gift to those who are identified with life and rejoice in its splendor and beauty. In turn, life endows them with love and grace. But God admonishes them, his unfallen sons and true believers: Though pleasure is ephemeral and insubstantial, hold fast to it in your mind, for it contains the meaning of life.

For most human beings, however, pleasure is a word that evokes mixed feelings. On one hand, it is associated in our minds with the idea of "good." Pleasurable sensations feel good, food that gives us pleasure tastes good, and a book that is a pleasure to read is said to be a good book. Yet most people would regard a life devoted to pleasure as a waste. Our positive reaction to the word is often hedged with misgivings. We fear that pleasure can lead a person into dangerous paths, make him

* Johann Wolfgang von Goethe, *Faust*, trans. by Bertram Jessup. New York, The Philosophical Library, 1958, p. 23.

13

forget his duties and obligations, and even corrupt his spirit if it is not controlled. To some people it has a lascivious connotation. Pleasure, especially carnal pleasure, has always been considered the main temptation of the devil. The Calvinists regarded most pleasures as sinful.

Each person in our culture shares these misgivings about pleasure. Modern culture is more ego-oriented than body-oriented, with the result that power has become the primary value, while pleasure is reduced to the position of a secondary value. Modern man's ambition is to master the world and command the self. At the same time, he is never free from the fear that this cannot be done, nor from the doubt whether it would be to his good if it could. Since pleasure, however, is the sustaining and creative force in his personality, his hope (or illusion) is that the achievement of these objectives will make a life of pleasure possible. Thus, he is driven by his ego to pursue goals which promise pleasure but demand a denial of pleasure. The situation of modern man is similar to that of Faust, who sold his soul to Mephistopheles for a promise that could not be redeemed. Though the promise of pleasure is the temptation of the devil, pleasure itself is not within the devil's power to give.

The Faustian story is no less significant today than it was in Goethe's time. As Bertram Jessup points out in the preface to his translation of Faust,* "Between the magic of the sixteenth century and the science of the twentieth there is no break in aspiration or intention to dominate and control life. If anything its significance has greatly increased with the decline of the moral authority of an omnipotent God." Elias Carretti says, "Man has stolen his own God." † He has gained the power to doom and destroy, a power that was formerly the prerogative of a punishing Deity. With seemingly unlimited power and without a restraining force, what will prevent man from destroying himself?

We must realize that we are all, like Dr. Faust, ready to accept the devil's inducements. The devil is in each one of us in the form of an ego that promises the fulfillment of desire on condition that we become subservient to its striving to domi-

* *Ibid.*, p. 7.
† Elias Carretti, *Crowds and Power*. New York, The Viking Press, 1963, p. 468.

nate. The domination of the personality by the ego is a diabolical perversion of the nature of man. The ego was never intended to be the master of the body, but its loyal and obedient servant. The body, as opposed to the ego, desires pleasure, not power. Bodily pleasure is the source from which all our good feelings and good thinking stems. If the bodily pleasure of an individual is destroyed, he becomes an angry, frustrated, and hateful person. His thinking becomes distorted, and his creative potential is lost. He develops self-destructive attitudes.

Pleasure is the creative force in life. It is the only force strong enough to oppose the potential destructiveness of power. Many people believe that this role belongs to love. But if love is to be more than a word, it must rest on the experience of pleasure. In this book I shall show how the experience of pleasure or pain determines our emotions, our thinking, and our behavior. I will discuss the psychology and the biology of pleasure and explore its roots in the body, in nature, and in the universe. We will then understand that pleasure is the key to a creative life.

PLEASURE

1 · The Psychology of Pleasure

The Morality of Fun

To the casual observer, it would seem that America is a land of pleasure. Its people seem intent upon having a good time. They spend much of their leisure time and money in the pursuit of pleasure. Their advertising reflects and exploits this preoccupation. Almost every product and service is sold with the promise that it will transform the routine of living into fun. A new detergent makes dishwashing fun, a new processed food makes meals easy to prepare, and a new car is supposed to make driving along our crowded highways fun. If these products of our technology fail to provide the pleasure they promise, one is exhorted to jet away to some distant place of enchantment where everyone has fun.

The question naturally arises: Do Americans really enjoy their lives? Most serious observers of the current scene believe that the answer is no. They feel that the obsession with fun betrays an absence of pleasure.* Norman M. Lobsenz published a study in 1960 of the American pursuit of good times under the title, *Is Anybody Happy?* Lobsenz did not find any happy people, and in his conclusion he wondered if man could achieve happiness. What he did find was that "behind the mask of gaiety hides a growing incapacity for true pleasure." † What he observed was America's new morality of fun, which he described as follows: "The important thing nowadays is to have fun, or look as if you are having fun, or to think you are having fun or

---

* Lewis Mumford notes, "Compulsive play is the only acceptable alternative to compulsive work." Norman M. Lobsenz, *Is Anybody Happy?*. Garden City Doubleday & Company, 1960, p. 75.
† *Ibid.*, p. 19.

at least to make believe you are having fun. . . . The man who is not having fun is suspect." *

He is suspected of being a heretic and a traitor to this new moral code. If he makes an effort to be one of the merrymakers but fails, the others will be sorry for him. Poor Joe! But if he finds the proceedings dull and boring, he had better offer a polite excuse and leave the group. He dare not expose the self-deception, and his presence in a sober and critical mood might do just that. He realizes that he has no right to destroy the illusions and break up the games people play with each other in the name of fun. If one is part of a crowd by choice or invitation, one cannot attack its values.

The morality of fun represents an attempt to recapture the pleasures of childhood by pretending. Much of children's play, especially that which imitates the activities of adults, contains the attitude, stated or implied, of "Let's pretend." The pretense may be that mud patties are real pies or that Johnny is a doctor. This pretense is necessary, because it enables a child to commit himself wholeheartedly to the play activity. The adult who joins children at their play must also accept their make-believe situations as real; otherwise he remains an outsider. Without make-believe, children could not make a serious commitment to their activity, and without such a commitment, there would be no pleasure.

The adult who participates in the "make-believe of having fun" reverses this process. He engages in such serious activities as drinking and sex with the attitude that he does so for fun. He tries to transform the serious affairs of life, like earning a living and raising a family, into fun. Of course he doesn't succeed. In the first place, these are activities which carry important responsibilities; and in the second place, the serious commitment which is so characteristic of children's play is avoided. The morality of fun seems designed specifically to prevent this commitment. If it's for fun, one need not be committed.

One of the main premises of this study is that a total commitment to what one is doing is the basic condition of pleasure. A partial commitment leaves one divided and in conflict. Children have the ability to commit themselves completely to their games

* *Ibid.*, p. 15.

and play activities. When a child says that his play was fun, he doesn't mean it was funny. He means that by virtue of a make-believe situation he entered wholeheartedly into a play activity from which he derived a great deal of pleasure through self-expression.

It is widely recognized that in their games and play children manifest the creative impulse at work in the human personality. Often a high degree of imagination is involved in these activities. The ease with which a child can pretend or make believe indicates that his world is largely an inner one containing a rich store of feelings upon which he can draw. Because he is relatively free from responsibilities and pressures, his imagination can transform his surroundings into a fairy world that offers unlimited opportunities for creative self-expression and pleasure.

Creativity in adults arises from the same sources and has the same motivations as the creative play of children. It stems from the desire for pleasure and the need for self-expression. It is marked by the same serious attitude that characterizes children's play. And like children's play, it is productive of pleasure. There is even an element of fun in the creative process, for all creativity starts with a make-believe—that is, it requires the suspension of what is known about external reality in order to allow the new and unexpected to emerge from the imagination. In this respect every creative individual is like a child.

Adults can and do engage in the same pretending and make-believe as children, though with less ease. Their imagination can transform the appearance of things for the purpose of play or work. For example, a woman will, in her imagination, re-decorate a room in her home and find considerable pleasure in this use of her creative talent. She may also describe this use of her creative talent as fun. Of course, when it comes down to making actual changes, the element of fun decreases as the consequences become more serious. It may and often does become work, but it can still be pleasurable. When both play and work involve the creative imagination and are pleasurable experiences, the difference between them is in the importance of the consequences. Adults can have fun when their activities are divorced from serious consequences and undertaken with the attitude "Let's pretend." Thus, a clown is funny when one can participate in the make-believe that he is serious. It would not be funny if he were serious. All humor is based on the capacity to suspend external reality to allow the imagination free play.

It is fun when reality is suspended in one's conscious imagination only and with a pleasurable effect. It is no fun when the pleasure disappears, as any child will tell you. Whatever the make-believe, a child remains in touch with his feelings and is aware of his body. This inner reality is never suspended: Should a child become hungry, get hurt, or for any reason lose his pleasure, the game is over for him. He does not engage in self-deception. This inner reality is never ignored by a child in his play; it is only the external appearance of things that is transformed in his imagination.

The denial of inner reality is a form of mental illness. The difference between imagination and illusion, between creative make-believe and self-deception, depends on the ability to remain true to one's inner reality, to know who one is and what one feels. It is the same difference that distinguishes fun as pleasure from so-called fun as an escape from life.

In my imagination I can picture myself as a great scientist, an intrepid explorer, or a gifted artist. But I trust that I have no illusions about these mental images. My imagination can explore the possibilities of becoming; my perceptions must confirm the facts of my existence. My thoughts may wander; my feet must stay on the ground. Only if a person is secure in his identity and rooted in the reality of his body is it fun to make believe. Without an adequate sense of self, the make-believe of fantasy becomes the delusion of paranoia, and that is no fun.

One reason for the lack of pleasure in our lives is that we try to make fun out of the things that are serious, while we are serious about those activities that should be fun. A ball game or a card game is an activity that does not ordinarily entail serious consequences; it could be played for fun, but people take these activities as seriously as if life or death depended on the outcome. It is not that they play seriously, for children play seriously, too; it is rather the seriousness with which they regard the outcome that dispels the pleasure. (How much pleasure is lost in a golf game because the score didn't measure up to expectations!) On the other hand, activities that are truly serious, like sex, the use of drugs and fast driving, are often engaged in for "kicks."

The current preoccupation with fun is a reaction to the grimness of life. This explains why New York, which may justifiably be described as the grimmest of cities, parades itself as the "Fun City." The search for fun stems from a need to escape from problems, conflicts, and feelings that seem intolerable and overwhelming. That is why fun for adults is associated so strongly with alcohol. For many people the idea of fun is to get high or drunk or escape their oppressive sense of emptiness and boredom through drugs. The use of LSD is called "taking a trip," which reveals its close connection with the idea of getting away. The drug user changes his inner reality, while the external situation remains the same. The child, as we saw, transforms his image of the outer world while retaining the reality of his inner experience.

The concept of fun as escape is related to the idea of the escapade. An escapade is a rejection of social reality, the reality of another person's property, feelings, or even life. An illicit drinking party, a ride in a stolen car, vandalism—all fall into the category of escapades which give the participant the illusion that he is having fun. The consequence of an escapade is often quite serious and its aftermath rarely pleasurable. Young people often engage in escapades to vent their resentments against a reality that has curbed their imaginations and limited their pleasure. When escapades are really innocent, that is, when they pose no dangers and are not destructive, they are part of the fun of teenage years and serve to bridge the period between childhood and adulthood. When, however, this is not the case, the escapade loses its character of fun and becomes a desperate move to escape reality.

The search for fun by adults undermines their capacity for pleasure. Pleasure demands a serious attitude toward life, a commitment to one's existence and work. It may be viewed as the business of life, whether one is playing as a child or working as an adult. An escapade, regardless of its apparent fun, must end in pain, as do all attempts to escape the commitment to life.

Sandor Rado remarked that "pleasure is the tie that binds."

To me this means that pleasure binds us to our bodies, to reality, to our friends, and to our work. If a person has pleasure in his daily life, he will have no desire to escape.

The morality of fun replaces the Puritan morality that governed the behavior of many Americans for several centuries. Puritanism was a strict creed that discouraged any frivolities. For example, card playing and dancing were prohibited. The manner of dress and the forms of address were severe. A Puritan was committed to the business of the Lord, which in practice meant being productive. But while it was easy to raise children, it was much harder to raise crops. Life was not easy for the Pilgrims and their descendants. Their struggle for survival left little time for fun or make-believe. Yet it would be a mistake to think that the Puritan way of life was devoid of pleasure. Their pleasures, however, were simple; they consisted of the good feelings one has when one's life flows smoothly and in harmony with the environment. The quiet charm of a New England village, still appreciated today, bears testimony to the pleasures they knew.

Many forces contributed to the breakdown of this morality. The immigrants from eastern Europe and the Mediterranean countries brought more color and new tastes to the American scene. Industry brought an affluence that slowly enlarged the Puritan view. And science with its handmaiden, technology, changed the concept of productivity from a personal expression to a mechanical process. The result has been a loss of those moral principles that in the past gave meaning to the Puritan ethic.

Reactions go to extremes. Today the morality of fun is based on the belief that "anything goes." To the believers in this proposition, the person who holds back is a renegade or traitor. He not only dampens their enthusiasm, he casts doubt on their basic assumption. On the other hand, the Puritans regarded the funlover with similar suspicion, but as a follower of the devil. The devil, they say, has all the fun, and there is, obviously, a place for the devil and his deviltry in our lives. Real fun adds greatly to the joy of living. But if we are to avoid becoming devils, we must not adopt the fun morality of "anything goes" as a code of behavior.

We have seen that pleasure is an essential ingredient of fun but that not everything that passes for fun is pleasurable. Happiness is also related to pleasure. In the following section we will explore the meaning of happiness and its relationship to pleasure.

The Dream of Happiness

Childhood has universally been regarded as the happiest time of one's life. Children, however, are not conscious of being happy. If you asked a child, "Are you happy?" he would be at a loss for an answer. I doubt very much that he would know the meaning of the word. He could very well tell you if he was having fun or not. Adults tend to see their early years as happy ones because in retrospect they appear cloudless, free from the worries and problems that plague maturity. But the past, like the future, is only a dream. Only the present has perceptual reality.

Is happiness a dream of the past or the future? Is it only a dream, or does it have a present reality? Are there people who are truly happy? These are questions I cannot honestly answer. A dedicated individual who has consecrated his life to a higher purpose may have this feeling. A nun, for example, doing God's work faithfully as she sees it, could consciously say, "I am happy." In many ways, however, her life parallels that of a child. Under the care of a mother superior, she has none of the responsibilities that fall upon the mature person in the world. Her consecration may remove all personal anxieties and leave her mind free to contemplate the majesty of her Lord. But her situation is unique and contains elements of unreality when compared with that of the average woman.

Confucius is reported to have said that he could not be happy as long as one person was suffering. One suffering individual was a cloud in his sky that would mar the bliss of perfection. If perfection is the criterion of happiness, then happiness is a dream that cannot be fully realized. It can, however, be the object of our striving, for we all seek perfection even when we recognize it as an unattainable ideal. The Declaration of Independence guarantees to all men the right to life, liberty, and the pursuit of happiness. It wisely refrains from assuring each man that they are more than legitimate goals.

I have heard people exclaim, "I am so happy," when some fortunate event has befallen them. And I have no doubt that the exclamation was genuine. The termination of the Vietnam war would make many people happy. For how long? For as long as the mood of euphoria following such an event would last. I remember the jubilation that resulted from the ending of World War II. For a day or two, or in some cases longer, people's spirits soared as the oppressive burden of this struggle was lifted from their shoulders and the weight of tragedy was removed from their hearts. Within a very short time, however, other struggles consumed their energies and other cares weighed their hearts. Their happiness was real but short-lived.

An Oriental monarch once remarked, "For more than thirty years I have done whatever I wanted, I have indulged my fancy freely, yet I cannot say that in all those years I experienced more than one or two moments of happiness." If a powerful ruler cannot achieve a state of happiness, how difficult must it be for an average person? I would not, however, agree with Loblenz that man was not meant to be happy. I don't know what he was meant to be. I would conclude that happiness is a feeling that arises in special situations and that it disappears when the situation changes.

The return of a son from war is a happy occasion for a mother. Prior to this event she will often remark, "How happy I will be when John comes home." His homecoming will fill her temporarily with a feeling of happiness, and she will then say, "I am so happy." What she means, however, is, "I am so happy that John is back." She may at the same time be very unhappy because another son is still fighting, or her husband may be ill, or . . . Her feeling of happiness is related to a special situation and is not a reflection of her total life.

If someone said today, "I am happy," it would be appropriate to ask, "What are you happy about? Did you win the lottery?" We take it for granted that a person must be happy about something. We are not so naïve as to believe that one can be happy for no reason. The reason will always be the avoidance of a tragedy or the gain of some fortune, monetary or otherwise.

It is a valid reason if it has the power to transport the individual, momentarily at least.

The feeling of happiness arises when one is transported beyond one's self or taken out of one's self. This is clear if we consider the happiness of the lover. The lover walks on a cloud, as it were; his feet do not seem to touch the ground. He is not only out of himself, he is also out of this world. For the time being the mundane world drops away or is shed like the cocoon of the butterfly. He feels released from all ego concerns, and it is this release that is the basis for his feeling of happiness.

The idea of release implies a prior confinement, which is to say that happiness is the release from a state of unhappiness. If some special situation makes us unhappy, the reversal of that situation will be experienced as happiness. Since we are unhappy about the war in Vietnam, we will be happy when that war terminates. The person who is unhappy about his financial condition would be happy if he learned that he had inherited a considerable sum of money. If the pursuit of happiness is a universal undertaking, this must mean that most human beings are troubled by cares that weigh heavily upon their spirits. They are also capable of imagining a future in which these cares are gone. This picture is their dream of happiness. Without a dream, it is impossible to know happiness.

When an unhappy situation changes, it is like a dream come true, and the euphoric mood that develops has some similarity to the dream state. One has difficulty in fully believing that it is true, it feels so much like a dream. When the sense of happiness is very intense, a person may say, "I can't believe it's true; it must be a dream." The mind, overwhelmed by the flood of excitation, loses its normal hold of reality. "Let me touch you again," says the overjoyed mother, "I can't believe you are real." Or one may pinch oneself to confirm one's wakefulness. And like a dream, happiness also fades away, leaving only a memory. The euphoric mood is quickly dispelled as the demands and problems of daily living assert their dominance in the mind.

Happiness and fun belong to the category of transcendental experiences. In both there is a suspension of the ordinary reality of a person's life. In each the spirit is released with a feeling of joy at its liberation. Unfortunately, all transcendental experiences are limited in time. The spirit does not and cannot stay free. It returns to the body, its physical abode, and to the prison of the self, where it comes again under the hegemony of the ego and its reality orientation.

We all sense that life should be more than a struggle for survival, that it should be a joyous experience, and that people are imbued with love. But when love and joy are missing from our life, we dream of happiness and run after fun. We fail to realize that the foundation for a joyful life is the pleasure we feel in our bodies, and that without this bodily pleasure of aliveness, living becomes the grim necessity of survival from which the threat of tragedy is never absent.

The Nature of Pleasure

Underlying any experience of true fun or happiness is a bodily sensation of pleasure. To be fun an activity must be pleasurable. If it were painful, it would be hard to describe it as fun. Because pleasure is missing, the "make-believe of fun" is a grim charade. The same thing is true of happiness. Without the feeling of pleasure, happiness is only an illusion. True fun and real happiness derive their meaning from the pleasure one feels in the situation. But it is not necessary to have fun or to be happy to experience pleasure. One can have pleasure in the ordinary circumstances of life, for pleasure is a mode of being. A person is in a state of pleasure when the movements of his body flow freely, rhythmically, and in harmony with his surroundings. I shall illustrate this concept with several examples.

Work is not ordinarily considered an occasion for fun or a reason to be happy, yet as everyone knows, it can be a source of pleasure. This depends, of course, on the conditions of the work situation and the attitude one has toward the task. I have known many people who found pleasure in their work, but not one of them would have said that it was fun or that it made him happy. Work is serious; it requires a certain discipline and a commitment to the activity. It aims at a desired result toward which one works, and it differs thereby from play, in which one can be indifferent to the outcome. But work can be a pleasure when the demands of a job freely and equitably engage the energies of an individual. No person can enjoy an activity to which he is constrained by an outside force or one that requires a greater expenditure of energy than he is capable of making. If, then, the work situation is voluntarily accepted, he will experience pleasure to the degree that his energies flow easily and rhythmically into the work activity. And quite apart from the satisfaction he will derive from his accomplishment, he will have a distinct feeling of pleasure in the rhythmic response of his body.

Watch a good carpenter at work, ard you can sense the pleasure he feels in the coordinated movements of his body. He seems to work effortlessly because his motions are so easy and smooth. If, on the contrary, his movements were awkward and poorly coordinated, it would be difficult to see how he could enjoy his work or be a good carpenter. It is unimportant whether we say that a man is a good worker because he has pleasure in his job or that he enjoys his work because he is good at it. The two are clearly related. The pleasure he feels in his body attaches itself to the product which reflects his pleasure in its quality of being good.

For the same reason, some women enjoy housework; even doing such chores as cleaning and dusting can be pleasurable to them. The woman who finds pleasure in cleaning actually enjoys the physical work involved. She gives herself to the task graciously, and her movements are relaxed and rhythmical. On the other hand, the woman who rushes through a chore or does it mechanically may achieve a positive result, but it will not be a pleasant experience for her. This is equally true for every other aspect of running a home. The pleasure of cooking is in the ease with which one does it, and this depends on one's identification with the activity. When one is identified with an activity, one flows out to it freely and spontaneously. The pleasure is this flow of feeling.

Conversation, to take another example, is one of the common pleasures of life, but not all conversation is pleasurable. The stutterer finds talking painful, and the listener is equally pained. Persons who are inhibited in expressing feeling are not good conversationalists. Nothing is more boring than to listen to a person talk in a monotone without feeling. We enjoy a conversation when there is a communication of feeling. We have pleasure in expressing our feelings, and we respond pleasurably to another person's expression of feeling. The voice, like the body, is a medium through which feeling flows, and when this flow occurs in an easy and rhythmic manner, it is a pleasure both to the speaker and listener.

Because pleasure is an outward flow of feeling in response to the environment, we generally attribute it to the object or situation that provokes this response. Thus people think of pleasure in terms of entertainment, having sexual relations, going to a restaurant, or engaging in some sport. Certainly there is pleasure in situations that stimulate the flow of feeling, but a view of pleasure that identifies it with the situation is limited and unrealistic. An entertainment is pleasurable only when one is in the mood to be entertained; it may actually be painful when one wishes to be quiet. And few situations are more distressing or painful than a sexual relationship in which the feeling fails to develop or flow. Even a gourmet meal is no delight to the person whose taste runs to simple food. Similarly, while poor conditions of work may take the pleasure out of a work activity, good conditions do not necessarily make work pleasurable.

To understand the nature of pleasure, we should contrast it with pain. Both describe the quality of an individual's response to situations. When this response is positive and feeling flows outward, he will speak of having pleasure. When the response is negative and there is no rhythmic flow of feeling, he will describe the situation as unpleasant or painful. But since the experience of pleasure or pain is determined by what happens in the body, any inner disturbance that blocks the flow of feeling will give rise to an experience of pain, regardless of the appeal of the external situation.

Pleasure and pain have a polar relationship, which is exemplified by the fact that the release from pain is invariably experienced as pleasure. And for the same reason, a loss of pleasure leaves one in a painful state. But because we associate pleasure with specific situations and pain with specific hurts, we do not realize that our conscious self-perception is always conditioned by these feelings. A normal individual is never without some awareness of the state of his body. In response to the question "How are you?" he will answer, "I feel fine, poorly, good, or bad." If he should say, "I feel nothing," it would be an admission of spiritual death. During all waking hours our feelings fluctuate along the pleasure-pain axis.

There are, however, other differences between pain and pleasure. Pain seems to have a substantial quality. Its severity is often directly related to the intensity of the noxious agent. A second-degree burn is invariably more painful than a first-degree burn. Pain is fairly consistent in that a given painful stimulus generally affects most people alike. While people have different thresholds to pain, very few would disagree as to the nature or effect of pain. Pain also tends to be localized, because the body contains specific pain receptors and nerves which serve to locate the source of the pain. If these nerves are blocked by an anesthetic agent, the pain disappears.

In contrast, pleasure seems to be insubstantial. If a good steak can excite our appetites, two good steaks can give us indigestion. It often happens that a dinner we enjoyed yesterday is unexciting when served again today. Pleasure depends greatly on one's mood. It is as difficult to enjoy a thing of beauty when one is depressed as it is to smell a rose when one has a cold. But a good mood, while indispensable to enjoyment, is no guarantee of pleasure. On too many occasions I have gone to the theater and cinema with keen anticipation and high spirits, only to emerge deflated and disappointed. Pleasure requires a concurrence between the inner state and the outer situation.

The differences in our reactions to pain and pleasure can be explained, in part at least, by the fact that pain is a danger signal. It denotes a threat to the integrity of the organism and calls forth a mobilization of conscious resources on an emergency basis. All the senses are alerted, and the musculature is tensed and ready for action. To meet the threat the exact location of the danger must be known, its intensity gauged, and all other activities suspended until safety is assured.

Pleasure has a large unconscious component, which accounts for its spontaneous character. It is not subject to command. It may appear in the most unexpected places: a flower that grows by the wayside, a conversation with a stranger, or an unwelcome social evening that turns out to be a delightful soirée. On the other hand, it may elude the most extensive preparations for a good time. In fact, the harder one looks for it, the less likely one is to find it. And if having found pleasure one grasps it too greedily, it disappears in one's grip. Robert Burns wrote:

> But pleasures are like poppies spread,
> You seize the flow'r, its bloom is shed.

In pleasure the will recedes and the ego surrenders its hegemony over the body. Like the listener at a concert who closes his eyes and lets himself be absorbed in the music, the person experiencing pleasure allows the sensation to dominate his being. The flow of feeling takes precedence over deliberation and volition. Pleasure cannot be possessed. One must give one's self over to the pleasure, that is, allow the pleasure to take possession of one's being.

Whereas the response of pain involves a heightening of self-consciousness, the response of pleasure entails and demands a decrease of self-consciousness. Pleasure eludes the self-conscious individual, as it is denied to the egotist. To have pleasure one has to "let go," that is, allow the body to respond freely. A person who is inhibited cannot easily experience pleasure because unconscious restraints restrict the flow of feeling in his body and block his natural bodily motility. In consequence, his movements are awkward and unrhythmical. The egotist, even though he seems to act without inhibitions, does not enjoy his exhibitionism, since all his attention and energies are focused upon the image he hopes to present. His behavior is dominated by his ego and is geared to the attainment of power, not the experience of pleasure.

The Creative Process

In this study I shall show that pleasure provides the motivation and the energy for a creative approach to life. Every creative act begins with a pleasurable excitation, goes through a phase of travail, and culminates in the joy of expression. The initial excitation is due to an inspiration. Something enters the person and takes possession of his spirit: a new vision, a new idea, an exciting substance, or a sperm which fertilizes an egg to start a new life. This produces a conception, which is then slowly given form and substance by the working through of the idea or vision. The completion of the creation is marked by the discharge of all tension, a sense of deep satisfaction, a feeling of fulfillment, and the joy of release. From start to finish the whole creative process is motivated by the striving for pleasure.

Not only does pleasure provide the motive force for the creative process, it is also the product of that process. A creative expression is a new way of experiencing the world. It introduces a new excitement and offers a new channel for self-expression. It literally creates a new pleasure, one that did not exist before, for all those who can share the vision of the new conception.

We generally think of creativity in terms of the production of a work of art which in its dynamic aspects parallels the basic creative act of life, the conception and birth of a child. We ordinarily assume, therefore, that creativity involves the transformation of a conception into an object, but it should be recognized that not every creative action is embodied in a material object. The minstrel or folk singer of yore created songs and poems that existed only in imagination and memory. The same is also true of dancers, prophets, and mathematicians, whose creativity consists of a new movement, a new insight, a new vision of relationships. The creative act may be defined as any form of expression that adds new pleasure and meaning to life.

No two experiences in life are the same, and no two pleasures are identical. Every pleasure is in a sense a new pleasure. It follows, therefore, that any action or any process that increases pleasure or adds to the enjoyment of life is part of the creative process. This concept broadens the scope of creative actions to include the myriad expressions of living organisms that promote pleasure and joy. The right word at the right time is a creative act. But even such simple things as a well-prepared meal, a new decor in a home, or a social evening can be creative expressions if they add pleasure to one's life. In this broad sense, every act of a person can be an opportunity for creative expression.

Pleasure and creativity are dialectically related. Without pleasure, there can be no creativity. Without a creative attitude to life, there will be no pleasure. This dialectic stems from the fact that both are positive aspects of life. An alive person is sensitive and creative. Through his sensitivity he is attuned to pleasure, and through his creative drive he seeks its realization. Pleasure in living encourages creativity and expansiveness, and creativity adds to the pleasure and joy of living.

2 · The Pleasure of Being Fully Alive

Breathing, Movement, and Feeling

Every person has experienced sometime in his life the sheer pleasure that attends the recovery from an illness or accident. On the first day that normal health is restored one senses with keen delight the joy of being alive. How exhilarating it is to breathe deeply! How exciting it is to move easily and freely! The loss of health makes a person aware of his body and conscious of the importance of good health. Unfortunately, this awareness is quickly lost, and the beautiful feeling that accompanied it fades fast. As soon as the individual resumes his usual activities, he becomes harnessed to drives that dissociate him from his body. He becomes preoccupied with events and objects in the external world and quickly forgets the revelation that pleasure is the perception of being fully alive in the here and now—which means to be fully alive in the bodily sense.

Having dissociated himself from his body, he no longer thinks in bodily terms. He ignores the simple truth that to be alive one must breathe and that the better one breathes, the more alive one is. He may become aware from time to time that his breathing is restricted, and on occasion, especially under stress, he may find that he is holding his breath, but he pays it no heed. He may even acknowledge with a resigned smile that the hectic pace of his life allows him no time to breathe. However, as he grows older he will make the sad discovery that this function, like other bodily functions, deteriorates if it is not properly used. Once breathing becomes difficult, a person would give anything to be able to breathe easily. He knows now that breath-

ing is a matter of life and death or, to put it positively, that life
is a matter of breath.

Another simple truth that should be self-evident is that an
individual's personality is expressed through his body as much
as through his mind. A person cannot be divided into a mind
and a body. Despite this truth, all studies of personality have
concentrated on the mind to the relative neglect of the body.
The body of a person tells us much about his personality. How
one holds himself, the look in his eyes, the tone of his voice, the
set of his jaw, the position of his shoulders, the ease of his movements, and the spontaneity of his gestures tell us not only who
he is but also whether he is enjoying life or is miserable and ill
at ease. We may close our eyes to these expressions of another's
personality, just as the person himself may close his mind to the
awareness of his body, but those who do so delude themselves
with an image that has no relation to the reality of existence.
The truth of a person's body may be painful, but blocking out
this pain closes the door to the possibility of pleasure.

A person enters therapy because he is not enjoying life. In
the forefront or the background of his mind he is aware that his
capacity for pleasure has been diminished or lost. The present-
ing complaint may be depression, anxiety, a sense of inadequacy, and so on, but these are the symptoms of a deeper disturbance, namely, the inability to enjoy life. In every case it can
be shown that this inability stems from the fact that the patient
is not fully alive in his body and in his mind. This problem cannot be fully resolved, therefore, by a purely mental approach. It
must be tackled on the physical and the psychological levels
simultaneously. Only when a person becomes fully alive is his
capacity for pleasure fully restored.

The principles and practices of bioenergetic therapy rest on
the functional identity of the mind and the body. This means
that any real change in a person's thinking and, therefore, in
his behavior and feeling, is conditioned upon a change in the
functioning of his body. The two functions that are most important in this regard are *breathing* and *movement*. Both of
these functions are disturbed in every person who has an emotional conflict by chronic muscular tensions that are the physical counterpart of psychological conflicts. Through these mus-

cular tensions conflicts become structured in the body. When this happens, they cannot be resolved until the tensions are released. To release these muscular tensions one must feel them as a limitation of self-expression. It is not enough to be aware of their pain. And most people are not even aware of that. When a muscular tension becomes chronic, it is removed from consciousness, and one loses an awareness of the tension.

Feeling is determined by breathing and movement. An organism feels only that which moves within its body. For example, when an arm is immobilized for a time, it becomes numb and without feeling. To recapture the feeling its motility must be restored. The motility of the whole body is reduced when breathing is restricted. Thus, holding the breath is the most effective way of cutting off feeling. This principle works in reverse, too. Just as strong emotions stimulate and deepen one's breathing, the stimulation and deepening of respiration can evoke strong emotion.

Death is an arrest of respiration, a cessation of movement, and a loss of feeling. To be wholly alive is to breathe deeply, to move freely, and to feel fully. These truths cannot be ignored if we value life and pleasure.

How to Breathe More Deeply

The importance of proper breathing to emotional and physical health is overlooked by most physicians and therapists. We know that breathing is necessary to life, that oxygen provides the energy to move the organism, but we do not realize that inadequate breathing reduces the vitality of the organism. The common complaints of tiredness and exhaustion are not generally attributed to poor breathing. Yet depression and fatigue are direct results of a depressed respiration. The metabolic fires burn low in the absence of sufficient oxygen, like a wood fire with a poor draft. Instead of glowing with life, the poor breather is cold, dull, and lifeless. He lacks warmth and energy. His circulation is directly affected by a lack of oxygen. In chronic cases of poor breathing the arterioles become constricted and the red blood count drops.

In a recent experiment, reported in the September 5, 1969, issue of *Medical World News*, a number of senile hospital patients were given increased oxygen by being placed in a hyperbaric oxygen chamber. The theory behind the experiment was that since a reduced supply of oxygen to the brain cells produces mental dysfunction, an increased supply might improve mental function. Most cases of senility are due to a sclerosis of the arteries in the brain, which reduces the flow of blood and oxygen to the brain cells. The positive results of the experiment surprised the doctors. Most patients showed a marked and definitive improvement in thinking and personality. "All those treated became more active, slept better, asked for newspapers and magazines to read, and, most importantly, resumed old habits of caring for themselves." In some cases the effects continued after the initial series of treatments ended. This was a preliminary study, as the experimenters themselves state. It will be repeated and subjected to further clarification. Its significance, however, is immense.

Most people are poor breathers. Their breathing is shallow, and they have a strong tendency to hold their breath in any situation of stress. Even in such simple stress situations as driving a car, typing a letter, or waiting for an interview people tend to limit their breathing. The result is to increase their tension. When people are made aware of breathing, they realize how often they hold their breath and how much they inhibit breathing. Patients commonly remark, "I notice how little I breathe."

I became aware of the relation between breathing and tension at college. As a member of the ROTC I participated in rifle practice at the local armory. My shooting was erratic, my aim uneven. One of the professional officers watching me advised, "Before you press the trigger, take three deep breaths. On the third breath let the air out slowly, and while doing so, squeeze the trigger gradually." I followed his advice and was amazed to find that my arm steadied and that I began to hit the bull's-eye. This experience proved valuable in other situations. I used to sit in the dentist's chair in a state of tension, gripping the arms tightly. This not only increased my fear but, as I discovered subsequently, also augmented the pain. When I focused my attention upon my breathing instead, I was pleasurably surprised to find that not only was I less afraid, but it seemed to hurt less. Breathing deeply had a similar relaxing effect upon my performance during examinations. By taking time to breathe, I could also organize my thoughts better.

Many years later, in my professional practice, I realized that the restriction of breathing was directly responsible for the inability to concentrate and the restlessness that trouble many students. I was often consulted by parents about the difficulties their children had with schoolwork. An examination of the child always revealed that his body was tense and his breathing minimal. The child became restless when he attempted to focus his attention for an extended period on a schoolbook. His mind wandered. He felt compelled to move. He sat and struggled, but he could not study easily. Adults who do not breathe well have the same trouble. Their concentration and effectiveness are decreased.

The inability to breathe fully and deeply is also responsible for the failure to achieve full satisfaction in sex. Holding the breath at the approach of climax cuts off the strong sexual sensations. Normally, the breath is exhaled with the forward swing of the pelvis. If inhalation occurs during the forward movement, the diaphragm contracts and prevents the giving in necessary for orgastic release. Any restriction on breathing during the sexual act cuts down the sexual pleasure.

Inadequate respiration produces anxiety, irritability, and tension. It underlies such symptoms as claustrophobia and agoraphobia. The claustrophobic person feels that he cannot get enough air in an enclosed space. The agoraphobic person becomes frightened in open spaces because they stimulate his breathing. Every difficulty in breathing creates anxiety. If the difficulty is severe, it may lead to panic or terror.

Why do so many people have difficulty in breathing fully and easily? The answer is that breathing creates feelings, and people are afraid to feel. They are afraid to feel their sadness, their anger, and their fear. As children they held their breath to stop crying, they drew back their shoulders and tightened their chests to contain their anger, and they constricted their throats to prevent screaming. The effect of each of these maneuvers is to limit and reduce respiration. Conversely, the suppression of any feeling results in some inhibition of respiration. Now, as adults, they inhibit their breathing to keep these feelings in repression. Thus the inability to breathe normally becomes the main obstacle to the recovery of emotional health.

Broadly speaking, since repression cannot be lifted until full respiration is restored, it is important to understand the mechanisms that block breathing. I shall discuss two typical disturbances of respiration. In one the breathing is more or less confined to the chest, to the relative exclusion of the abdomen. In the second the breathing is mainly diaphragmatic, with relatively little movement in the chest. The first type of breathing is typical of the schizoid personality, the second of the neurotic personality.

In the schizoid individual the diaphragm is immobilized, and the abdominal muscles are tightly contracted. These tensions cut off sensations in the lower half of the body, especially the sexual feelings in the pelvis. The chest is held in the deflated position and is generally narrow and constricted. Breathing in is limited, and the result is an inadequate oxygen supply and a lowered metabolism. Breathing in is literally a sucking in of air and requires an aggressive attitude to the environment. Aggression, however, is reduced in the schizoid individual, who is closed off emotionally from the world. He manifests an unconscious reluctance to breathe because he is fixated at the uterine level, where his oxygen needs were met without his effort. To overcome the schizoid block to breathing in, his terror must be released and his aggression mobilized. He must feel that he has a right to make demands on life; in the most primitive sense, that he has a right to suck life in.

On the other hand, in the neurotic individual, whose aggression is not as blocked as in the schizoid, the chest is immobilized, while the diaphragm and upper abdomen are relatively free. The chest is generally held in an expanded position, and the lungs contain a large amount of reserve air. The neurotic person finds it difficult to breathe out fully. He holds on to his reserve air as a security measure. Breathing out is a passive procedure; it is the equivalent of "letting go." Full expiration is a giving in, a surrender to the body. Letting go of the air is experienced as a letting go of control, which the neurotic individual fears. The diaphragmatic respiration of the neurotic is a more effective type of breathing than the thoracic respiration of the schizoid. Diaphragmatic breathing provides maximum air for a minimal effort and is adequate for ordinary purposes. However, unless both the chest and the abdomen are engaged in the respiratory effort, the unity of the body is split, and emotional responsiveness is limited.

Normal or healthy breathing has a unitary and total quality. Inspiration begins with an outward movement of the abdomen as the diaphragm contracts and the abdominal muscles relax. The wave of expansion then spreads upward to embrace the thorax. It is not cut off in the middle, as in disturbed people. Expiration starts as a letting down in the chest and proceeds as a wave of contraction to the pelvis. It produces a sensation of flow along the front of the body which ends in the genitals. In healthy breathing the front of the body moves as one piece in a wavelike motion. This kind of breathing is seen in young children and animals, whose emotions are not blocked. Such breathing actually involves the whole body, and tension in any part of the body disturbs this normal pattern. For example, pelvic immobility disrupts this pattern. Normally there is a slight backward movement of the pelvis in inspiration and a slight forward movement in expiration. This is what Reich called the orgasm reflex. If the pelvis is locked in the forward or backward position, this balance-wheel action of the pelvis is prevented.

The head is also actively involved in the breathing process. Together with the throat it forms a great sucking organ which brings the air into the lungs. If the throat is constricted, this sucking action is reduced. When the air is not sucked in, the breathing is shallow. It has been observed in infants that any disturbance of their sucking impulse affects their breathing. I have observed that as soon as patients suck the air, their breathing becomes deeper.

The connection between sucking and breathing is clearly seen in cigarette smoking. The first drag on a cigarette is a strong sucking action which draws in the smoke as one would draw in air. There is a temporary feeling of satisfaction as the smoke fills the throat and lungs, and the person feels his lungs come alive in response to the irritant of the tobacco.

This use of the cigarette to excite the respiratory movements creates a dependence on the smoke. The first drag is followed by a second and a third, and so on. Smoking then becomes a compulsion. The smoke itself has a depressing effect on respiratory activity, apart from its initial stimulation. The more a person smokes, the less he breathes. However, because of his first experience, he cannot get away from the feeling that the cigarette is essential to help him breathe.

The function of smoking to stimulate breathing is seen in two situations, the morning cigarette and smoking under stress. The morning cigarette starts the day for some people, but it also hangs them up on cigarettes the rest of the day. In situations of stress the average person tends to hold his breath. This makes him anxious. To start breathing and overcome his anxiety, he takes a cigarette. Thus a habit is established: Reach for a cigarette when under stress. The motto for compulsive smokers should be: Take a breath instead of a puff.

Depth of breathing is measured by the length of the respiratory wave, not by its amplitude. The deeper the breathing, the more the wave extends into the lower abdomen. In truly deep breathing the respiratory movements reach and involve the floor of the pelvis, and one can actually feel sensations in that area. The downward expansion of the lungs is limited by the diaphragm, which separates the thorax from the abdomen. When we speak, therefore, of abdominal breathing, we do not mean that any air penetrates the abdomen. Abdominal breathing describes the bodily movements in breathing. It denotes that the abdomen is actively engaged in the inspiratory process. Its expansion and relaxation allow the diaphragm to descend. But of even greater importance is the fact that only through abdominal respiration does the wave of excitation associated with breathing embrace the whole body.

In the remarks above I commented on the difference between schizoid breathing and neurotic breathing. The former is mostly confined to the thorax, while the latter is mainly limited to the diaphragmatic area. Diaphragmatic breathing extends only into the upper part of the abdomen, and thus while it is deeper than the more shallow breathing of the schizoid individual, it does not qualify as truly deep breathing. From this point of view the depth of breathing is a reflection of the emotional health of a person. The healthy person breathes with his whole body, or more specifically, his breathing movements extend deep down into his body. In a man it could be said, broadly speaking, that he "breathes into his balls."

Breathing cannot be dissociated from sexuality. Indirectly it provides the energy for the sexual discharge. The heat of passion is one aspect of the metabolic fires, of which oxygen is an important element. Since the metabolic processes provide the energy for all living functions, the strength of the sexual drive is ultimately determined by these processes. The depth of respiration directly determines the quality of the sexual discharge. Unitary or total breathing, a respiration that involves the whole body, leads to an orgasm that includes the whole body. It is common knowledge that breathing is stimulated and its depth increased by sexual excitation. It is not generally recognized, however, that shallow or inadequate breathing reduces the level of sexual excitation. Restricted breathing prevents the spread of the excitation and keeps the sexual feeling localized in the genital area. Conversely, sexual inhibition, the fear of allowing sexual feelings to flood the pelvis and the body, is one of the causes of shallow and limited breathing.

The respiratory wave normally flows from the mouth to the genitals. In the upper end of the body it is connected to the erotic pleasure of sucking and nursing. In the lower end of the body it is tied to the sexual movements and sexual pleasure. Breathing is the basic pulsation (expansion and contraction) of the whole body; it is therefore the foundation for the experience of pleasure and pain. Deep breathing is a sign that the organism experienced full erotic gratification in the oral stage and is capable of full sexual satisfaction in the genital stage.

Deep breathing charges the body and literally makes it come alive. And one of the self-evident truths about an alive body is that it looks alive: The eyes sparkle, the muscle tone is good, the skin has a bright color, and the body is warm. All this happens when a person breathes deeply.

Simple breathing exercises are ordinarily of little help in overcoming the problems associated with a disturbed respiration. The muscular tensions and the psychological conflicts that prevent deep breathing are not affected by such exercises. And the greater volume of inspired air which such exercises produce does not fully enter the blood stream and is not absorbed by the tissues. Only when the body feels the need for more oxygen and makes a spontaneous effort to breathe more deeply does a person become more alive through breathing. This is not to say that people should ignore the conscious component of breathing. We should try to be aware of the common tendency to hold our breath when under some stress and make an effort to breathe easily and deeply. By taking time to breathe, we can counter to some extent the pressures that force us to keep going all the time.

Patients in bioenergetic therapy are encouraged to do special exercises which relax the muscular tensions of the body and stimulate its breathing. These exercises can also be recommended to the general public, with a word of caution to the effect that they can release feelings or produce some anxiety. They will also promote a greater self-awareness, but in this process the person may feel pain in those parts of his body that were previously immobilized. This is especially true of the lower back. Neither the released feelings nor the anxiety or pain are any cause for alarm. These exercises should not be done compulsively or pushed to an extreme, since in themselves they will not solve the complicated personality problems that trouble most people.

Patients in therapy who do these special exercises designed to deepen breathing almost invariably develop tingling sensations in various parts of the body: the feet, the hands, and the face, and very occasionally over the whole body. If the tingling sensations become intense, feelings of numbness and paralysis may also supervene. These sensations, known as parasthesias in medicine, are regarded as symptoms of the hyperventilation syndrome. Doctors interpret these symptoms as being due to the discharge of too much carbon dioxide from the blood through intensive breathing. I do not believe this interpretation is fully accurate. Runners who breathe heavily do not develop these symptoms. I regard them as a sign that the person's body has become overcharged with oxygen, which he is unable to utilize. He may also become dizzy because of this excess charge, which disturbs his customary equilibrium. Both the dizziness and the parasthesias disappear when the breathing returns to normal.

As the patient's capacity to tolerate higher levels of excitation and oxygen increases, the parasthesias and dizziness diminish and disappear. The tingling is a superficial excitation which tends to deepen into specific feelings with continued work on the breathing. Sadness, longing, and crying frequently emerge and reach expression. These may give way in turn to anger. Numbness and paralysis are indications of fear and contraction in the face of the increased excitation. These reactions, too, disappear as the patient's tolerance for feeling grows.

The basic bioenergetic breathing exercise is done by arching backward over a rolled up blanket on a stool two feet high. This is shown in Figure 1.

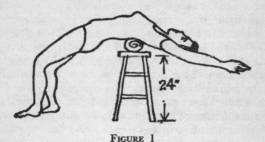

24"

FIGURE 1

When done at home the stool should be placed alongside a bed so that the head and arms, which are extended backward, hang over or touch the bed. Since this is a stress position, the mouth should be open and the breathing allowed to develop freely and easily. Most people tend to hold their breath in this position, as they do in most stress situations. This tendency must be consciously countered. The legs should be parallel, the feet resting flatly on the floor about twelve inches apart, and the pelvis should be allowed to hang freely. If this position induces some pain in the lower back, it is an indication of tension in that area. If one relaxes to the position, the breathing will become deeper and fuller (more abdominal and of greater amplitude). The rolled up blanket is placed between the shoulder blades, but this position can be varied to mobilize the different muscles of the back.

The position should not be held if it becomes too uncomfortable or if one feels choked. It is advisable that the beginner start slowly and, except in special circumstances, hold a stress position for no longer than two minutes. The purpose of this exercise is to promote one's breathing, not to test one's endurance.

The effectiveness of this exercise is shown by the fact that in many people it will induce crying or a feeling of anxiety. I recall a case in which a patient in her first experience with the stool developed panic. She had taken several deep breaths when suddenly she was on her feet gasping for air. A moment later she burst into sobs, and her panic disappeared. The deep breathing, for which she was unprepared, had opened the way for a feeling of sadness, which welled up in her throat. Unconsciously her throat closed as she tried to choke the feeling off, and she could not breathe. This was the only time I saw a patient react in this way to the exercise, but it indicates the potential power of the exercise.

I use this exercise regularly to further my own breathing and to relax the tension between my shoulders. I keep a stool in my bedroom and lie over it most mornings before breakfast. It helps overcome the tendency to round the shoulders and hunch forward which is found in most people. The exercise itself is the development of the natural tendency to stretch backward over the back of a chair, which many people do spontaneously after they have been sitting hunched forward for some time. All animals stretch upon rising, and this exercise is a most effective form of stretching. After lying over the stool for a minute or so and breathing deeply, I reverse the position with another exercise.

In this second exercise the person bends forward to touch the ground with his fingertips. His feet are about twelve inches apart, the toes turned slightly inward and the knees slightly bent. There should be no weight on the hands; the whole weight of the body rests on the legs and feet. The head hangs down as loosely as possible. The weight of the body should fall midway between the heel and ball of the foot. This position is illustrated in Figure 2.

FIGURE 2

We use this position in bioenergetic therapy to bring a person into a feeling of contact with his legs and feet. At the same time it stimulates abdominal respiration by relaxing the front wall of the body, especially the abdominal musculature, which was stretched by the first exercise. Again the mouth should be open and the breathing allowed to develop easily and freely. If a person holds his breath in any exercise, its value is lost.

When this exercise is done correctly, the legs should begin to vibrate or tremble, and they will continue as long as the breathing continues, sometimes even increasing in intensity. This vibration is normal. All alive bodies vibrate in stress positions.

Normally, breathing is an involuntary rhythmic activity of the body under the control of the vegetative nervous system. It is also subject to conscious control, so that the person can deliberately increase or decrease the rate and depth of his respiration. Conscious breathing, however, does not influence the typical involuntary pattern of respiration, which is closely tied to the emotional responsiveness of the individual. The involuntary vibrations of the body, on the other hand, have an immediate effect on the respiratory pattern. The vibrations of the legs and other parts of the body stimulate and release the breathing movements. When a body is in a state of vibration, breathing deepens spontaneously. This is because the vibratory state of a body is a manifestation of its emotional responsiveness.

Breathing is also directly involved in voice production, which is another vibratory activity of the body. Inhibitions in crying, screaming, and yelling are structured in tensions which restrict respiration. The child who has been taught that "children are to be seen, not heard" does not breathe freely. The natural tendency to speak up, cry out, or scream is choked off by spasms in the musculature of the neck. These tensions affect the quality of the voice, producing a speaking voice that is too thin, too low, too flat, or too sibilant. The voice must be restored to its full range and the specific neck tensions released if the breathing is to recover its full depth.

Releasing Muscular Tension

Every chronic muscular spasm is a restriction of an individual's freedom of movement and expression. It is therefore a limitation on his capacity for pleasure. The aim of bioenergetic therapy, then, is to restore the natural motility of the body. Motility refers to the spontaneous or involuntary movements of the body upon which the larger conscious movements are superimposed. A person's motility is reflected in the aliveness of his facial expression, in the quality of his gestures, and in the range of his emotional responsiveness. Body motility is the basis of all spontaneity, which is the essential ingredient of both pleasure and creativity. Spontaneity is an expression of the child within us, and its loss indicates that a person is cut off from the child and removed from his childhood.

Bioenergetic therapy starts with breathing, since this provides the energy for movement. Furthermore, the restriction of breathing imposes a restraint upon the body's motility. The respiratory waves associated with the movements of breathing are the basic pulsatory waves of the body. As these waves pass through the body, they activate the entire muscular system. Their free movement guarantees the spontaneity of feeling and expression. This means that as long as one's respiration is full and deep, there are no blocks to the flow of feeling. Breathing induces movement, which is the vehicle for the expression of feeling.

In all people the deepening of respiration sets up vibrations in the body. These start in the legs, and if they become strong enough, they can extend to the whole body. The vibrations may actually become so strong that one feels he is going to "fall apart." The fear of falling apart is the physical counterpart of the fear of letting go of one's ego defenses and being one's real self. No one actually falls apart, nor for that matter do one's ego defenses completely crumble, although they are shaken by the experience. Through these vibrations in his body a person becomes aware of the powerful forces in his personality that are immobilized by chronic muscular tensions. And he also experiences how the liberation of these forces makes him feel more alive and contributes to his pleasure.

A healthy personality is a vibrant personality. A healthy body is a pulsating and vibrant body. In the state of health the body's vibrations are relatively fine and steady, like the hum of a smooth running automobile. When the motor in an automobile goes dead, we sense it by the absence of vibration. In a similar way, it can be said that individuals whose bodies do not vibrate are emotionally dead. On the other hand, a body that shakes too violently is like a car whose spark plugs are fouled, whose valves are corroded, or whose bearings are dry. When these bugs in a car are ironed out, its vibration becomes a purr. A purr is the sound of a smooth running car. It is also the feeling of a smoothly functioning body—a body that moves with the ease and grace of an animal's.

The "bugs" in a human body are chronic muscular tensions. They develop as inhibitions of impulses and cannot be worked out definitively except by the release of the inhibited movement. But before this can happen they have to be made conscious and charged with feeling. This is what the vibrations accomplish. Every chronically tense muscle is a contracted muscle that has to be stretched to activate its potential for movement. Stretching a contracted muscle, which is elastic tissue, sets it into vibration, which may vary from a fine fibrillation to gross shaking depending on the degree of tension and the amount of stretch. Regardless of its quality, the vibration serves to loosen the chronic spasticity of muscles. It is often said of some people that they need a good shaking. This is what the body attempts to do through its involuntary vibrations and clonisms—namely, to shake the person loose from his fixed and rigid patterns of movement.

Have you noticed how a baby's chin quivers just before he starts to cry? The quiver is a prelude to the larger vibrations or convulsive movements that occur with crying. It frequently happens with patients that when the vibrations which begin with their legs extend to the chest and throat, they break into sobs. The vibrations may also release other spontaneous expressions. I have seen spontaneous kicking movements grow out of intense vibrations in the legs when the patient was lying on his back with his legs extended upward. This infantile position is one that easily induces a vibratory tremor in the legs. It is illustrated in Figure 3.

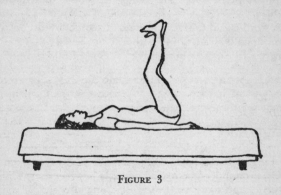

FIGURE 3

The person lies on a bed with his legs extended upward, knees slightly bent and the feet in extreme flexion. The head is held loosely backward to get it "out of picture," that is, to reduce ego control. The arms rest at the sides. If an upward thrust is maintained in the heels, this will stretch the calf muscles and the legs will begin to vibrate. Holding one's breath stops the vibrations; breathing easily and deeply increases them.

In addition to the involuntary vibratory movements, which are the foundation of the bioenergetic work with the body, a number of expressive movements are also used to mobilize and release suppressed impulses and feelings. These movements start consciously and are voluntarily performed, but they can often become involuntary when an emotional charge is aroused that infuses the movement.

One of the simplest and easiest expressive movements used to reduce muscular tension is kicking a bed. The person lies flat on a bed with his legs outstretched and kicks up and down in a rhythmic manner. The kicking should be done with the foot relaxed, so that the leg comes down flat on the bed. When the body is relatively free from tension, the breathing becomes synchronized with the kicking, and the head is whipped up and down with each kick as the wave of the movement passes through the body. This total bodily response will not occur if the body is held stiffly or if strong neck tensions prevent the head from moving. With continued exercise one learns to give in to the movement, which then becomes freer and more coordinated.

Kicking is an expressive movement. To kick is to protest, and every person has something to protest or kick about. It is a movement, therefore, which everyone can do. I recommend it to all my patients and suggest that they do 50 to 200 kicks a day, counting each kick separately. The best bed for this purpose is one that has a four-inch-thick foam-rubber mattress, but any bed will do. Patients who do this exercise regularly report that it has a pronounced beneficial effect. They feel more alive, more energetic, and more relaxed after doing this simple exercise. I have no hesitation in recommending it to all my readers, for there is no way in which it can be done wrong and no danger in its use. One may discover that his movements are awkward and uncoordinated, that he tires rapidly, and that his kicks have an impotent quality. This is an indication that a person's self-expression was blocked as a child. It is all the more reason to keep kicking. Figure 4 illustrates this activity.

To make the kicking even more meaningful in the therapy situation, the patient is often directed to express in words an appropriate feeling. He can say "No" or "I won't" or "Leave

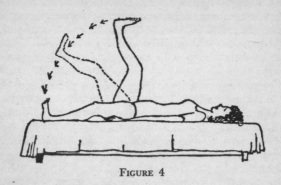

FIGURE 4

me alone." These utterances are made in a loud voice, with the o-sound sustained for a long period. Using the voice in this way mobilizes a deeper breathing which often adds an emotional quality to the action. The use of sound and words with the movement also serves to integrate the ego attitude with the bodily expression, promoting coordination and control. When patients give themselves freely to the sound and the movement, the kicking becomes more rapid and the voice rises in pitch. The kicking takes on an involuntary aspect, at which point the patient experiences the action as an emotional expression. Yet no matter how intense the feeling becomes, he is fully aware of himself and can stop the movements at will.

A similarly expressive movement can be made with the arms. In this exercise the patient lies on the bed with his knees bent. Then with both fists clenched the arms are raised over the head and brought down alongside the body in a blow. While doing this the patient is encouraged to say "No" or "I won't." The movement is repeated a number of times to make the voice sound more convincing and the blows more effective. Most patients have difficulty in expressing this negative feeling strongly. The voice often has an undertone of pleading, crying, or fear, and the arm movements are mechanical or impotent. If one challenges the patient by saying, "You will," during the exercise, the strength of his ability to oppose authority can be gauged. Some patients stop in confusion, while others change their statement to "I will." A few accept the challenge and confront the therapist with an intensified "I won't."

These movements not only arouse feeling but also stimulate breathing and set the body in vibration if the patient can allow himself to experience and express a negative or hostile attitude. Many other expressions can be used with these movements, such as "Go to hell" and "I hate you." Any unconscious holding back is manifested directly as a lack of coordination. This incoordination is especially evident when the patient tries to execute the movements of a temper tantrum. In this exercise the legs, knees bent, are drummed into the bed one after the other. At the same time the arms flail the bed alternately. When this movement is coordinated, the right arm and right leg move together, each side alternating with the other. The head rotates to the side that is making the movement downward. A lack of coordination is manifest when the rhythm of the leg movements differs from that of the arm movements. In this case the arms tend to speed up, while the leg movements become slower. Or there is a crossing phenomenon; the right arm moves synchronously with the left leg, while the left arm moves with the right leg. The crossing phenomenon is due to the noninvolvement of the body; the limbs are moving independently, like the vanes on a windmill. Not infrequently the head turns in the opposite direction to the movement of arm and leg, indicating some degree of dissociation between head and body. Uncoordinated movements generally leave a patient feeling dissatisfied.

Hitting a bed, like kicking, can be recommended to everyone. I have made it a personal practice to do this exercise whenever I feel tension building in my body or when I feel a surge of anger that I do not want to let out on somebody. I will hit the bed rhythmically fifty or more times, using one arm after the other. This has a stronger action than kicking in reducing tensions in the upper part of the body, especially around the shoulders, and it also deepens one's respiration. When the exercise is done gracefully, with a full stretch of the arms upward and backward, it leaves one feeling relaxed and exhilarated.

Many mothers have told me that rather than hit their children when they feel provoked they go up to the bedroom and let their anger out on a bed. In this way they get their release without a feeling of guilt. Needless to say, it also makes for a more pleasant home.

In addition to the above exercises, which develop the ability to express negativity, hostility, and anger, bioenergetic therapy also uses movements which express tenderness, affection, and desire. Reaching out with the mouth and arms to kiss, to suck, to touch, and to embrace is not easy for many people. Muscular spasticities in the jaw, throat, and arms often make these movements look and feel awkward. As a result the person is hesitant about making such a movement and insecure when he does attempt it. And since a hesitant movement often evokes an ambiguous response, the person ends up with a greater sense of being inadequate and rejected. Self-confidence is the awareness that one can express himself fully and freely in any situation with appropriate and graceful movements.

It may seem surprising that spontaneity and self-control are, despite their seeming contradiction, both facets of natural motility. Self-control implies self-possession, which is the attribute of a person who is in touch with his feelings and in command of his movements. He has self-control because he can choose how to express himself, since his motility is not limited or constricted by chronic muscular tensions. He differs thereby from the controlled individual, the compulsive personality, whose behavior is dictated by his tensions, and from the impulsive individual, whose behavior is a reaction to his tensions. It is a common experience in bioenergetic therapy that the freer a person becomes in his movements, the more self-control he gains.

Grace describes the quality of an individual whose body is free from chronic tension. His movements are graceful because they are spontaneous yet fully coordinated and effective. Since spontaneity is an essential element of grace, true grace cannot be achieved by practice. The exercises outlined above will have little value if they are done without an awareness of what they are designed to accomplish, namely, the release of muscular tension. When these tensions are released, grace is the natural result.

Feeling and Self-Awareness

It is an axiom of bioenergetic analysis that what a person really feels is his body. He cannot feel the environment except through its action upon his body. He feels how his body reacts to stimuli proceeding from the environment, and then he projects this feeling on the stimuli. Thus, when I sense that your hand is warm as it rests upon my arm, what I feel is the warmth in my arm that is produced by your hand. All feelings are body perceptions. If a person's body does not respond to the environment, he feels nothing.

Self-awareness is a function of feeling. It is the summation of all body sensations at any one time. Through his self-awareness a person knows who he is. He is aware of what is going on in every part of his body; in other words, he is in touch with himself. For example, he senses the flow of feeling in his body associated with breathing, and he senses all other spontaneous or involuntary body movements. But he is also aware of the muscular tensions that restrict his movements, for these too create sensations. The person who lacks self-awareness suffers from self-consciousness. Instead of a feeling of contact with his body, he sees it from without as it were, with his mind's eye. Not being in touch with his body from within, it feels strange and awkward to him, which makes him feel self-conscious in his expression and movement.

In the unaware person there are areas of his body that lack sensation and are therefore missing from his consciousness. For example, most people are generally unaware of the expressions on their faces. They do not know if they look sad, angry, or disgusted. Some faces have such an obvious expression of pain that the observer is surprised that the person is unaware of it. Other areas of the body of which people are commonly unaware are the legs, the buttocks, the back, and the shoulders. Every person knows that he has legs, buttocks, back, and shoulders, but he doesn't feel them as living parts of his body. He cannot tell whether his legs are relaxed or contracted, whether his buttocks are pulled backward or tucked forward, whether his back is up or down, and whether his shoulders are raised or lowered.

Such a lack of awareness means that the person has lost the full scope of the function of those parts of the body which are missing from consciousness. The person who doesn't feel his legs lacks a sense of security, because he doesn't have the feeling that his legs will hold him up. He is not emotionally secure on his own feet and feels the need for someone or something to support him. The buttocks function as counterweights to maintain the normal erect posture. When the buttocks are pulled forward, the upper half of the body tends to collapse. This can only be prevented then by extruding the chest and stiffening the back. Tucked in buttocks make one's posture resemble that of a dog with its tail between its legs. The individual who carries himself in this posture has lost his natural cockiness, which can only be compensated then by an exaggerated ego pose based on rigidity. On the other hand, if the buttocks are retracted, the person loses the ability to swing his pelvis forward in a sexually aggressive manner. His body reveals a lordosis, which is an exaggerated hollow in the small of the back. He suffers from sexual inadequacy because of an inability to discharge fully and freely his sexual feeling.

Normally the pelvis is suspended freely and moves spontaneously forward and back with breathing. This movement is intensified in intercourse and results in the involuntary movements of the orgasm. The backward movement charges the pelvis with sensation and feeling, while the forward movement discharges the feeling to the genitals. Chronic pelvic tensions, which restrict pelvic motility, reduce a person's orgastic potency. The sad thing about these tensions is that they also decrease a person's awareness, so that he doesn't know what is wrong with his sexual functioning. He may blame himself or his partner, without any understanding of the cause of his difficulties.

Because of chronic tensions, the average person has little feeling in his back. One commonly finds that the back is either so rigid as to be unbending or so pliable as to offer no support for the body. In both cases the person loses the ability to "back up his feelings" or to hold them back. Too much rigidity leads to compulsiveness, too great a flaccidity to impulsiveness. Lacking sensation in his back, he cannot mobilize his anger to overcome his frustrations. In an animal like a dog or a cat, one can literally see the back rise when the animal is angry. Even the hair along its back stands up as this part of his body is charged with feeling. Disturbed human beings become irritable or go into a state of rage, but they lack the animal ability to express anger in a direct way.

Tension in the back is generally associated with tensions which immobilize the shoulders. Two important functions are affected by shoulder tensions. One is the ability to reach out, and the other is the ability to strike out. When the shoulders are fixed in a raised position, the person is "hung up" as if he were suspended by a clothes hanger. Raised shoulders are an expression of fear, because the shoulders go up in fright. The person with raised shoulders is hung up by his inability to reach out or strike out and is unable, therefore, to let down.

The unaware person is also unwary. His image of himself does not coincide with the picture he presents to others, and his naïve acceptance of this image leaves him open to unexpected responses. The person who thinks he presents a manly appearance because his chest is inflated is shocked when he learns that other people can see this as a pose. By the same token he is easily fooled by the poses and facades which other people erect. Only to the degree that you are aware of yourself are you aware of others, and only to the extent that you feel yourself as a person can you feel for another person.

Loss of self-awareness is caused by chronic muscle tension. This tension differs from the normal tensions of living by the fact that it is a persistent, unconscious muscular spasticity that has become part of the body's structure or way of being. Because of this fact, the person is unaware that he has such chronic tensions until they begin to cause him pain. When this happens, he may sense the underlying tension, but he has no awareness of what it means and why it developed. And he is completely helpless to do anything to relieve the tension. In the absence of pain, however, most people are completely oblivious to the way they hold themselves or move. They feel comfortable in their structured attitudes, unaware of the limitations which these attitudes impose upon their potential for living.

A muscle becomes tense only under stress. When a body is moving easily, it feels no strain. Stresses are of two kinds, physical and emotional. Supporting a heavy weight is a physical stress, as is the continuation of a movement or activity when a muscle is tired. Feeling the pain of the tension, the person stops the activity or drops the weight. If, however, there is no way to remove the stress, the muscle will go into spasm. An emotional stress is just like a physical one; the muscles are charged with a feeling that they cannot release. They contract to hold or contain the feeling just as they do to support a weight, and if the feeling persists long enough, the muscle will go into spasm because it cannot get rid of the tension.

Any emotion which cannot be released is a stress for the muscles. This is true because an emotion is a charge which presses outward for release. A few examples will illustrate these ideas. Sadness or hurt feelings are released through crying. If the crying is inhibited because of parental objections or for other reasons, the muscles which normally react in crying become tense. These are the muscles of the mouth, throat, chest, and abdomen. If the feeling which cannot be released is one of anger, the muscles of the back and shoulders become tense. Inhibited biting impulses lead to jaw tensions, inhibited kicking impulses to leg tensions. The correlation between muscle tension and inhibition is so exact that one can tell what impulses or feelings are inhibited in a person from a study of his muscular tensions.

As far as the muscle is concerned, there is little difference between an external stress and an internal stress. Both place the muscle under tension. Physical stresses are generally of shorter duration than emotional stresses, which tend to persist and become unconscious.

When a muscle goes into spasm, it contracts and stays contracted until the stress is removed. You will find this to be true of a leg cramp, for instance. To get rid of the cramp you must change your position and move the cramped muscle. A cramp, however, is a very acute tension which allows no alternative. The tensions that arise through inhibition are chronic tensions which develop slowly, through repeated experiences, and so insidiously that the person is hardly conscious of the tension. Even if he is conscious of the tension, he knows no way to release it. He has to live with it, and the only way to live with a tension is to forget about it.

A relaxed muscle is a muscle charged with energy. It is like a loaded gun ready for firing. The trigger which discharges the muscle is an impulse from its effector nerve. The discharge of the muscle produces a contraction, which is translated into movement. A contracted muscle cannot move until it is recharged with energy. This energy is brought to the muscle in the form of oxygen and sugar. Without a supply of additional energy, it is impossible to release contracted muscles. The important factor in this process is oxygen, since without sufficient oxygen the metabolic process in the muscle comes to a halt. This fact points up the importance of breathing for relaxation and for the lifting of repressions. When a patient's breathing is deepened, his tense muscles will go into spontaneous vibration as they become charged with energy.

In some patients the vibrations may turn into spontaneous expressive movements as the body itself releases its repressed impulses. Generally, movements are started consciously, and the repressed impulses are evoked when the movements take on a total quality. A patient may begin by kicking the couch as an exercise, but as he lets go to the movement, it takes over the whole body, producing an emotional release. Tense muscles can only be released by expressive movements, that is, movements in which the activity expresses the repressed feeling. As long as a movement is mechanically performed, the repressed impulses are held back and no release of the tension is effected.

What role does analysis play in bioenergetic therapy? The emphasis in this chapter has been on the physical aspects of this therapy, and this may give the reader the impression that the analytic understanding of character plays a secondary role. This, of course, is not true. It is as important for a patient to know the origin of his conflicts as it is for him to gain self-awareness through bodily activity. The two approaches must be attuned to each other for effective therapy. All the modalities of psychotherapy and psychoanalysis are used in bioenergetic therapy to further self-understanding and self-expression. This includes the interpretation of dreams and the working through of the transference situation. In contrast to other forms of therapy, however, the work with the body is the foundation on which the ego functions of self-understanding and self-awareness are erected.

The basic bioenergetic concept is that each chronic muscle tension pattern must be dealt with on three levels: (1) its history or origin in the infantile or childhood situation, (2) its present-day meaning in terms of the individual's character, and (3) its effect on bodily functioning. Only this holistic view of the phenomenon of muscle tension can produce those changes in the personality that can have a lasting value. This leads to several important propositions.

1. Every chronically tense muscle group represents an emotional conflict which is unresolved and probably repressed. The tension results from an impulse seeking expression that meets a restraint based on fear. A jaw tension may represent the conflict between an impulse to bite and the fear that such action would lead to punitive measures by the parent. The same tension could also be related to an impulse to cry and the fear that it would provoke the parent's anger or rejection. Tensions have multiple determinations, since all parts of the body are involved in every emotional expression. This means that every tension must be worked through in terms of all the movements in which the tense muscle can participate. If possible, the specific conflicts involving the tense muscle group should become conscious both as to the impulse it holds and the fear it represents.

2. Every chronically contracted muscle represents a negative attitude. Since it is blocking the expression of some impulse, it is in effect saying, "No, I won't." Unaware of the impulse and the tension that blocks it, all the individual can sense is "I can't." And without awareness, he really can't move the part of the body controlled by the muscle. The "I can't" becomes changed into an "I won't" when the person becomes aware of the holding expressed in the tension. By expressing his negative attitude consciously, he frees the muscle from the necessity of unconsciously blocking the impulse, and through this maneuver he gains the choice of expressing the impulse or withholding its expression. For example, many patients are inhibited in crying

and *can't* give in to their sadness. I will ask them, then, to hit their fists into the bed, as described in the previous section, and say, "I won't cry." It is surprising how often this leads immediately to sobbing.

The generalized negative attitude expressed in the holding action of tense muscles extends to and includes the therapist and the therapeutic situation. It is covered by a facade of politeness and cooperation. One can get through this facade by the painstaking analysis of the transference or move immediately by making the expression of negativity the first order of business in therapy. Every patient in bioenergetic therapy confronts his concealed negativity by working with the expression of hostility and negativity both physically and vocally.

3. The biological aspect of muscle tension is its relation to the capacity for pleasure. The total tension of death manifested in the condition of rigor mortis is the complete absence of any capacity for feeling pleasure or pain. To the degree that chronic tensions immobilize our bodies, our capacity for pleasure is reduced. This knowledge can provide the motivation for the sometimes painful task of releasing these tensions. Without this knowledge and the understanding of the bioenergetic dynamics of breathing, movement, and feeling, one is impotent to recapture the joy of living. In desperation one develops the illusion that success and power can transform a joyless existence into a pleasurable life.

3 · The Biology of Pleasure

Excitation and Lumination

In the first chapter I made some observations about the nature of pleasure from a psychological point of view. This was followed by a discussion of breathing, movement, and feeling and an analysis of their importance to the pleasure of being fully alive. In this chapter I shall return to the phenomenon of pleasure and examine it as a biological process.

Everyone knows that pleasure results from the satisfaction of needs. To eat when one is hungry and to sleep when one is sleepy are the kinds of pleasurable experiences that illustrate this principle. The need creates a state of tension which when discharged through the satisfaction of the need produces a pleasurable feeling of relief. This view of pleasure was accepted by Freud. However, a concept of pleasure that limits it to the discharge of tension or the satisfaction of needs, though obviously valid, is too narrow to comprehend human behavior.

People actually enjoy a certain amount and kind of tension. They find pleasure in challenging situations, such as competitive sports, because the tension increases the amount of excitation. The buildup of excitation is in itself a pleasurable sensation when it is associated with the prospect of its release. In sex this intensification of excitation is called forepleasure, in contrast to the endpleasure, or satisfaction of release, or orgasm. When, however, the prospect of release is missing or the satisfaction is unduly postponed, desire and need become painful states. Thus, both need and fulfillment are aspects of the experience of pleasure in the absence of conflict and disturbance.

Since the primary needs of an organism have to do with the maintenance of its integrity, pleasure is associated with the sense of well-being that arises when this integrity is assured.

In its simplest form, pleasure reflects the healthy operation of the vital processes of the body. Leslie Stephen makes the same point when he says: "We must suppose, then, that pleasure and pain are correlatives of certain states which may be roughly regarded as the smooth and distorted working of the physical machinery and given these states, the sensations must always be present." There is no neutral state. A person feels either good or bad according to his state of physical functioning. If his feelings are suppressed, he will be depressed. Pleasure may be defined, then, as the sensation that develops from the smooth operation of the ongoing process of life.

The ongoing process of life, however, is more than mere survival; that is, it is more than the maintenance of the physical integrity of the organism. The ability to survive is found in many emotionally disturbed individuals who complain that they have no pleasure in living. In these cases the processes of life have stopped going onward. Pleasure and survival are not identical. Life does not aim at a static equilibrium, for that is death. Life includes the phenomena of growth and creativity. That is why novelty is such an essential ingredient of pleasure. The repetition of identical experiences is boring, and we use the expression "bored to death" to indicate how life-negating a lack of excitement is.

Biologically, pleasure is closely tied to the phenomenon of growth, which is an important expression of the ongoing process of life. We grow by incorporating the environment into our beings both physically and psychologically. This involves a reaching out and a taking in of air, food, and impressions. We enjoy the expansion and extension of our beings: the increase of our strength, the development of motor coordination and skills, the broadening of social relationships, and the enrichment of our lives. The healthy person has an appetite for life, for learning, and for the assimilation of new experiences into his personality.

The relationship between pleasure and growth explains why youth, a period of active physical and mental growth, is closer to pleasure than age. It also explains why the pleasures of older people take a more intellectual form, since this aspect of their personalities is still capable of growth. Young people, as everyone knows, have a greater capacity for excitement than older people.

The secret of pleasure is hidden in the phenomenon of excitation. A living organism has the inherent capacity to hold and increase its level of excitation; it does not change from inertness to responsiveness, like a machine when its motor is started or the current is turned on. There is a continuous excitation in the living organism which increases or decreases in response to stimuli proceeding from the environment. Broadly speaking, an increase of excitation leads to pleasure, a decrease to boredom and depression.

Excitatory phenomena occur in nonliving nature, too. In physics an electron is said to become excited when it moves to an outer orbit, a "more excited" state. The electron changes its position by capturing a photon, a particle of light energy. When the electron releases this energy, again in the form of light, it returns to its former orbit, a less excited state. The lumination of the earth's atmosphere is another example of an excitatory process in nature. As the sun rises above the horizon, its energy bombards the gaseous envelope surrounding our planet. This energy is picked up by the electrons in the atoms of the atmosphere, which become excited and emit light. The fact that space is dark shows that daylight is an excitatory process in our own atmosphere produced by the sun's energy. The lumination of an electric light bulb may be viewed as due to the same process. As the electric current passes through the filament of the light bulb, it excites the electrons of the filament, causing them to give off light.

Lumination is also an aspect of excitation in living organisms. We light up with pleasure, shine with joy, and glow with ecstasy. The radiance of an alive person is most clearly seen in the brightness of his eyes, but it may also be manifested in a glowing complexion. I recall the remark made by my son when his mother commented on the fact that he was not smiling when his school picture was taken. "But, Mom," he said, "my eyes are sparkling like diamonds." In the intense pleasure of the full sexual orgasm a sensation develops in the body which is perceived as a glow. The radiance of a person in love is a direct expression of his joy.

The lumination of the human body is not just a metaphorical way of speaking. The human body is surrounded by a "force field" which has been described as an aura or atmosphere. It has been observed and commented on by many writers, including Paracelsus, Mesmer, Kilner, and Reich. My associate, Dr. John C. Pierrakos, has made a special study of this phenomenon for the past fifteen years. This field or aura can be seen by the naked eye under certain conditions. It is shown in early Renaissance paintings as a glow about the heads of saints.

The significance of this field for our present discussion is that it reflects the level of excitation in the body. As the inner excitement mounts with pleasurable feelings, the color of the field becomes more intensely blue and the width of the envelope increases. There is a depression of the whole field in states of pain, probably due to the action of the sympathetic-adrenal systems in withdrawing blood from the surface of the body. The field also pulsates, that is, it appears and disappears at an average rate of fifteen to twenty-five times per minute under normal conditions. The rate of pulsation, like the color of the field, is related to the degree of excitation in the body. When the body goes into involuntary vibratory movements as a result of deeper respiration and more feeling, the rate of pulsation may reach forty or fifty per minute; at the same time, the width of the field extends farther, and its color becomes brighter.

Excitation in a living organism differs from that in nonliving nature, generally because it is contained within a closed system. The body is enclosed by a skin that acts both as a shield to protect the organism against overwhelming stimuli from without and as an envelope to hold the inner charge. A living organism has the ability not only to maintain its level of excitation above that of its environment, but also to increase this level at the expense of the environment. Life runs counter to the second law of thermodynamics, the law of entropy. Evolution and the growth of each individual bear witness to the fact that life is an ongoing process toward greater organization and more energy.

Individuals vary in their capacity to become excited and in their ability to contain excitation. Some people are glum, too serious and constrained. Nothing seems to excite them. Others are overexcitable, high-strung, restless, and hyperactive. They cannot hold excitation and yield to every impulse. These differences can be related to the patterns of muscular tension in the body which determine a person's character structure. This thesis is explored and elaborated in my book *The Physical Dynamics of Character Structure*.

Because it is a closed system containing an inner charge or excitation, the living body has an inherent motility. It is in constant motion, awake or asleep. The heart beats, the blood flows, the lungs expand and contract, digestion proceeds continuously, and so on. It moves independently through space. It is, in other words, alive. When it loses its inherent motility, it is dead.

In the higher organisms, especially man, the body's movements are divided into two classes, the voluntary movements, which are consciously made and ego-directed, and the involuntary movements, of which a person may or may not be conscious. The distinction between these two classes is not sharp, however. All voluntary movements are superimposed on underlying involuntary movements. The decision to walk, for example, is consciously made; the specific movements that go into walking are largely involuntary and unconscious. If our responses to stimuli or situations contain a large unconscious or involuntary component, we describe them as spontaneous. A high degree of motility and spontaneity characterizes the healthy person. Both motility and spontaneity are decreased in depressed states.

These considerations show the direct connection between the ongoing process of life and pleasure. Life (energy process)→excitation→motion→pleasure. These connections are directly visible in a child, who literally jumps for joy when he is excited. In a state of excitement one cannot sit still. One is moved to dance, run, or sing. The experience of being moved from within, as opposed to the deliberate action of moving, is the basis of all feeling.

The Pleasure-Pain Spectrum

Feelings of pleasure or pain reflect the quality of the body's involuntary movements. These in turn express the kind and degree of inner excitation. There are painful states of excitation as well as pleasurable ones. Each state is manifested in certain involuntary movements which enable the observer to distinguish among them.

Subjectively, what one experiences in pleasure or pain is the quality of the body's motility. This is what is meant by the smooth or disturbed working of the physical machinery. The hypothesis underlying this concept is that one can only feel that which moves. A feeling is the sensory perception of an internal movement.

An analysis of the movements underlying the different sensations in the pleasure-pain spectrum will make these concepts clearer. This spectrum is shown below. It ranges from agony as the extreme of pain to ecstasy as the extreme of pleasure. The midpoint of the spectrum, "good feelings," represents the normal state of bodily function.

AGONY—PAIN—DISTRESS—GOOD FEELINGS—PLEASURE—JOY—ECSTASY

a. Agony denotes a painful condition that is beyond the tolerance of the organism. In agony the body twists and contorts in a series of convulsive movements. The final agony of death is such a convulsion.

b. Pain, in contrast to agony, implies that the disturbance has not exceeded the body's tolerance. In agony the integrity of the organism is at stake; in pain it is only threatened. Pain is expressed by writhing and jerking movements less convulsive than those of agony. The difference, however, is only one of degree.

c. Distress is a milder form of painful agitation. The body wriggles or squirms with distress, but its movements are not as spasmodic as those in the above conditions.

d. "Good feelings" represent a state of ease and relaxation in the body manifested by quiet and harmonious movements. This is the basic pleasure state expressed in the remark "I feel good."

e. As excitement mounts on the pleasure side of the spectrum, the movements of the body become more intense and more rapid, maintaining, however, their coordination and rhythm. In pleasure the person feels soft, vibrant, and buoyant; his eyes are bright and his skin warm. It can be said that the body *purrs* with pleasure.

f. Joy denotes increased pleasurable excitement such that the body seems to dance. Its movements are lively and graceful.

g. In ecstasy, the highest form of pleasurable excitement, the currents in the body are so strong that the person is "lit up" like a star. He feels transported (from the earth to the cosmos). Ecstasy is experienced in the full sexual orgasm, in which the movements also take on a convulsive character but are unified and rhythmic.

The difference between the movements on the two sides of the spectrum is the presence or absence of coordination and rhythmicity. In all painful states the body's movements are uncoordinated and spasmodic; in pleasure the movements are smooth and rhythmical. Movement is the language of the body. From the quality of a person's movements one can determine his state of feeling. Mothers can tell from the expression and body movements of an infant whether he is in a state of distress or whether he is comfortable and experiencing pleasure. The logical reason for the differences noted above is that one struggles to get away from pain, whereas one flows out to pleasure.

From this analysis it is obvious that pleasure cannot be defined as the absence of pain. While it is true that relief from pain often produces a feeling of pleasure, this is a rebound phenomenon. The pain has made one conscious of his body, and for a short time following its release one is also conscious of the pleasure of being alive. As soon as the pain is forgotten, the pleasure of its release is gone. Under the pressure of our ego drives for success and status we quickly lose consciousness of our bodies. They become harnessed to the will, and their motility and spontaneity are reduced. Unfortunately, our common experience is, as Samuel Johnson expressed it, that "life is a progression from want to want, not from enjoyment to enjoyment."

It is more logical to define pain in terms of pleasure than the other way around. Pleasure, in the form of a good feeling, is the basic state of a healthy body. Pain denotes some disturbance of this basic state. Pain therefore represents a loss of pleasure, just as illness is a loss of health. Psychologically, we experience pain as a loss of pleasure, as when we say, "I am pained by your rejection." On the other hand, when a relationship holds no promise of pleasure, its disruption is not experienced as painfully.

There is no neutral state in nature, and there is no neutral condition in the human organism that corresponds to an absence of pleasure or pain. An absence of feeling is pathological. This condition, which is not uncommon, indicates that feeling has been suppressed. Suppression of feeling is produced by chronic muscular tensions which restrict and limit the motility of the body, thereby reducing sensation. In the absence of movement, there is nothing to sense or to feel.

Characterological and physical rigidity resulting from chronic muscular tension develops out of the need to suppress painful sensations. Obviously, no one would want to suppress pleasurable ones. When chronic muscular tensions are resolved in the course of bioenergetic therapy, it is to be expected that painful memories and feelings will emerge into consciousness. The ability of a patient to accept and tolerate these painful feelings will determine his capacity to experience pleasurable ones. The dictum "No pleasure without pain" should be interpreted to mean that the capacity to experience pleasure is tied to the ability to feel the painfulness of a disturbing situation.

The Nervous Regulation of Response

The human organism is equipped with two nervous systems to integrate and regulate its responses. One, the cerebrospinal system, coordinates the action of the voluntary muscles with the proprioceptive and exteroceptive sensory input. It also regulates muscle tone and maintains posture. To a varying degree in different people the movements it controls are under conscious control. For example, some people can consciously wiggle their ears; others can make the biceps muscle contract at will.

The muscles on which this system acts are the striated, skeletal muscles of the body.

The second system is the autonomic or vegetative nervous system, which regulates such basic bodily processes as breathing, circulation, heart action, digestion, elimination, glandular activity, and pupillary reactions. The muscles on which it acts are called smooth muscles because they lack the striatious characteristic of the larger, skeletal muscles. Its action is not under conscious control, whence the name "autonomic system." It is composed of two subdivisions, known as the sympathetic and parasympathetic divisions, which act antagonistically. For example, the sympathetic nerves speed up the action of the heart, while the parasympathetic nerves slow it down.

In *The Function of the Orgasm,* Wilhelm Reich pointed out that "the parasympathetic [is] operative whenever there is *expansion, elongation, hyperemia, turgor and pleasure*. Conversely, the sympathetic is found functioning whenever the organism *contracts,* withdraws blood from the periphery, when it shows pallor, *anxiety or pain*." * The identity of parasympathetic innervation with feelings of pleasure is clear. In pleasure the body expands, the superficial tissues are filled with fluid and charged with blood, and the pupils of the eyes narrow to sharpen the focus. The sympathetic division, through its innervation of the adrenal glands, mobilizes the body to meet the emergency created by pain or the threat of danger. It prepares the organism for fight or flight; in the process the senses are alerted (the pupils are dilated), the heart muscle is stimulated, blood pressure is raised, and oxygen consumption is increased.

The two divisions have opposite effects on the direction of blood flow. Parasympathetic action dilates the peripheral arterioles, increasing the blood flow to the surface and producing greater surface warmth. The heart slows to a relaxed and easy beat. Sympathetic action contracts the superficial arterioles, forcing blood to the interior of the body to provide more oxygen for the vital organs and the musculature. Thus, parasympathetic action promotes an expansion of the organism and a

* W. Reich, *The Function of the Orgasm*. New York, Orgone Institute Press, 1942, p. 251.

reaching out to the environment, that is, a pleasurable response. Sympathetic action produces a contraction and a withdrawal from the environment, a response to pain.

Every painful situation is an emergency to which a person reacts via the sympathetic-adrenal system by increasing his state of tension and his consciousness of the environment. This tension results from a state of hypertonicity in the muscles as they prepare to act. It differs from the chronic muscular tension described in the preceding section, which is unconscious and represents the persistence of a state of preparedness arising from a past emergency. The heightened consciousness involves an active engagement of the will. In an emergency an individual does not act spontaneously; every action is a calculated move designed to remove the danger.

The will is an emergency mechanism. It is activated whenever a more than natural effort is required to meet a crisis. For example, it requires willpower to charge an enemy position in war, since the natural reaction is to escape if possible. Similarly, it requires willpower to persist in a painful undertaking, since one's natural tendency is to drop the venture. The will serves the function of survival in the face of what appear to be overwhelming odds. When the will is activated, the voluntary musculature of the body is mobilized, just as the citizens of a nation are mobilized in time of war. Normal behavior is suspended as the conscious ego takes full command. In an emergency one has neither the inclination nor the time for pleasure. The rhythmic and graceful involuntary movements that express pleasure must give way to controlled movements that express one's determination. The difference can be illustrated by a horseman who has been enjoying his ride, allowing his horse great latitude in its movements. Faced with an emergency, the rider takes full control of the horse, which then can be pushed beyond its natural limits; but in this situation the pleasure of riding is gone for both the horseman and his horse.

The will is antithetical to pleasure. Its use implies that one is in a painful situation that requires a mobilization of the organism's total resources. When the will is employed to achieve even a minor goal, the body reacts as if it were in a state of emergency; the sympathetic-adrenal system is stimulated to provide the extra energy for the effort. If the goal is imperative, the sense of emergency increases on the bodily level, more adrenalin is secreted, muscular tension increases, and more blood is withdrawn from the surface of the body. Whether the goal is physical, such as lifting a heavy weight, or psychological, such as writing an article for a deadline, it creates a state of tension that belongs to the pain side of the spectrum. The familiar picture of the reporter at his typewriter, tense, nervous, frustrated, and smoking one cigarette after another, illustrates the intensity of the physical strain that can be imposed by a psychological goal.

By its nature, every goal creates an emergency situation, since it would be meaningless if it didn't pose a challenge and require an effort. But setting goals is also a function of the creative process. As soon as an inspiration has crystallized into a conception, a goal is formulated, namely, that of expressing the conception in appropriate form. Setting goals is also part of the reality principle, which under the aegis of the ego modifies the pleasure principle. The reality principle states that an individual will postpone an immediate pleasure or tolerate a pain for the sake of a greater pleasure in the future. In effect, the reality principle is a different formulation of the creative process. Both envisage a greater pleasure and a keener enjoyment of life as a result of the effort required to achieve the goal. If, however, one loses sight of this objective, the goal becomes meaningless.

For a great many people the achievement of goals becomes the criterion of life. No sooner is one goal realized than another is proposed. Each achievement provides a momentary thrill of satisfaction that soon fades, thereby necessitating a new goal: a new car, a better house, more prestige, more money, and so on. Our culture is obsessed with achievement. Striving constantly to meet goals, living continually in a state of emergency, people necessarily develop high blood pressure, ulcers, tension, and anxiety. We pride ourselves on our drive, forgetting that every push requires the activation of the sympathetic-adrenal system.

Not every goal demands a postponement of pleasure. We have seen that a state of tension can be pleasurable if it is associated with the prospect of its release and the fulfillment of the underlying need or desire. The anticipation of pleasure is itself a pleasurable experience. Under this condition the necessary effort is easy and relaxed, the activity proceeds smoothly, and the body's movements retain a high degree of coordination and rhythmicity. Work of this kind is pleasurable. But one can only work in this fashion when there is no desperation, when the activity is as important as the goal, and when the end does not dominate the means. We do not live to produce, we produce in order to live. A preoccupation with goals and achievement characterizes people who are afraid of pleasure.

The Fear of Pleasure

To speak of the fear of pleasure seems like a contradiction. How can anyone be afraid of that which is beneficial and desirable? Yet many people avoid pleasure; some develop acute anxiety in pleasurable situations, and others actually experience pain when the pleasurable excitation becomes too intense. When I presented this material in a lecture, someone asked, "How do you explain the remark 'It feels so good it hurts'?" This question reminded me of a remark a patient once made: "It hurts good." It is well known that some people seem to find pleasure in pain. This seemingly masochistic reaction requires some explanation.

Consider the situation of a person who finds that he has become stiff from being in one position too long. Stretching his cramped muscles is painful, yet doing so restores his circulation and gives him a good feeling. Another example is that of the person who squeezes a boil that has come to a head in order to release the pressure. The procedure is painful, but as the boil bursts and discharges its contents, the feeling is one of pleasure and satisfaction. In both cases pleasure is derived from the release of tension, which could not be achieved without undergoing some pain. Almost every visit to a doctor or dentist involves some pain, which is voluntarily accepted for the sake of feeling better. Supporting pain in the interest of pleasure is part of the reality principle. There is nothing masochistic about it. It is the pleasure we seek, not the pain.

The sexual masochist who obtains pleasure from being beaten

is similarly motivated. He needs the pain to release the pressure. His body is so contracted and the muscles of his buttocks and pelvis are so tense that the sexual excitation does not get through to the genitals strongly enough. The beating, apart from its psychological meanings, breaks the tension and relaxes the muscles, allowing the sexual excitation to flow. Reich in his study of masochism showed that the masochist is not interested in the pain *per se* but seeks the pleasure that becomes available through the pain.

What differentiates the masochist from a normal person is his continued need of pain to experience pleasure. Again and again the same painful situations are provoked in his desperate attempts to gain a feeling of pleasure. He seems not to learn from his experiences. His approach is uncreative.

Masochistic behavior is motivated more by the desire for approval than by the desire for pleasure. Approval requires submission, which to the masochist is a prerequisite for pleasure. The submissive attitude that underlies the masochistic personality undermines any creative activity. In turn, his submissiveness forces him into provocative behavior which brings about his castigation. If the deep-seated guilt and fear that pervade his personality are not resolved, the masochist goes round and round in the same vicious circle, constantly seeking pain to get some pleasure but ending with more pain than pleasure.

It is important to note that traumas are not always immediately perceived as painful. Often a cut that is inflicted by the slip of a sharp knife is not felt until moments later, when there is sudden pain as waves of feeling flood the injured area. The knife cut induces a localized shock which leaves the traumatized part momentarily stunned. The same thing happens with psychological traumas. An insult is not often perceived as soon as it is uttered. The pain of the insult seems to strike us later, and we then react with a surge of anger. It could be that the insult caught us off guard and we were unprepared to react. But this interpretation does not explain the delayed reaction to physical injury.

Pain, like any other feeling, is the perception of a movement. In contrast to pleasure, when the movement flows smoothly and rhythmically, the movement that gives rise to the sensation of pain is interrupted and spasmodic. A cut is painful until new channels are established that allow the blood to flow freely through the injured area. Then the pain subsides. An insult is painful because it provokes an anger that cannot be immediately expressed. The release of this anger assuages the pain. Until the normal flow of feeling is restored, a situation of pressure exists (a moving force or energy builds up behind an obstacle), and this pressure or tension is experienced as painful.

The best illustration of this concept of pain is the condition of frostbite. The trauma of frostbite is generally painless, but the recovery is very painful. The person who has frostbite may actually be unaware of the condition until he enters a warm room. Then the pain begins, and it becomes increasingly severe as the blood returns to the frozen extremity. Freezing a part of the body is often used as an anesthetic procedure because it cuts off sensation. Thus the pain of frostbite is due to the pressure that arises when the energy-bearing fluids of the body, blood and lymph, attempt to force their way into the constricted spaces of the frozen extremity.

Pain is a warning of trouble, a danger signal. In the case of frostbite, it is a sign that the thawing-out process must be gradual to avoid any permanent damage to the tissues. If the pressure builds up too high, the contracted, frozen cells burst, resulting in necrosis of the affected part. The treatment of frostbite requires a progressive elevation of temperature to avoid this danger. Even following this procedure, some pain will be encountered, and it is unavoidable if the restoration of function is to occur.

Fear of pleasure is fear of the pain that inevitably develops when an outward-flowing, expansive impulse meets a contracted and bound area of the body. Reich had described the masochistic fear of pleasure as a fear of bursting if the excitation should become too strong. To understand this statement we must look at the individual whose body is tense and tightly held as being in a condition similar to that of frostbite. He is frozen in his immobility and lack of spontaneity. In a situation of pleasure he is exposed to the warmth produced by the flow of blood to the periphery of his body through the action of the parasympathetic nerves. His body tries to expand, but the expansion becomes painful when it encounters the resistance of chronically spastic muscles. The sensation may even be frightening. The individual feels that he will burst or "fall apart." His immediate impulse is to get out of the situation.

If a person could tolerate the pain and stay in the situation, allowing the pleasurable movements to flow through his body, he would experience the "falling apart" physically. He would begin to tremble and shake. His whole body might vibrate. He would feel that he was losing control over his body. His movements would become awkward, and his sense of self-possession would be gone. When this happens to people outside of therapy, they become so nervous that they feel forced to withdraw from the situation.

However, the trembling and shaking represent the breakdown of muscular tensions and their psychological counterpart, the ego defenses. It is a therapeutic reaction, an attempt on the part of the body to shake itself loose from the rigidities that limit its motility and inhibit the expression of feeling. It is a manifestation of the body's self-healing property. If it is encouraged, as is done in bioenergetic therapy, and allowed to proceed, it generally ends in crying. An overwhelming pleasure will frequently produce crying, as it breaks down the rigidity of the body. Examples of this reaction are numerous. Many women cry following a pleasurable sex experience. People cry when they encounter long lost friends or relatives. The expression is "I'm so happy I could cry."

As adults we have many inhibitions against crying. We feel it to be an expression of weakness, of femininity, of childishness. The person who is blocked against crying is blocked against pleasure. He cannot "let go" to his sadness, and so he cannot "let go" to his gladness. He becomes anxious in situations of pleasure. His anxiety stems from the conflict between the desire to let go and the fear of letting go. This conflict must arise whenever the pleasure is strong enough to threaten his rigidity.

The convulsive discharge of crying is the primary mechanism for the release of tension in the human being. Most infants cry when they are in distress, and all infants cry when in pain. On the interpersonal or psychological level their crying is a call for the mother. Biologically, it is a reaction to a state of contraction in the body. If one observes a baby in a state of distress or pain, one will notice that his body has become stiff and rigid. But in contrast to adults, his vibrant and alive young body cannot maintain this rigidity. First his jaw begins to quiver, then his chin crumbles, and in a moment his whole body is convulsed with sobs. Mothers know that the crying of a baby is a signal of distress and hasten to remove the disturbance. The baby, however, does not cry to summon his mother, for he will often continue to cry after she comes until the tension is released.

The function of crying to reduce tension is seen in psychiatric practice. Patients invariably declare that they feel better after a good cry. Some will even say, "I need to cry." After crying the patient's body is softer, his breathing easier and deeper, his eyes brighter, and his skin color better. One can sense the tension leave the patient's body as he gives in to the crying. When crying fails to have this effect, it is because the patient was too inhibited to allow the involuntary movements of crying to take over. In this situation a sympathetic touch or an understanding remark may remove the inhibition sufficiently to allow a full discharge to occur.

The fear of pleasure is the fear of pain, not only the physical pain that pleasure evokes in the contracted and rigid body but the psychological pain of loss, of frustration, and of humiliation. In the course of growing up we overcome these pains by suppressing our sadness, our fear, and our anger. In the process we diminish our capacity for love, for joy, and for pleasure. Feelings are suppressed by bodily tensions in the form of chronic muscular spasticities. What we do, in effect, is suppress all feeling, which lays the basis for a depressive tendency in the personality. By deadening ourselves to pain, we deaden ourselves to pleasure.

We cannot recover the capacity for joy without reexperiencing our sorrow. And we cannot feel pleasure without going through the pain of rebirth. And we are reborn again when we have the courage to face the pains of our lives without recourse to illusion. There is a dual aspect to pain. Although it is a danger signal and represents a threat to the integrity of the organism, it also represents the body's attempt to repair the effect of an injury and to restore the integrity of the organism.

I am reminded of a story I read about a surgeon in Vietnam. He was operating in a frontline hospital, treating the casualties as they came off the battlefield. The more seriously injured were given temporary treatment preliminary to being shipped out to a base hospital. As he was operating, a young wounded soldier lay on a cot crying with pain while waiting his turn.

"Please, doctor," cried the soldier, "give me some morphine. I can't stand the pain." But the doctor did not heed this request. A reporter observing the scene asked the doctor why he did not alleviate the soldier's suffering.

"Pain," said the doctor, "is the only thing that keeps those men alive." Morphine would have depressed the soldier's vital functioning and made his death inevitable.

If we are afraid of pain, we will be afraid of pleasure. This is not to say that one must seek pain to find pleasure, as the masochist does. Unable to face the pain within himself, the masochist projects his pain into external situations. It is to say that we must not run away from the pain of facing ourselves honestly if we wish to have joy in our lives.

4 · Power Versus Pleasure

The Mass Individual

An organism's natural striving for pleasure is normally suspended in only two situations: in the interest of survival and for the sake of a greater pleasure. In circumstances that threaten an individual's life, pleasure and creativity become irrelevant values. The important thing is to survive, and a person will endure pain and forego pleasure to stay alive. Apart from this situation, an individual will postpone an immediate gratification of a need or desire if this will lead to a greater pleasure in the future. He will also tolerate a certain amount of pain to achieve a goal that promises significant pleasure. The creative process often entails some pain in the effort to bring a conception to fruition. In neither of these two situations can the sacrifice of pleasure be considered a destructive act. Pleasure is still the main objective of the individual.

There is one condition, however, which leads to self-destructive behavior. That condition is crowding, or more specifically, overcrowding. It is known that when an animal group exceeds an optimal density in terms of its living space, destructive forces are set in motion to reduce the number of animals. It has been shown experimentally that a rat population confined to a limited area becomes self-destructive when its density exceeds a certain figure. Neurotic behavior patterns develop; there is a loss of interest in cleanliness; mother rats abandon or destroy their young; and stronger males attack and kill weaker ones.

The explanation that is given for this behavior is that the animals become disturbed by the excessive number of contacts they have with each other in the condition of excessive density. On the one hand they are excited and stimulated by these contacts, but on the other they are restricted in the discharge and release of the excitation by their overcrowded condition. Thus they become tense, nervous, and self-destructive.

The parallel between the neurotic behavior of rats and that of modern man, who also lives in overcrowded conditions, has not escaped attention. Psychiatrists, however, hesitate to accept the single fact of overcrowding as the cause of the emotional ills they see in their offices. First, these illnesses develop in persons who do not live in overcrowded conditions. Second, not every person in an area of high density becomes self-destructive. And third, most emotional problems have been definitely traced to early childhood experiences in the family. The parallelism is, however, so striking that it cannot be ignored. Further, many studies have shown that the incidence of emotional illness is higher in low-income areas of high density.

I would suggest that the common denominator in all neurotic behavior patterns is a diminution of the sense of self. This includes a loss of the feeling of identity, a reduced awareness of one's individuality, a decrease in self-expression, and a diminished capacity for pleasure. Overcrowding will certainly contribute to this limitation of personality as a disposing cause, while the family situation acts as the effective cause. The family, as Wilhelm Reich has pointed out, is the operative agent of society.

Although no one knows the optimal density for the human population, it cannot be denied that we are living in a mass society and that its members exhibit a degree of self-destructive behavior. Instead of striving for pleasure, which is the normal pattern, they are driven to achieve success, and they are obsessed with the idea of power. Neither the drive nor the obsession promotes a creative approach to life. They are destructive forces in the personality.

In a mass society success is the mark that distinguishes the individual from the crowd. The successful person is said to "have it made." What he has made is a name for himself. Having achieved this distinction, he is supposed to be able to sit back and enjoy life while the rest of the crowd, the nameless ones, must continue their struggle for success. The successful individual is envied by the crowd, which sees in his success an aura of power and imagines that through success all problems will disappear or at least be significantly reduced.

We know rationally that success contains no magical properties. Emotionally, however, we are all more or less committed to success in some form or other, financial, political, athletic, social, and even marital. Whatever area we choose for our endeavor, we attach such importance to success that it often becomes the dominant drive in our lives.

This is understandable, since thinking in terms of success or failure is natural in our goal-oriented culture. From the moment we enter school our public life is marked with the record of our successes and failures. Progress through school is represented by the achievements of successive goals, and this then becomes the pattern of our adult life. Since goals are inherent in planning (every plan has a goal), we shall have to follow such a pattern as long as the need to plan our activities on the personal or social scale exists. I cannot envision the disappearance of this need in a complex society.

The problem that concerns us here, however, is the increasing tendency for success itself to become the overriding goal. If, for example, I plan to write a book, my goal is to have it published. When this goal is achieved, I can say that I have succeeded. But in the public mind this is no success. Should the book, however, by any chance reach the best seller list, I will really have achieved success. I will have gained the recognition that is somehow essential to the image of success.

Can it be said that the struggle for success is a striving for recognition? There is considerable evidence to support this view. In every field of endeavor procedures and practices have been developed to provide the acclaim that success requires. In the movies it is the Academy Award, in the New York theater it is the Tony Award. Baseball has its Hall of Fame, football its All-American teams. The successful businessman is honored at luncheons and dinners, the artist at receptions and openings. All of these activities are attended with as much publicity as possible, to enhance the image of the successful individual.

This image as it is presented to the public in the mass media pictures the successful person as a happy individual. He is surrounded by a smiling family, each member of which seems to bask in the sunshine of his success. No cloud darkens the horizon of his good fortune. This image may become tarnished later as the problems of his personal life erupt into the public consciousness, but by that time other successful individuals will have captured the public attention to add new luster to the image of success. The public seems to need figures to admire, and the mass media cater to this need. The successful person is the hero of the technological age.

Heroes are not new. Every age produces its quota of individuals who distinguish themselves from other members of their community by some achievement. Their acclaim serves as an inspiration for others to follow their example. The image of the hero is that of an individual who embodies a virtue to the highest degree. That virtue may be courage, wisdom, or faith, but it is always a personal attribute that is made evident by the hero's achievements. The hero does not strive for recognition. The motivation for his actions cannot be egotistic or he would not be a true hero.

In our culture success in itself implies no superior virtue. A book is not necessarily a superior one because it makes the best-seller lists. Most books that achieve this distinction appeal to the mass market and are generally supported by extensive publicity. While success in the business world may require a high degree of business acumen, this quality has never before been considered a personal virtue. Today it is the achievement that counts, not the personal qualities of the individual. Sometimes success is achieved by qualities that are anything but virtuous. Until his downfall Hitler was considered a success by a great many people throughout the world. Of course, success may attend the individual with superior abilities; however, what is acknowledged is not the personal virtue of the individual but his achievement.

The actual accomplishment is often relatively unimportant. The author of six good books may be less of a success than the writer of one best seller. What does count is the recognition. Without recognition one cannot be considered a public success.

To achieve success means to rise above the crowd, to stand out from the mass of people and be recognized as an individual. For the writer it means that what he says or writes is now re-

garded as important. "He counts" is the way one successful author was described. Before his success, he didn't "count," although what he wrote before his success may have had greater
value than his subsequent work. Through success he had become important. We see this all the time. As soon as a person
becomes successful he is listened to with respect. Since he has
"made it," his words may tell the rest of us who are still strug-
gling the secret of his good fortune. The successful person is
important to all who wish to be successful.

The image of success as a driving force in people's lives is
relatively new. Images have always played an important role in
people's lives. In the past, however, the dominant images have
been those of a religious nature or of an all-powerful ruler.
These shared images have served to unite people and to relate
them to a higher—that is, supra—individual purpose. An image
can do this because it focuses a person's thinking and directs his
energies. It can be used, therefore, to control a person's behavior. We have learned how to manipulate the process of image
formation through advertising or by controlling the means of
communication. This power enables those who are in power
and have easier access to the means of communication to shape
the values of a society. Since these values will be their own
values, it can be expected that success and power will be among
the more important ones.

Success is the spotlight that singles out the one from the
many. Actually, in today's world it is not necessary to achieve
anything special to be successful; if the spotlight singles out
an individual, he is on his way to success. If you are written
up and photographed by *Life,* you can be considered a success.
If you appear on a nationwide television show, you "have it
made." The spotlights have become so powerful that the person
on whom they rest for a moment is distinguished for life. But
by the same process, the rest of the people are cast into a deeper
shadow.

Since success is the symbol that distinguishes the individual
from the mass in the public eye, it is a product of the system
that creates the mass. It may seem like a contradiction, therefore, to say that the striving for success is also one of the important forces that create a mass culture. But true relationships

are always dialectical. If a mass society breeds a striving for success, then it is equally true that the image of success becomes one of the cohesive forces in a mass society.

The mass media are not the only force that creates the mass individual, that is, the person with no public identity. Mass entertainment and mass production are other parts of the system. What individuality can one feel through driving a Ford or a Chevrolet? There are close to a million of each on the highways. To overcome this handicap some aggressive individuals try to be the first with the newest model. If we are forced to buy identical products and live in identical homes, these important areas of self-expression are closed. But mass production even requires us to work in identical jobs. We may be one of twenty secretaries in an office, one of a hundred salesmen in a division, one of a thousand production workers in a factory; we are mass individuals who can be replaced without disturbing the routine.

Mass entertainment has an even more insidious effect, for it enters into our private lives. As viewers of television, we are not even known. We sit in semidarkness watching an image, and we are not related to the performer by even so much as the buying of a ticket. We are deprived of the opportunity to express our response by giving or withholding applause. We are the great unknown public, which does not count except in terms of numbers. The only outlet for our egos is through identification with the limelighted individuals, the successful ones.

In addition to the striving for success, a mass society also induces in its members an obsession with power. The striving for success develops out of the need to gain recognition, to achieve an identity even if it is only a public one, and to feel important. The struggle for power stems from a need to overcome an inner feeling of helplessness and to compensate for an inner feeling of despair. For a person there are two aspects to power. One is wealth, and the other is authority. Both can confer upon their possessor a sense of power that can serve to create a pseudo-individuality similar to that of the successful person. Wealth and authority seem to provide opportunities for self-expression that are denied people of limited means or lesser position.

But self-expression presupposes that one has a self to express.

Neither wealth nor authority can create a self where one doesn't exist. I am not unique among psychiatrists in treating rich people who suffer from severe emotional disturbances that make them and their families miserable. Many of them actually feel guilty about possessing wealth, which, despite its seeming advantages, often proves to be a burden. Authority may be even more of a handicap, since it imposes upon its possessor an obligation to maintain a posture and position that conflicts with his feelings and desires. The man in authority believes that he owes loyalty to the system that gave him authority, regardless of the fact that it may undermine his personal integrity.

The self-destructive quality of the striving for success often becomes manifest when success is achieved. Some time ago I treated a businessman who after some years of effort had attained the success he had hoped for. He consulted me because he was depressed. His success had not produced the good feelings or the sense of liberation he had anticipated. Another case was that of an actress who had struggled hard to gain the recognition she wanted. When it finally came, she became depressed. These incidents are so common that I have come to the realization that depression develops when an illusion collapses. The illusion in these cases was that success leads to happiness or promotes pleasure.

Since the values of a mass society are success and power, the person who accepts them becomes a mass individual and loses his true individuality. He no longer thinks of himself as a person apart from the crowd, since his primary interest is to rise above the crowd. At the same time it is very important to be accepted by the crowd. He abandons the discriminating attitude of the true individual in favor of conformity. His behavior is oriented away from pleasure and toward prestige; he becomes a status-seeker and a social climber. What is worse is that these values infiltrate his home life. They become the criteria by which he judges his children, who must measure up by being both acceptable and outstanding.

The blame for this state of affairs cannot be placed on the people who run the system. The television producer is not responsible for turning us into mass individuals. The fault is not the lack of quality in television shows. The system itself is all wrong, for its aim is to appeal to the greatest number, and its means is to employ the lowest common emotional denominator.

We become mass individuals when we identify with the system, accepting its values. Yet we cannot easily isolate ourselves from the system, for it pervades every aspect of our culture. We must buy some mass-produced products, for they are cheaper though not necessarily better. We must read the papers occasionally, though I have found that they add little to my feeling of well-being. And if we do not wish to be without a radio or television set, we should at least be discriminating in our choice of programs. We must be discriminating if we wish to avoid being brainwashed by the overwhelming propaganda and advertising that are hurled at us in favor of the system. We can only do this if we guard our true individuality and not let ourselves be seduced by the rewards which the system offers to those who achieve success.

The system does provide opportunities for the aggressive individual to become one of the actors in the drama and not remain part of the unseen and unheard audience. Someone has to run the show, or at least so it appears. Those individuals who rise to the top in the hierarchy of power are considered to be the successful ones. There are hierarchies in every field of endeavor: business, politics, society, art, and so on. And there are hierarchies within each segment of the field. Every organized activity creates a hierarchy of power. In each hierarchy, large or small, the person who is at the top and wields the greater power is regarded as a success by those lower on the scale.

Yet no one truly runs the show; no one really wields the power. Those at the top are as much part of the system as the lowest man on the totem pole. They can be replaced as easily as one of their subordinates. They are not creative people whose work bears the stamp of their individuality. Their function, like that of each mass individual, is to keep the show going, to keep the system operating, to keep the machine running. Sure, it's different at the top, but only in terms of power, not in terms of pleasure. At the top one may have the ego satisfaction that he stands out from the mass, but it is not because he is an individual. He stands on the shoulders of the mass of people, whose support is necessary for his position. He is not different from them. He is a mass individual upon whom the spotlight has focused for a time. He is an individual committed to the struggle for power and dissociated from his body and its orientation toward pleasure.

True Individuality

In the preceding section I have sketched some of the sociological factors that are operative in the development of the mass individual. Fortunately, no human being is totally a mass individual. Each of us retains some portion of his individuality that the system has not destroyed. Each of us is capable of experiencing some degree of pleasure and, therefore, of distinguishing that which is personally meaningful from the how-to-be-successful propaganda. Without a sense of pleasure, discrimination is impossible.

We are not accustomed to thinking of pleasure as the foundation of individuality. In the public mind the individual is the person who stands out from the crowd. But the public doesn't know the person, it is acquainted only with his image. Magnified by the mass media, the image looks large and impressive. It comes as quite a shock to find that the real person is not at all like his image. The famous author turns out to be a shy and hesitant conversationalist. The well-known actress proves to be withdrawn and emotionally unresponsive offstage. The successful businessman has little to contribute apart from the details of his business life, and so forth. If we do not let ourselves become blinded by the image, we soon realize that there is something lacking in the personal lives of these individuals. Not infrequently their success is a compensation for the lack of meaning in their private lives. On the personal level they fail to impress us with a sense of their individuality.

As a psychiatrist I have had the occasion to treat many persons who could be considered successful. Their need for my help was an indication that they had lost a sense of themselves, a feeling of individuality and of personal identity. I was once consulted by a famous artist who had reached the point where he asked himself, "Who am I?" His work was judged to be individualistic and expressive. He was well known and highly regarded, but within himself he was confused and insecure, unsure of his identity and deficient in a sense of self. He felt unreal because he was out of touch with his body. And while his artistic work provided a good measure of ego satisfaction, he lacked the feeling of pleasure in being alive which alone gives meaning to existence.

I have also known some people who had a feeling of excitement about living. They were not enthusiasts who proclaimed their devotion to life. Such proclamations are suspect of being attempts to convince one's self that life is worth living. They were not followers of a cause or fanatics of some creed. They were not consecrated to a great achievement. The significant thing about them was that when you met them, you knew immediately that you were in the presence of an individual. It was not what they said or did that gave this impression but something about the person, something physical.

They radiated a strong feeling of pleasure. Their eyes were bright, their manner alert. They looked at you with interest and listened with attention. When they spoke, they expressed their feelings and what they said made sense. They moved easily, because their bodies were relaxed. If you observed their bodies, you became aware of an inner vitality manifested by a good skin and good muscle tone. You knew intuitively that these were people who enjoyed life. Of course, these people did not need treatment.

When I say that such people radiate pleasure, it is to express the fact that one feels good in their company. It is a pleasure to be around them, just as it is depressing to be with a depressed person, sad to be with a sad person, and so on. Pleasure is after all a rhythmic vibration of the body which communicates itself to the atmosphere and affects others in the immediate environment. I could also describe such individuals as vibrant personalities, for it is this quality which makes one conscious of them. It should go without saying that they are individuals, for no two organisms have identical rhythmic patterns. Each is unique in the subtle variations with which nature endows each new being.

Of equal importance is the fact that such people feel their individuality and know their identities. They are directly in touch with their feelings at all times and therefore know what they want and what they do not want. When they speak, their views are always special, for no two people have identical feelings. And knowing what they feel, they are rarely at a loss to express the subjective reason for a personal judgment. This is expressed as "I like the play because . . . ," or "I dislike that actress; she was too self-conscious, too stiff, and too dependent on mannerisms," and so on. Such people have taste. Without taste one cannot claim to be an individual. True individuals do not stand out in a crowd, they stand apart from crowds.

There are other people who have what are called "magnetic" personalities. You are drawn to them by the feeling of power that emanates from them. They dominate all gatherings because they override all competition. There is a tension in their bodies that creates an aura of suspense in the atmosphere. You feel excited, as if something important were going to happen, and you become tense and a little anxious. These individuals also radiate, but the radiation is not pleasurable. It is a force that is constrained, and its effect is to constrain their audience.

Power creates a sense of individuality, but only in terms of other people. The "magnetic" personality or, as I shall call him hereafter, the power individual, falls flat when he is alone, since the force cannot be experienced except by its power to attract. It turns to hostility when the response is negative, for a negative response is a denial of the "individuality" of this person. These individuals must be part of a crowd, where they stand out by their dominance. Yet they are not true individuals, for apart from their role—to dominate—they have no real identity.

The distinguishing characteristic of the power individual is egotism. He projects the image of a superior person, a sort of superman, and every action is designed to enhance this image. He must be a success, for failure is unthinkable; it is too human and, therefore, an expression of weakness. This type of individual is not identified with his body, which may appear to be in superb condition. It cannot appear otherwise if it is to uphold his image. It is an instrument of his will, and it is perfected like a machine for the work it has to do, namely, support the massive ego that rests upon it. He may be a successful executive, and he is generally a successful athlete and always a successful lover. What he doesn't see is that he has failed as a human being.

Talk to an egotist about pleasure, and he will recount his exploits. Discuss your feelings, and he will describe his plans and projects. He finds no lack of words with which to talk about himself, but never on the intimate level where two people exchange their deepest feelings. I have known some of these people, too. Occasionally they come into my office for a consultation. Not one has ever remained as a patient. The thought of submitting to another person, even a therapist, is too frightening to these papier-mâché egos.

For many people the price of success is too high, and therefore the rewards become meaningless. They reject the system, or the establishment as they call it, and refuse to be mass individuals. Their way out is to eschew the power struggle and disclaim any personal ambition. They drop out of the competitive race, and together with others of similar views they form the "hippy" communities of New York, San Francisco, and elsewhere.

The hippy belongs to a long tradition of rebellion against the values and mores of a mass society. It is a tradition that goes back at least as far as Jean-Jacques Rousseau, but the rebellion has never been so widespread or so vociferous as it is today. In the past it was limited to the artistic and intellectual circles. The present rebellion is anti-intellectual as well as anti-materialistic and is, or has been, strongly drug-oriented.

Like all human beings, a hippy needs an identity and must try to assert his individuality. He does this by a style of dress and a manner of life that are unusual. He wears his hair long to distinguish himself from the crowd. One of my young patients said about his shoulder-length hair, "It makes people look at me, and I like it." Cut his hair, and you destroy his image. The same thing is true of his dress. It is both a dissent and a form of self-assertion. The more bizarre it is, the more attention it draws to its wearer. The hippies have certainly created some bizarre outfits.

Is the hippy, then, a true individual? I have treated a number of these people, and their main problem was a deficient sense of self and an insecure and frightened ego. To understand the hippy we must not be taken in by his talk of love. A "love-in" sounds exciting, but apart from the music it is a gathering of forlorn people desperately in need of some contact with other human beings. If love is to be more than a word, it must manifest itself in feeling, specifically in a feeling of pleasure, and this is sadly lacking in the hippy.

It may seem that my criticism is too severe. I base it on the hippies I have known and seen. Those who have come into my office looked rather lifeless, were depleted of energy, and lacked vitality. Their bodies were tight, their breathing severely restricted, and their sexual function disturbed. In fact, some of them consulted me because of their sexual impotence.

The hippy often begins as a dropout from school, where he finds the pressure too intense and the demands too heavy. His abandonment of the struggle is caused by an inability to sustain the effort; later it becomes rationalized by the language of dissent and opposition. Distraught parents have brought more than one young man to me who was failing or had failed in school and who had adopted the hippy mode in self-defense. Parents tend to place the blame for this situation on bad companions who have turned their son onto false paths. They fail to see the physical condition and the personality problem that made this move inevitable.

I shall illustrate this problem with the case of one young man of seventeen who couldn't make it. His parents were affronted by his uncut hair and unkempt clothing. No threat or force could induce him to change his appearance or take a greater interest in his schoolwork. What disturbed them most was the fact that he had the mental capacity to do the work. He lacked the physical stamina to concentrate on his studies, but this of course they didn't know.

He was a thin young man with a narrow face and blank eyes. His chest was small and tight. It required an effort for him to take a deep breath. His body showed an exaggerated flexibility. His musculature was poorly developed. He spoke to me in a flat voice, without raising his lowered eyes. He offered no information and answered my questions with a yes or no. Later, as the therapy progressed, communication between us improved.

Studying was difficult for this patient. When he tried to concentrate on a book, his eyes felt heavy and he became drowsy. His mind wandered from the subject, and his will wasn't strong enough to keep his attention focused. He slept long hours every day. He simply didn't have the energy to push himself. The basic mechanism responsible for the production of energy in his body was defective. He didn't breathe enough, and without an adequate oxygen intake, his energy was low. He showed the typical disturbance of a schizoid personality, the causes and effects of which have been elaborated in a previous book.*

My patient had no choice but to drop out of school. He had no alternative but to associate with others who experienced similar difficulties. He became a hippy because it offered a way out. He did not go as far out as some hippies. He had smoked marijuana, but he had not taken any trips on LSD.

The connections I have outlined above between bodily function and behavior made sense to this patient. I made few references to his appearance. I am neither for nor against long hair, but an unkempt appearance is an expression of a lack of feeling for the body. One cannot feel anything for a body that is not a source of pleasure, and consequently one ignores the body and its appearance.

This young man had very little pleasure in his body, which is the same thing as saying that he had little pleasure. His body was in a contracted state, and its rhythmic activities markedly reduced. The therapy was directed to this problem as well as to his psychological conflicts. But it was the physical therapy that affected him most. When his breathing became stimulated and his body began to vibrate, he exclaimed, "Gee, it feels good. I never knew it could feel good."

Generally speaking, the hippy is not connected with his body in a pleasurable way. His orientation is away from his body. His use of drugs, from marijuana to LSD, is an escape from the body. These drugs deaden the body while they overexcite the mind. They may increase the range of sensory awareness, but they limit the range and intensity of movement. Hippies are generally pictured lying around. Their love is erotic, that is, sensual, but it is not genital passion. That too requires energy.

The hippy's rejection of the values of a mass society is valid, but we must recognize that it is based on an inability to com-

* Alexander Lowen, *The Betrayal of the Body*. New York, The Macmillan Company, 1966.

pete. In his role as the opposition, the hippy achieves a pseudo-individuality that rests on a negative attitude rather than a positive one. His way of life is not grounded in an identification with bodily pleasure. It eschews the pain that cannot be avoided when pleasure is the desideratum. In escaping from the mass society, the hippy escapes from life itself. The hippy's way is not a creative approach to the problem.

The Illusion of Power

The appeal of power seems tremendous, especially to those who feel deprived of it. Unions strike for power, students riot for power, nations go to war for power. No prospect has aroused the Negroes of this country to such fervor as the slogan "Black Power." People seem willing to fight and die for power; they cannot or will not make a similar commitment to pleasure. What is the mystique of power?

Let us look at the meaning of power. Broadly speaking, power is the ability to manipulate or control the environment. In this sense all animals possess some power; they all manipulate the environment to satisfy their needs. The beaver builds a dam, the woodchuck excavates a hole, and the bird constructs a nest. Man is the greatest manipulator of all, but as long as his power remained a personal power, he was no different from the other animals. When man hunted with spears or bows and arrows, the balance in nature was undisturbed. That situation changed when power became an impersonal force that man could harness to his will.

The growth of power is the story of civilization. Civilization and power began with the domestication of animals and the development of agriculture, that is, with the production of wealth. The first real power was in the hands of a ruler and lay in his control over the stored food surpluses in his domain. Through this control he could exercise command over his subjects, who would then lend their energies to his purposes in return for the security he offered. Power gradually increased as man learned to harness the natural forces and direct their energies to his ends. And it increased in proportion as tribes became states and states were united to form nations. It grew faster when he discovered the steam engine and tapped the latent energy in coal. Then by rapid steps came the internal combustion engine, electricity, and nuclear energy.

The amount of power that man has at his disposal is frightening. At this point in his history I believe that he has unleashed a genie that could very easily destroy him if he does not understand its mode of operation. There is an old saying that power corrupts a person. This has generally been applied to rulers or persons in positions of authority, since they were the only ones who had power in the past, but the adage is broad enough to cover all aspects of power. When we think of the destructive aspects of power, we picture the horrors of modern warfare: napalm, anti-personnel shells, and ultimately nuclear weapons. Frightening as this is, I am more concerned with the insidious effects of power upon the human personality.

Power is antithetical to pleasure. It bears the same relationship to pleasure that the ego does to the body. Pleasure stems from the free flow of feeling or energy within the body and between the body and its environment. Power develops through the damming and control of energy. This describes the basic distinction between the pleasure individual and the power individual. Power develops from control and operates through control. It has no other mode of operation. I shall illustrate this concept with several examples. The leader of a thousand free men has no power, though the men may be an effective fighting force when they are united in a common purpose. His leadership is based on influence. On the other hand, the commander of a thousand soldiers has power, because he can control and direct their actions at his will. Wind has no power; it is only a force. It has energy. It is when we control the force of wind by making it turn a windmill that we generate power. Similarly, a swift-flowing river has no power. The power arises when the force of the moving water is channeled and directed to turn the wheels of a turbine.

Pleasure is the feeling of harmony between an organism and its environment. This is not a static concept, for the environment is constantly changing or being changed, thereby providing opportunities for new and greater pleasures. Power, on the other hand, is both controlling and disruptive. It erects a wall between man and his natural surroundings. It protects him, but it also isolates him. The person who lives in a modern city apartment, heated in the winter and air-conditioned in the summer, and goes to work in a similar kind of office building is like an animal in a zoo or a fish in an aquarium. His survival is assured and his comforts are provided, but the excitement and pleasure of the open field, the stimulation of the changing seasons, and the freedom of unlimited space are denied him. It is a poor fish that would exchange the freedom and the dangers of the sea and river for the security of the aquarium.

In gaining power over nature, man has become subject to the very controls he has imposed upon his environment.

The insidious danger of power is its disruptive effect on human relationships. The person who wields power becomes a superior figure, while the person subject to power is correspondingly reduced to an object. The use of power denies the equality of human beings and must lead to conflict and hostility. This is especially true in the close, personal relationships that exist in a home.

The moment the question of power enters into the relationship of a husband and wife, the couple is in for trouble. The weaker person always feels threatened, and an undercover struggle for power develops that will corrode the good feelings and affection each has for the other. But it is in the relationship between parents and children that the most damaging effects of power are found. Power is always used to control a child, supposedly in its own interest but really in the interest of the parents. The effect of power, and every punishment is an exercise of power, negates the child's individuality, suppresses his self-expression, and denies him the right of dissent.

I am often consulted by parents who complain that their children lack discretion and don't know what they want to do. One young man brought to see me by his parents suffered from an inability to make up his mind. The story that unfolded was the following. Every desire the young man had had as a child had to be submitted to his parents and justified by a good reason. If he wanted something, he had to explain why he wanted it. His desire for pleasure was not of sufficient importance. In the name of rationality they used their power to control his actions, and the result was a suppression of his striving for pleasure and with it of the creative impulse in his personality. This is a story that I have heard repeated in too many homes.

Parents use power to control their children because they were similarly controlled when they were young. Having been the objects of power, they are now determined to exercise power even over their children, which is the easiest way to exercise power. The exercise of power seems to restore, in their minds the idea that they are individuals who have a right to make demands and express them. Psychoanalytic theory offers us some understanding of how this association develops.

It is generally accepted in psychoanalytic thinking that the infant comes into the world with a sense of omnipotence. This feeling derives from his intrauterine existence, where all his needs were automatically fulfilled. The feeling of omnipotence is further strengthened by breast-feeding. The young consciousness of the infant sees the world in terms of the breast. If it is readily available to him, he feels that he possesses the world. Later he will become aware that there is a second breast, which he will fondle with his hands as he nurses on the first one. At this time he literally has his world in his hands. His expanding consciousness will gradually make him aware of his mother. Her body, which he at first perceived as an extension of himself, becomes an independent object. But as long as his mother responds fully to his demands to be held and to be nursed, he will still feel omnipotent in his ability to command this larger world.

In a healthy mother-child relationship, the pleasure the infant experiences at the breast is shared by the mother. She too enjoys the experience. And as the baby's eyes meet his mother's eyes, the feeling that passes between them can be described as joy and love. No other contact between mother and child can be as intimate or as fulfilling as nursing. And if this process could follow its natural course, it would continue for about three years or longer. When the child grows older, he nurses only on getting up, going to bed, and when he needs some reassurance that his world is still intact and his power to command this personal world undiminished.

As he grows up, the child will necessarily be weaned. The

weaning may or may not be a traumatic experience, but it is as inevitable as the trauma of birth. The child then steps into a new world in which he slowly recognizes that he is no longer omnipotent, that other individuals have needs which must be met, and that mutual cooperation is necessary. To the degree that nursing has fulfilled his oral needs, he will accept this new world with its different conditions and its prospects of different pleasures.

The child that is not fulfilled in this way is a deprived child. He is deprived emotionally of a pleasure that is the right of every human infant, and he is deprived psychologically of the feeling of importance and omnipotence. The deprivation is lessened if the mother holds her baby and handles him with tender loving care, but in any case the loss of the pleasure at the breast is a deprivation.

It may be argued that I make too much of breast-feeding. It was argued that Freud and Reich gave too much importance to sex. But nursing and sex are the primary expressions of our mammalian nature. To reject them is to deny our animal heritage, and this constitutes a denial of the body.

I have seen the advantages of breast-feeding in my own child and in the children of some of my patients. I cannot claim that it solves all problems. I will state categorically that the fulfilled child is less of a problem than the deprived child. There are many other advantages to breast-feeding. I would refer those of my readers who are interested in this function to an organization of mothers who have nursed or are nursing their children, known as La Leche League. It has offices in most cities of the United States.

Whenever a child feels deprived of pleasure, he will fight to gain it. This can very easily give rise to a conflict with the parents. The issue quickly becomes transformed into one of power. The parent, feeling that his right to control the situation is being challenged, does not hesitate to use his superior power to enforce his will. He may have recourse to punishment or use the threat of a withdrawal of love to bring about the child's submission. Once this happens, the lines are drawn for a power struggle between parents and children which may continue intermittently for many years but in which the children are always the losers since they are dependent on their parents. In the end the parents, too, will be losers. They will lose the deep affection and love that only develop through the sharing of pleasure and joy. Growing up in such homes, children long for the day when they will have the power to do as they wish. Since the lack of power is associated in the child's mind with the deprivation of pleasure, it seems logical that pleasure can be attained through power.

The image of success is an illusory fulfillment of the infant's deprivation at the breast. The person who seeks power and strives for success has a fixation at the infantile level. His dream is that once he attains power or achieves success, he can lie back and have his wants taken care of by others. He will have the power to command his environment to cater to his needs. He will be able to indulge himself as he was unable to do when young. His aim is regressive, and the goal when attained must prove a bitter disappointment. Having gotten the recognition and the power, his unconscious fantasy is that he can turn to his mother for fulfillment. But it is too late. The milk has gone from her breasts, and the impulse to suck has become frozen in his tight mouth.

Since power is antithetical to pleasure, it can increase the experience of pleasure. To do this it must be in a creative relationship to pleasure. Through power we can make our surroundings more beautiful, we can make many of life's tasks easier, and we can extend our contacts with the universe. Power enhances and enlarges man's ego. This can be a positive development if the ego remains identified with the body and oriented toward the expression and satisfaction of its animal instincts. I am not advocating, therefore, a return to nature. We would not, and probably could not, surrender the potential that lies in power. It can be constructive as well as destructive. The only people who can handle power constructively, however, are those who have been fulfilled in childhood and know how to enjoy life.

Power carries with it the enormous responsibility of not abusing it for ego purposes. In our greed we could easily destroy the beauty of the earth. We are not too far from doing so now. When power comes into the hands of a deprived person, the situation is dangerous. Whether that power is money, a high-powered automobile, or a rifle, the risk to human welfare is great. The deprived person worships power; his new idols are the personifications of power: James Bond, Superman, and so on. What are these but the fantasies that run through the mind of a deprived child?

In proportion as our power grows bigger, the roots of pleasure must sink deeper and more firmly into the earth. In this direction lies our hope.

5 · The Ego: Self-Expression Versus Egotism

Self-Expression

The process of evolution among animals has led through an increasing complexity and greater organization of structure to a heightened sense of individuality. A concomitant effect of this development is the need to express this individuality. In the preceding chapter we saw that when this need is frustrated by the conditions of social living, such as overcrowding or the formation of a mass society, self-destructive tendencies develop. Under these conditions the need for self-expression in man takes on neurotic forms. It becomes a striving for success and a desire for power.

Biologists are beginning to recognize that the need for self-expression is only slightly less important than the need for survival. If one asks, "Survival for what?" the only meaningful answer is the pleasure and joy of living, which cannot be dissociated from self-expression. Adolph Portmann in his interesting study *New Paths in Biology*, makes this point in the following sentence: "Metabolism may serve the survival of the individual, but however important it is, we must remember that an individual is not there for the sake of its metabolism but rather that metabolism serves manifest individual existence." * Self-expression is the manifestation of individual existence.

The emphasis on self-expression adds a new dimension to biology. The behavior of animals cannot be evaluated solely in terms of its survival value. Survival and self-expression are closely related functions. Portmann makes this clear in his book.

* Adolph Portmann, *New Paths in Biology*. New York, Harper & Row, 1964, p. 152.

103

He notes that "there are countless examples of how self-preservation and self-expression combine in one and the same organ." * He mentions the larynx as one example, and his reference is to song and speech. Biologists, following Konrad Lorenz's observations, have come to regard the song of birds as serving the function of proclaiming a territory rather than as an expression of inner feeling. For those of us who have found delight in the singing of birds, it is nice to know that it serves both functions.

Psychology is the new dimension that is added to biology by the emphasis on the significance of self-expression. What is expressed on the outside reflects what is going on inside the organism. Self-expression as the manifest aspect of individuality corresponds to self-awareness and self-perception as the inner or psychic aspects of individual existence. According to Portmann, "a rich appearance [among the animals] is always a reflection of a rich inner world." † But this inner world is not solely a mental phenomenon. To quote Portmann again: "No one can localize the inner world, for though we appreciate the central importance of the brain, we know that the inner life as a whole involves the body as a whole." **

Human beings, who are more highly developed than the other animals, have a greater need to express themselves. And since they are also more conscious of their individuality, their self-expression has a more conscious component. If we lack the brilliant plumage of birds or the colorful fur of other mammals, we have more than replaced them with the color and variety of our creative products. The clothes we wear, the homes we build, our arts and crafts, our songs and dances are all manifestations of this basic impulse to self-expression. Whatever utilitarian values these things serve, their role in the fulfillment of the need for self-expression cannot be ignored.

Self-expression on the conscious level is a function of the ego and of the body. It differs thereby from the forms of self-expression that are unconscious, because they are manifestations only

* *Ibid.*, p. 151.
† *Ibid.*, p. 155.
** *Ibid.*, p. 35.

of the bodily self. The color of one's hair or of one's eyes is a form of bodily self-expression, which does not involve the ego. All creative actions, however, are necessarily conscious, and the ego therefore plays an important role in formulating and executing the creative impulse. This impulse, however, does not arise in the ego. It has its genesis in the body, its motivation in the striving for pleasure, and its inspiration in the unconscious.

Self-expression, creativity, and pleasure are closely related. Every form of self-expression has a creative element and leads to pleasure and satisfaction. A woman who bakes a cake, for example, is expressing her individuality in this creative act. She has pleasure in the activity and a feeling of satisfaction in the accomplishment. In addition, there is a special satisfaction that attends the achievement. "I *made* a cake" is self-expression on the bodily level, which fulfills the bodily need to do something active and creative. "*I* made the cake" is self-expression on the ego level and provides a special ego satisfaction. I shall explore the relation of these two satisfactions in this section.

The acquisition of knowledge and the mastery of skills are important ego functions and are a major source of ego satisfactions. The "I" wants to know, and it wants to be able to do. It wants to be an active force in shaping its life. Very few of us can recall the excitement we experienced when we learned to walk or speak or read, but most of us have experienced the excitement that accompanies such achievements as learning to ride a bicycle, bake a cake, ski, drive a car, or speak a foreign language. These accomplishments provide ego satisfactions which should not, however, be separated from the pleasure of the learning process or from the pleasures which these skills promise to yield in the future.

Every project that we undertake and complete provides these dual satisfactions, one on the physical level through the pleasure of the activity and the other on the ego level through a consciousness of the achievement. This double reward corresponds to a duality in man's nature. On one hand we are conscious actors in the drama of life and therefore aware of our individual roles. Too often, however, this self-consciousness blinds us to the fact that on the other hand, like the animals, we are part of the scheme of nature, living in our bodies and dependent for our bodily pleasure on a harmonious relationship with nature.

When we are thus blinded, we become ego-conscious, that is, egotistical. An egotist confuses the ego with the self and believes that whatever promotes his ego furthers the interest of the self. This is true only within narrow limits, which I shall define later. Putting the ego first reverses the normal relationship between the ego and the bodily self and can lead to destructive behavior. The bodily self is the foundation on which the ego rests. Strengthening the foundation improves the whole structure of the personality. Repairing the roof does little for the foundation. When pleasure is sacrificed for an ego drive like success, the result can be disastrous.

Consider, for example, the person who lives beyond his means in order to impress his neighbors. Owning a big house or an expensive car will inflate his ego, but it will also cause him considerable pain and distress when he has to pay for its upkeep. He can ignore the pain only by dissociating from reality. If he suppresses the pain, he also cuts off all possibility of pleasure. The sacrifice of pleasure makes the value of the ego satisfaction he derives from his possessions questionable.

Even if a person can make the necessary money through his efforts to buy and maintain an elaborate establishment, the ego satisfactions it will afford him are hardly worth his investment of time and energy. It is one thing to work for something that will provide real pleasure; it is another thing when the object serves simply to enhance a person's image. Since we humans are self-conscious beings with egos, we are not unmindful of the images we present. The image is important because it represents the person, but it is not the person. The individual who identifies with his image rather than with his bodily self is an egotist.

No image is big enough to provide the bodily satisfactions that make life meaningful. The ego that is not fed at its roots by bodily pleasure develops an insatiable hunger. The individual dominated by an insatiable ego is under constant pressure to expand his image. His ego drive takes on a relentless quality that overrides all personal considerations to achieve its aims. The person who takes off in this direction cannot stop. If he makes one million dollars, he must strive just as hard to gain a second million, then a third, and so on. The additional money can hardly increase his security or contribute materially to his pleasure, yet the drive to continue making money seems to gain momentum with each increase in wealth. His ego is like a gas balloon that must rise higher and higher, expanding as it does so until it bursts.

Money has a strong appeal to the ego because it represents power. Each increase in wealth or power yields a measure of ego satisfaction. It enables the ego to think that it is the master of its world. It may seem only a short distance from the acquisition of knowledge and the mastery of skills to the conquest of nature, but it is the difference that separates the integrated man from the egotistic, alienated man obsessed by power. The need for power is a reflection of man's insecurity and a sign of the inadequacy of his ego. While power and wealth can add to the pleasure of life, they do so only when they are not the goals of life.

Money is not the only area in which ego drives operate. The field of spectator sports is highly charged with ego interests, and we can gain further insight into the nature of these interests from an analysis of this phenomenon. A spectator at a sporting event who is partial to one of the teams derives considerable satisfaction from the victory of his team. If he is a fan, it is not even necessary for him to watch the event in person or on TV. Just the idea of his team winning or losing carries a strong emotional charge. For a fan, the pleasure of watching the performance is often of secondary value. If his team loses, he may be plunged into a dejection that completely wipes out this pleasure. Such strong reactions are understandable if one has a personal stake in the outcome. Obviously, many people make a big ego investment in their favorite players or favorite teams and feel vindicated or let down by their performance.

A fan is identified on the ego level with the object of his admiration. Through this identification the achievements of his hero become, in a sense, his own. He gets a personal satisfaction, therefore, from his hero's achievement, although he has not participated in the activity. For the fan, identification with the hero serves the function of self-expression in a vicarious way. For the athlete, the performance is a true form of self-expression; his total being is involved in the contest. Since it is only the fan's ego that is involved, his commitment is limited and his role is confined to that of a spectator, but he reacts emotionally, as if he were totally involved. He is, in fact, expressing himself through his ego identifications.

Every ego identification is a form of self-expression. The person in our first example who bought a large house is saying to the world, "Look. *I* am the owner of this house. I am identified with it." However, it is only his ego that is identified with the house unless the person himself has taken an active part in the design or construction of the house. Similarly, the person who has amassed a large sum of money feels identified with his money. When he says, "I am worth two million dollars," he means "I am two million dollars." And the fan who is identified on an ego level with the New York Giants reacts with the feeling, "I am the New York Giants." What he actually does say is, "*We* won the game."

Self-expression through ego identifications may seem like a poor substitute for the real thing, which is self-expression through creative activity. Such, however, is the power of the ego to affect behavior that it feels like the real thing to the person making the identification. There must be some aspect of reality to all kinds of identifications. If one is a member of a club, it is valid to feel a sense of personal pride in the successes of the club. Many people are identified with their schools and feel that the achievements or failures of their graduates reflect upon themselves. While this identification can be excessive in some cases, of which the old school tie is an example, it has a legitimate basis in the fact that as a member of the student body one was involved actively in the programs and affairs of the school. Patriotism in the modern state is another ego identification that has a real basis, because it stems from one's own membership in a community.

Through his ego identifications an individual feels himself to be part of society, involved in its strivings and sharing its accomplishments and failures. Without such ego identifications, a person would feel cut off from the currents and movements in the social situation and isolated from the interests of the community. He would be forced to find his pleasure and meaning within the boundaries of the self, which no one can fully do, since pleasure depends on a harmonious relationship with the environment. By its identifications the ego extends the boundaries of the self, increasing thereby the possibilities for pleasure and satisfaction.

Problems arise when a person becomes overextended, that is, when his ego identifications compensate for a lack of self-identification. In a healthy person the ego is grounded in the feelings of the body and identified with the bodily self. Self-expression is then primarily in the form of creative living and only secondarily through ego identifications. When the identification with the body is weak and tenuous, a person's identity is vague, and his self-expression in creative living is greatly reduced. Such an individual, who is alienated from his bodily self, must seek an identity and a means of self-expression through ego identifications. This becomes his main mode of self-expression, and in this case it is a poor substitute for the real thing.

Too great an investment in ego identifications diverts energy from the self, which becomes more depleted in proportion as the ego becomes more inflated. The ego satisfactions that one gets from these investments do not contribute to the enjoyment of life. Like illusions, another function of the dissociated ego, they may sustain the spirit, but they do nothing for the body. I have heard many successful people complain that they got no "real satisfaction" from their seeming success.

There is another aspect to the ego's role in self-expression, and this is the need for recognition. Every conscious act of self-expression feels incomplete until it evokes a response from the other members of the community. If the response is favorable, one gets an extra measure of satisfaction from the achievement. If it is negative, one's satisfaction is reduced. A creative action that goes unnoticed generally leaves one with a feeling of frustration. A writer is disappointed if no one reads his book, an artist is discouraged if no one reacts to his paintings, and a cook is unhappy if her work is unnoticed. It seems we all need some recognition of our individuality. Without this recognition it is difficult to maintain one's identity or to sustain the sense of self.

Having an ego, one is conscious of being an individual, but one is also conscious of being separate and alone. As much as one wants to be an individual, one also wants to be accepted as part of the group. The first desire is satisfied through an act of self-expression, the second through the recognition given to this act. Since both desires flow through the ego, their fulfillment leads to ego satisfactions. We can also discern a quantitative factor in this process. A stronger ego is associated with a higher degree of individuality, a greater need for self-expression, and a more intense need for recognition. A weaker ego has a lesser drive for self-expression and is content with lesser recognition.

The desire for recognition underlies the phenomenon of status. The amount of recognition determines one's status, and the drive for status derives from the ego's need of recognition. Status is a phenomenon which we humans share with many animals. The pecking order among barnyard fowl, the feeding order in a hunting pack, the priority in the selection of mates are often determined by status. For the species, status serves to insure the survival of the fittest. In terms of the individual, it furthers his sense of identity and supports his ego. As long as the ego is identified with the body, as in the animal, status reflects the individual's physical endowment. Among human beings, however, many factors unconnected with the body determine an individual's standing or status in the community. Hereditary position, wealth, manner of speech, family relationships play important roles in determining status.

When status is not a true indication of an individual's personal qualities, it acts as a disruptive force, dissociating the ego from the body. Status shapes an individual's ego image. The higher the status, the bigger the image, for we can *see* ourselves only through the eyes of others. However, we *feel* ourselves from within if we are in touch with our bodies. No difficulty arises when the image corresponds to the reality of the body, that is, when the way we see ourselves corresponds to what we feel. A lack of correspondence disturbs our sense of identity. We become confused about who we are. The conscious mind is tempted to identify with the image and reject the reality of the body. This dissociation of the ego from the body leads to unreality in living. The person becomes obsessed with his image, concerned about his position, and committed to the struggle for power to enhance his status. Pleasure and creativity fade into the background of his life.

The Role of the Ego in Pleasure

The ego plays an important role in pleasure when the ego is identified with the body. A strong ego permits a greater enjoyment of life. A weak ego diminishes the capacity for pleasure. These statements can be understood if one pictures the body as a bow and the ego as the conscious force that draws the bowstring and bends the bow. In this picture the flight of the arrow is the experience of pleasure, for it represents the release of the tension in the bow. A strong ego will create a greater tension in the bow or support a greater tension in the body. It will therefore produce a fuller flight of the arrow when it lets go. When the bow is not fully extended because the ego is weak, the arrow falls impotently to the ground. Ignoring for a moment the question of whether the arrow finds its mark or not, we should realize that pleasure is represented by the free flight of the arrow. And actually, it is a pleasure to shoot an arrow into the air and to sense its flight as an expression of one's effort.

> I shot an arrow into the air.
> It fell to earth I know not where.

Most people are too ego-conscious to be content with simple pleasure. If they shoot arrows, they demand targets that will challenge their skills. Shooting at a target adds another element to this picture. If one hits the target, one gets an additional ego satisfaction from the success that increases the pleasure of the activity. A failure to hit the target produces an ego disappointment that blunts the simple pleasure of shooting arrows. The extra satisfaction that success provides also serves as an incentive to greater effort. The ego is enhanced by success and can in subsequent undertakings exert a greater force. It is diminished by failure, which weakens the will. When the ego is identified with the body, success increases the body's capacity to tolerate tension and therefore to experience pleasure. When this identification does not exist, however, success goes to a person's head, inflating his ego and tempting him to extend himself beyond his capabilities.

The ego can also be compared with a general. It is the head

of the personality, but unlike the general, who is the head of an army, it is in the forefront of every contact with the external world. I have located it in the forebrain, close to the eyes and the other sense organs. This area is the part of the body that receives the most stimulation from the environment, which facilitates the ego's function of perception. And through its control of voluntary movement the ego sets the tone of our relationship to the environment. Normally, an expansion of the ego in reaction to a positive response from the environment (recognition of one's self-expression) irradiates the whole body with excitement. When the ego collapses because its foundation in the body is weak and it is not sustained from the outside by recognition, depression results.

At the opposite end of the body is the genital apparatus, the center for the sexual functions. Sex is the epitome of pleasure and creativity. This is not to say that all pleasure is sexual or that all sexual activities are pleasurable. Sexuality is the body's main channel for the discharge of tension and the individual's most important creative expression. Between these two poles of the organism there is a pulsation of energy. This polarity is based on the obvious fact that the upper or fore end of the body is primarily concerned with intake or charging up, while the lower or hind end is involved in the processes of elimination and discharge. The flow of energy or feeling between the two poles of the body is pendular. Its rhythm is determined by the energetic processes of the body. When a pleasurable contact is made with the environment, energy and feeling flow into the upper half of the body. The ego becomes stimulated, and the body becomes excited. After the excitation reaches a certain intensity, the direction of flow is reversed. Energy and feeling flow downward into the channels of discharge, either sexually or through other movements. As land animals we move in relation to the ground. Thus, when a child is excited, he jumps for joy. Animals in the same situation leap and bound, and adult humans dance. All energy is ultimately discharged into the earth.

In all pendular phenomena, the movement in one direction is equal to that in the opposite direction. The flow of feeling into the sexual organs is no greater, therefore, than the flow of feeling upward into the head and vice versa. This means that the strength of the ego determines the intensity of the sexual drive and that the amount of sexual pleasure and satisfaction influences the strength of the ego.

This relationship between the ego and the sexual function can be extended to all forms of pleasure. The stronger the ego, the greater the pleasure. In turn, pleasure feeds the ego. The more pleasure one has, the stronger does his ego become. A stronger ego can support a greater excitation, which is then transformed into pleasure and satisfaction when release occurs.

The pendular swing of energy between the two poles of the body, that is, between the upper and the lower halves of the body, is continuous during our waking hours. Every step we take involves a consciousness of direction and a feeling of contact with the ground. If the latter is absent, we either walk mechanically or float like spirits. When this pulsation of energy or feeling flows freely, each step and every movement is a pleasure. In more intense activities the pulsation increases in degree and rhythm. A higher degree of excitation is generally paralleled by a quicker rhythm, as in running and dancing. Both of these activities, in comparison with walking, entail a greater consciousness of the aim of the activity and a greater sense of the body in motion. There is more ego involvement on one hand and greater pleasurable release on the other. The presence of this pulsation guarantees that whatever one does, mind and body function together harmoniously to promote the timing and effectiveness of the action and to insure pleasure and satisfaction from its consummation.

Pleasure is experienced when a total commitment of mind and body is made to any activity. It is the result of a total surrender to impulse and feeling coupled with the awareness that the aim and timing of the action are right. If, in addition, the goal is achieved, one has a deep-seated sense of satisfaction. Three factors combine to produce this special feeling of full satisfaction: an inner surge of excitation, the conscious coordination and timing of the movement, and the outer desired result. When body, mind, and movement coalesce in a moment of personal truth, the feeling is one of fulfillment. At the moment of fusion the excitement transcends the boundaries of the self and transports the individual to the heights of joy.

Those who have experienced these moments know that they have an almost mystical quality. Moments before the final event, one intuitively senses that it will happen. Before the ball meets the bat the batter may sense the home run coming. Before the climax of sex actually occurs the lover may know inwardly that the orgasm will be ecstatic. Before the words are put on paper the writer may become aware that they will form a beautiful phrase. Perhaps the most common example is bowling, in which one can feel that he will make a strike as soon as the ball leaves his hand. When these things happen, it seems as if strange forces have guided our actions.

The ball player may call it timing, the lover may speak of his feeling, and the writer may ascribe his achievement to imagination. These terms merely denote that a perfect harmony was attained between the self and the world, which made the action appear effortless and the result inevitable. In its more limited activities the wild animal knows this joy of perfect harmony. Its movements are generally unerring, its timing is incredibly accurate, and its commitment to life is always total. The wild animal lives, of course, in a far greater harmony with its environment than we humans do with ours.

The feeling of complete harmony with the environment that can lead to the perfect action is the underlying principle of Zen mastery. The Zen master has attained a degree of integration in which he is one with his actions and with his world. He is fully himself and yet completely selfless at the same time. This contradiction can be explained by the total identification of the ego with the body. The distinction between will and want is eliminated. Only when the ego wills what the body wants does the body respond unerringly and unhesitatingly to the will of the ego.

It would be naïve to believe that this perfect harmony can be achieved in all areas of life and at all times. Fortunate are the people who have attained it in any one sphere of activity. Within that sphere their actions have the mark of the master. Others have known it at moments, and it has been what Abraham Maslow calls a "peak experience." It is the basis of the feeling of joy. And it is the principle that underlies the creative approach to life.

The Role of the Ego in Pain

The ego operates with images, and its satisfactions are derived from the realization of its images. For example, we all have a self-image that we are constantly striving to realize. This image represents a potential that we hope to achieve. It inspires our efforts, and it directs and coordinates our activities. Its realization promises happiness. A hardworking man may dream of a life of leisure, a mother may dream of the future of her children, a writer may dream of the great novel he will write, and so on. Images are a part of the life of every individual. They are created by the upward and outward flow of feeling into the ego and toward the world. They enlarge our outlooks and expand our spirits. They excite the body and create sensations of pleasure—anticipatory pleasure, because the true pleasure awaits the realization of the image and the discharge of the excitation which then occurs.

Every project one undertakes involves an image. The businessman starting a new venture already pictures himself running it. The housewife planning new decor imagines herself living with it. These images are exciting because one anticipates that life will be more enjoyable after their realization. But this may not happen.

If the ego is dissociated from the body, the downward flow of excitation does not take place. A pleasurable discharge of excitation does not occur. Release of excitation through coordinated and graceful body movement is blocked by chronic muscular tensions that represent suppressed negative and hostile impulses. It is prevented from finding its natural outlet in love by repressed sexual anxieties. It is disturbed by latent insecurities, stemming from one's early relationship to his mother, which later affect one's relationship to the earth and the ground, symbolic extensions of the mother. The person who is not well grounded, literally and figuratively, is afraid to "let down" or "let go." He is, as we say today, "hung up." The result is an inability to experience pleasure and an increase in the states of tension and pain.

Excitation that is blocked from flowing downward overcharges the ego and creates new images that have to be realized before pleasure can be experienced. New projects are undertaken, further efforts are made, but their effect is only to increase the tension and the pain. It is easy to see how a self-destructive spiral develops. One has to climb higher and higher on the social ladder, each step of which produces a momentary ego satisfaction that soon fades into discontent. One has to make more money, buy a bigger house, attain a higher political position, write more books, and so on. Each move upward that is not followed by a corresponding flow downward and discharge of the excitation serves only to increase the state of pain, which then furthers the dissociation of the ego from the body.

The dissociated ego confuses the image with reality. It sees the image as an end rather than as a means to an end. Its goals take on a compulsive quality, and the pleasure of living is lost. It is sadly true, as psychologists point out, that we are a goal-oriented people. We mistake the goal for the pleasure and fail to see that the goal is a promise of pleasure, not a guarantee of it. We tend to regard the achievement of the goal as the reward itself. Inevitably, then, one goal is replaced by another, while the postponement of pleasure continues indefinitely. Progress *per se* becomes the final objective, and our lives become harnessed to a statistical table or a graph.

The end result of ego striving is depression or death. The postponement of bodily pleasure drains a person's good feelings and saps his energies. Sooner or later the effort collapses and the ego, like a balloon that has risen too high, falls, plunging the individual into a depression. If this happens, the person's life is spared, for the depression stops the senseless striving and allows the body to recuperate. In some people, however, the ego holds on to the bitter end. The collapse that occurs in this situation is physical rather than psychological. How often we hear of people who seemingly at the summit of their achievement die of a heart attack, cancer, or some similar cause. I have personally known of several cases in which this happened. There is a limit to the body's tolerance of stress, and when this limit is passed, illness develops.

Egotism

Psychiatrists are often referred to as "headshrinkers." This designation indicates that one of their main tasks is to reduce the inflated egos of their patients. What they actually do, of course, is bring the patient down to earth. By eliminating his illusions the patient comes into better contact with reality and his functioning is improved. In the popular mind this is viewed as a shrinking process; the ego is cut down to the size of the body and is grounded in the functions of the body. The patient's ego is not attacked directly by the psychotherapist. Such an approach can have a disastrous effect, since the person is identified with his ego. The collapse of the ego, as I mentioned above, can plunge an individual into depression or suicide. Instead, the patient is brought into contact with the reality of his existence as a physical being, that is, with his body and his feelings. To the degree that a patient can accept his feelings and identify with his body, he is released from the pain of trying to fulfill an image that was imposed upon him by his parents and society.

The image that dominates most individuals today is that of success. In one form or another most people strive for success. Women strive to be successful wives, successful mothers, or successful socialites. Men strive to be successful lovers, successful businessmen, or successful professionals. If one doesn't achieve success, one may be considered a failure. This tendency to judge one's life in terms of success and failure shows the degree to which we are dominated by our egos. Passing such a judgment on life is a destructive action far more serious than the judgments that are involved in the conceptual emotions of guilt, shame, and vanity. It seems that as we escape from the burden of guilt that plagued our forefathers, we subject ourselves to the greater burden of responsibility for success and failure.

By assuming this responsibility, man becomes an egotist. He sees himself as ruler of the world and master of his soul. Never before in his history has man had such hubris. In all previous times he has seen himself as subject to a higher law, as part of a larger order, and as the instrument of a superior power. There have always been some individuals whose egotism set them above moral principles, who assumed a divine authority. Their conquests carved a trail of pain and suffering. The wounds they inflicted have not yet fully healed. But these conquerors were a passing phenomenon. Their power faded with their deaths, and their influence was offset by the deep religious convictions of people.

This situation changed with dramatic suddenness in the twentieth century. Science ended and technology undermined man's belief in a supernatural force that had the power to mold his life and shape his destiny. Two world wars shattered his faith in moral law and natural justice. And the rise of psychology made him conscious of the emotional factors that determine his thinking. Finally, with the advent of the automobile and the breakup of community living, each person became an individual who felt responsible for his own life. This is an awesome responsibility, one that only an egotist can face with equanimity. Yet naïvely and blindly modern man stepped into the role vacated by God, unaware that in the process he was losing his soul.

Speaking of the soul is a tricky affair. No one knows what it is, and many will argue that it doesn't exist. I shall describe it as a quality of being. A person who does not feel that he is part of a larger scheme, who does not sense that his life is part of a natural process that is bigger than himself, can be said to be without a soul. The soul of a man is that which unites him to the past and commits him to the future. It binds him to the earth and relates him to all living creatures. It is the basis for his identification with cosmic phenomena and the source of the oceanic feeling of unity with the cosmos. If he has a soul, a man can break through the narrow boundaries of the self and experience the joy and ecstasy of oneness with the universal. If he doesn't have a soul, a man is locked in the prison of his mind and his pleasures are limited to ego satisfactions.

A person without a soul is an egotist. He sees the world only in terms of himself. His wife and children are extensions of his self-image. His interests reflect his ego needs. If he skis, for example, it is done to prove his ability and to impress others with his skill. The magnificence of the mountain with its covering of snow, its solitude, its frosted trees doesn't touch him. If he makes love to a woman, it is done with little feeling. The ego satisfaction of conquest or of satisfying the woman is more important to him than the experience of love. He may be socially conscious, but his participation in causes stems from his ego identifications. He may be a "successful" person or he may consider himself a failure, for his ego is the arbiter of all his actions.

The egotist thinks of himself as a creative person, since he is constantly expressing himself. What he is actually expressing is his image of himself, an image that is devoid of beauty, grace, or truth. These qualities belong to the individual who is in touch with the deeper forces of life, the forces that create and sustain life, not just human life and certainly not just the life of a single human being. Truth, beauty, and grace define an organism's relationship to its environment. They express the fact that the relationship is a harmonious one, productive of pleasure and oriented toward the enjoyment of living. Every animal, from the worm in the earth to the porpoise frolicking in the sea, has these qualities. It has a soul, and therefore it is self-expressive and creative. Without a soul there can be no true creativity, no true art. But where an animal lives its art, man projects his. In both cases true art is the expression of an organism's deep feelings, a manifestation of its soul.

The twentieth century saw the birth of egotistical man and the demise of true art. This is a big statement and a broad generalization, but there is ample evidence to support it. Since twentieth century art is expressionistic, any expression can be considered art. It no longer matters what is expressed. Beauty, grace, and truth are irrelevant. The situation would be ludicrous, were it not for the fact that the artist as egoist is supported by critics and art dealers who are also egoists. The critics decide what is significant on the basis of their own ideas, and the dealers decide what is salable on the basis of popularity and fashion. The art market has become a fashion market in which no one knows who sets the trends but in which a trend that catches on determines success.

Not only in his art but in his architecture, in his economy, in his treatment of nature, egotistical man has the arrogance to think that whatever he does is expressive and significant. He knows that his cities are ugly, that his countryside is despoiled, that his rivers are dirty and his air polluted, but he naïvely believes that given enough power and enough money he can create a paradise. Does he not realize that his quest of power over nature has destroyed the basis of a creative relationship between himself and nature? That his technology has alienated him from the living process? And that his science has robbed him of spirituality?

No, he does not fully realize these things. He sees the mind as the essence of his personality, while the body is regarded as merely the setting in which the jewel of the mind shines and glitters. The corollary of this attitude is that the body is merely a mechanism which reflects the operation of the mind. It is possible, of course, to extend the concept of mind to include the body, to make the psychic self synonymous with the somatic self. But such extensions are often merely rationalizations to cover man's bias in favor of the mind and prejudice against the body.

The soul of a man is in his body. Through his body a person is part of life and part of nature. In the growth and organization of his body he passes through all the stages of evolution. Ontogeny, we say, recapitulates phylogeny. His body incorporates, therefore, the history of life on earth. It includes many of the common elements of nature, although they are combined in unique ways. It is subject to the laws of nature, of which it is truly a part. Then why the bias against the body? Why is it derogated in favor of the mind?

Many answers suggest themselves, although none seems definitive. Man's body is not greatly different from those of the other mammals, whereas his conscious mind is unique. Having discovered this fact only lately in the course of his evolutionary history, man lords it over all other animals, with disdain and contempt for their stupidity and ignorance. He has turned against his body because it represents his animal nature. He has also turned against it because it is part of nature, while his mind is solely his own. A man can believe that he possesses his mind, but he never fully possesses his body. There are processes in the body which the mind can never comprehend or control—the beat of the heart, the surge of feeling, the longing for love. And because the mind cannot fully control the body, it is afraid of the body as it is of the unknown forces in nature.

The body is corporeal; it grows and decays. The mind, so it seems, is ethereal, pure, and incorruptible. The body is heavy and subject to the law of gravity. The mind is light, and its thoughts transcend time and space. The body is vulnerable; it can be hurt and broken. In contrast, the mind seems impregnable. Children have a saying that illustrates this idea. When taunted by their playmates, they answer: "Sticks and stones may break my bones, but words can never hurt me." Compared to the animals that were his predators in his early history, man's body was weak and relatively helpless. His conscious mind, however, was powerful. He could outwit them, and in the end he did outdo them.

But the body has feeling, and it alone can experience pleasure, joy, and ecstasy. It alone has beauty and grace, for apart from the body these terms are meaningless. Try to define beauty without referring to the body, and you will see how impossible it is. If you say that beauty is something pleasing to the eyes, you have incorporated two body referents, pleasure and eyes, in your definition. It is our bodies that appreciate the freshness of a stream, the sweet taste of pure water, the sight of blue sky, the song of a bird, the smell of a flower, and so on. If we are in touch with our bodies, we enjoy being part of nature and being able to share its splendors. If we are identified with our bodies, we have souls, for through our bodies we are identified with all creation.

As a psychiatrist, I daily see the suffering of the egotistic human being. Whether he considers himself a success or regards himself as a failure, his basic complaint is that he is dissatisfied, unfulfilled, and unable to experience pleasure and joy. Being out of touch with his body, he does not sense its painful condition; he is unaware of the chronic muscular tensions that block his self-expression. His problems stem from the dissociation of thinking from feeling, from a distrust of feeling as a guide to behavior, and from fear of the body's involuntary responses. Placing his faith in a dissociated ego, he relies on "rational" thought and will for responses that should be emotional and motivated by pleasurable feelings. It is not surprising that sooner or later he becomes depressed and finds life empty and meaningless.

I call this patient an egotist, because he wants to know how to perform better, how to achieve his ego image. This emphasis on the "how" rather than the "why" which is typical of our current approach to life characterizes the egotistical attitude. It assumes that man can do anything if he has the right information. It denotes the arrogance of the mind, for it ignores the fact that thinking is conditioned by feeling and that creativity is a function of the body's quest for pleasure. Like all psychiatrists, I have to reduce the patient's inflated ego, but my patients do not describe me as a "headshrinker." This is because I work with the body as well as the mind. The aim of bioenergetic therapy is to restore the unity of the personality, to reestablish the identification of the ego with the body, and to free the body from the chronic muscular tensions that block its motility and restrict its respiration.

In the integrated personality the distinctions I have drawn between thinking and feeling, between the voluntary and the involuntary movements of the body, and between the ego and the body do not exist except as artificial constructs, artifacts of speech and discussion. The different levels of functioning are not discernible to the naked eye. No thought is uttered without some note of feeling in the voice. No word is written that doesn't carry an emotional charge. No bodily movement occurs that isn't perceived as pleasure or pain. The ego doesn't function as a separate entity. It is part of the unitary structure that we call an individual. It is one aspect or view (the view from the top) of a person's unique personality.

The individual exists, simply that. Like all other animal organisms, he tries to make this existence as enjoyable as possible. He can, however, approach this aim from two directions. If he approaches it from the body, he will realize that pleasure is a state of harmony with the natural and the human environment. He will sense that joy is the merger of the inner and the outer and that in ecstasy the boundaries of the self completely dissolve. He will know that the ego, in defining his individuality, potentiates its surrender. This is the approach of a person with a soul. If, on the other hand, he approaches this aim from the point of view of the ego, he will strive for power and success. His achievements will give him a momentary sense of ego satisfaction, but his pleasure will be minimal and limited to sensual gratification. Overconscious of his ego, he will never know the joy of surrender. He will confuse the image of individuality with true individuality. This is the approach of the egotist, the person without a soul.

6 · Truth, Beauty, and Grace

Truth and Deception

Biologists have been impressed for some time with man's rise to dominance in the animal kingdom. In view of the immense power at his command today, no one questions his dominance now. But this was not always so. Before he gained this power he was at a relative disadvantage physically compared to the animals he hunted or which hunted him. He had neither great speed nor great strength. He lacked the long canine teeth with which a baboon protects itself. He was naked, exposed, and vulnerable. Sometime in the course of his development he learned to use a club and a stone knife, but these were not formidable weapons. The big advantage man had in the struggle for survival was his better brain. If he could not outfight the other animals or outrun them, he could and did outwit them.

More than any other animal man lives by his wits. In any natural environment survival often depends on keeping one's wits. The hunted must always be alert to the possibility of danger and aware of avenues of escape. The hunter must know the way of the prey, how to approach it, and how to make a kill. But the hunter also has to be adept in the use of stealth and deceit, for the wary prey often has to be caught off guard. In this struggle for survival man has outmatched his rivals.

In any discussion of truth and deception we must recognize that deceit has an important part to play in the affairs of man and beast. In many areas of life it has a positive value. In the game of football, for example, we greatly admire the player who knows how to use deceit to throw his opponent off balance and gain the advantage. Plays are hidden and camouflaged for the same reason. In the sport of boxing the smoothness of a feint which misleads an opponent is regarded as the mark of a master.

A major part of the strategy of warfare is based on the use of deception. No general with his wits about him would telegraph his attack to the enemy; he would, on the contrary, make every effort to hide and mask his moves. But it is not only in the realm of physical combat that deceit plays an important role. The game of poker would lose its excitement if deceit were prohibited. And chess would not be the challenge it is if deceit were not an integral aspect of the game. In many situations the proper use of deceit can spell the difference between victory and defeat.

Generally speaking, the ability to be deceitful is an important asset in all situations of opposition or contention. Thus in every situation where dominance or power is an issue one would be naïve not to be on guard against the possibility of deceit. Deception is out of place and has an obvious negative value in situations that call for cooperation and understanding. To deceive a person whom one claims to love is an act of betrayal. The deception destroys the pleasure which the relationship was designed to promote. Of even more serious import is deceit of the self: Self-deception is disastrous.

In situations of conflict the conscious use of deceit demands a degree of objectivity that increases the level of consciousness. To evaluate properly the worth of a deception one has to place himself in the position of the opponent. Uppermost in the mind of the person planning a deception is his opponent's response. "If I move so or say this, what will he do or think?" And the success of the deception depends on how accurately one has gauged this response. The effective use of deceit requires that one step outside the self and become conscious of both the other and of the self.

The significance of deceit for self-consciousness was brought to my attention by an observation by one of my patients. She told me that she recalled the moment when she first became self-conscious, or conscious of her individuality. She was about four or five years old, and her parents had demanded an explanation from her for something she did of which they did not approve. Quickly the thought flashed through her mind that she did not have to answer them truthfully. "At that moment," she said, "I became aware of myself as an independent being. I realized that

I had the power to deceive them." Although I heard this statement more than twenty years ago, I have not forgotten it, because it struck me as containing an important insight into
the human personality.

Consciousness arises from the recognition of differences. This
concept is stated and developed by Erich Neumann in his book
*The Origin and History of Consciousness.** It means that if
one is to be conscious of light, one must have experienced
the dark. A person or animal living only in light or darkness
would not be conscious of either. Similarly, to know what "up"
is one must also know what "down" represents. To be aware of
one's self one must be equally aware of the other. Self-consciousness must depend, likewise, on the recognition of a pair of opposites or alternatives of self-expression. If an individual can only
speak the truth, he lacks a choice. Without a choice, his self-
expression is limited and his consciousness reduced. Recogniz-
ing that one has a choice whether or not to answer truthfully
strengthens the ego's mastery of behavior, since the ego, operating through the intellect, is the judge of truth. This choice in
effect places the ego in the driver's seat of the personality.
Through its ability to discriminate between truth and deception, right and wrong, the ego, which is identified with the intellect, becomes the center of self-consciousness.

Can a person gain this ability to discriminate truth from
falsehood without exploring the realm of deceit? I believe not.
Many children go through an early phase of development in
which they tell lies. The lie often is a denial of some action
which the parents would regard as wrong. For example, a child
may take some money that is lying around and hide it. When
confronted by his parents with their conviction that he took the
money, the child, in his most innocent manner, denies any
knowledge of the matter. Some time later he may admit the
action, or the money may be discovered among his possessions.
Most parents would make a horrible scene and punish the child
for lying, but if they are wise, they will regard the incident as
a childhood exploration of deceit and trust that he will learn
to use it properly.

* Erich Neumann, *Origins and History of Consciousness,* trans. by R. F. C.
Hull. Princeton, Princeton University Press, 1954.

The suppression of a child's ability to be deceitful must have a destructive effect on its developing personality. I had not given this problem much thought until a patient brought it up following a public lecture I gave on the role of deceit in thinking. This patient suffered from a serious deficiency in her sense of self. She even lacked the normal facade with which most people confront the world. She was very open in her expression of feeling, but her feelings were insincere. Her repeated avowals of her intent to improve, to take better care of herself, for example, had no effect on her behavior. Despite my repeated contrast of her statements with her behavior, she could not see that her words were empty phrases designed solely to gain my approval. Her attitude was unique in the degree to which she resisted any suggestion that her seeming cooperation covered an underlying negativity. My lecture touched a chord in the patient and produced the following material. I will quote her statements.

"I have never been able to tell a lie. I've always had to tell the truth. Everything I thought or felt or wished was my mother's concern, and I was very flattered by her interest. I don't know how she got the idea across to me that I couldn't withhold anything from her.

"I could not be deceptive, but I always admired this ability. I was not afraid of being a bad girl but of being a withholding girl. I felt I had no right to withhold anything from my mother. She was always right. She had an uncanny knack for spotting a withholding. I kept a dairy which she read. I wanted approval, but my mother never approved. The only way I knew to get love was to play along. I didn't feel I had the right to any privacy."

What happened to this patient was that her need for privacy, to withhold personal information, to maintain a sense of self, and to be deceitful if necessary to protect this self, turned into self-deception through the suppression of this natural tendency. Having surrendered her privacy, she lost her sense of self. Unable to lie, she didn't know the truth. I have rarely run into a more difficult case in the course of my practice.

While my patient was denied the right to be deceitful, her mother practiced this art on her child. Her pretended interest was a cover for her desire to dominate. "I was brought up as an experiment. I had to be unusual," my patient said. Despite these statements, she could not recognize the extent of her mother's destructiveness. She never saw her mother's deceit.

Children in our culture are brought up to regard the telling of a lie as bad, wrong, or sinful. This practice is based on the fact that it is destructive to lie in relationships that are based on trust and affection or in situations that require a cooperative effort to achieve a common end. A lie undermines trust and introduces antagonisms which destroy the pleasure these relationships offer. However, if honesty exposes a person to punishment and pain, it will require an effort of will to be honest, since the natural tendency of all organisms is to avoid pain. One will make this effort if the threat of pain is mild. When the threat of pain exceeds an acceptable level, forcing a person to tell the truth against his own interest puts him into conflict with himself and disrupts the integrity of his personality. Democratic governments protect their citizens against this harmful effect by providing constitutional guarantees against self-incrimination. Unfortunately, the relationship between parents and children contains no such safeguards.

There is a well-known maxim that rules are made to be broken, and young children are especially notorious for their disregard of rules. Desiring freedom and seeking pleasure, children naturally rebel against restraints. If parents use punishments to enforce rules, it is difficult to see how children can avoid telling lies. The only alternative for the child who has broken a rule is to say nothing at all. Unfortunately, the right to silence is not respected in most homes. The result is either a child who lies or a child who cannot lie because he has been deprived of his sense of self.

The right to set rules and inflict punishment is an exercise of power. It is based on the assumption that hostile and negative forces in a community can only be controlled by such means. But power in itself creates antagonisms that interfere with cooperative and community living. We must accept the fact that such forces exist in the larger communities in which we live and that, realistically, some laws and power are necessary for the smooth operation of large societies. But if we introduce this concept into the home and family situation, we undermine the basis for pleasure and joy in these relationships. When power enters a home by the front door in the form of punishing parents, distrust and deceit enter by the back door in the form of rebellious and lying children.

The home that is governed by the pleasure principle, in contrast to one that is ruled by power, produces children who are sure of themselves, who know the difference between truth and deception, and who can cooperate to promote pleasure and joy. This is not to say that such children may not occasionally lie. In every home there are some rules; there is always some threat of punishment, some exercise of power. To maintain the trust and affection that bind the family together, the rules are kept to a minimum and are designed to further the pleasure of all members. The use of punishment and power is a clear manifestation that trust and affection have weakened and that cooperation and mutual pleasure have diminished. The lie itself is never punished, for it is a clear indication that more trust must be extended.

The right to punish a child is a betrayal of the trust a child places in his parent. The child trusts that the parent will do nothing to cause it pain but will do everything to give it pleasure and promote its happiness. When, however, the parents proclaim this aim in words but inflict pain and punishment, the child feels betrayed and deceived. The idea that punishment is inflicted for the victim's good is recognized today as a rationalization. We incarcerate a convict to protect society, and we punish a child to insure his submission to the will and power of the parents. Yet many parents believe that punishment is good for the child. Spare the rod and spoil the child is an old maxim that belonged to a sex-negative and pleasure-denying culture. It represents an uncreative approach to life.

No single factor is more responsible for the loss of a person's creative potential than self-deception. This takes many forms. In the first chapter I pointed out how we deceive ourselves through the morality of fun. Faith in power is another form of self-deception, egotism is a third, and the belief that punishment has a positive effect is a fourth. A person deceives himself each time he is not true to himself. But to be true to himself a person must know who he is and what he feels. If his feelings are suppressed, his behavior will be a reflection of ideas that have been instilled in him and will not be an expression of his true being or self.

Self-deception is the result of a loss of contact with the bodily self. The person who does not sense what is going on in his body is out of touch with himself. His sensing and therefore his senses are awry. Unable to rely on his senses, he believes what he is told or what he reads when it is presented as objective fact because he has no way of assessing truth. He is susceptible to advertising and slogans and vulnerable to the big lie. In following all the current fads he thinks he is being an individual, whereas he is really only a mass individual. No one chooses to deceive himself. Self-deception develops when a person has been so deeply deceived in his personal relationships that he no longer trusts his own senses.

Thinking and Feeling

Thinking is ordinarily regarded as being opposed to feeling. The thinking person is contrasted to the impulsive person, the individual who acts on his feelings without thinking. "Stop to think" is the command of reason. It may seem like a contradiction, therefore, to say that what one feels is intimately connected with what one thinks. Yet if we examine our thought processes, we will be surprised at how much of our thinking is related to our feelings, how much of our thinking has an emotional basis. Most of our ordinary thinking is subjective: We think about ourselves, how we feel, what we are going to do, how we will do it, and so on. It requires an effort of will for us to become objective in our thought processes.

Thinking plays a dual role with regard to feeling. When a person is trying to think objectively, thinking is opposed to feeling. At other times thinking is subjective and is highly colored by feeling. In subjective thinking the line of thought runs parallel to the feeling. In objective thinking it runs contrary to the feeling; that is, one looks at the feeling critically. This dual role of thinking in relation to feeling suggests that there is a dialectical relationship between these two processes. It can be shown that they have a common origin in the unconscious but diverge and become antithetical on the level of consciousness.

From the point of view of consciousness, thinking and feeling represent different aspects of the function of perception. A feeling is a sensory perception of a bodily process and carries an energetic charge or affect. Feelings can be quantitatively differentiated. Anger, for example, has a different intensity, or affective charge, from rage. These quantitative differences permit us to construct an emotional spectrum of anger feelings. But even anger itself is subject to variations of intensity. One can be more angry or less. A thought, on the other hand, is a psychic perception of a bodily process in the form of an image. The image, or thought, itself carries no charge and has no quantitative aspect. But since no two images are identical, they are qualitatively different. The motive power or charge behind a thought is due to the feeling that accompanies it. These relationships between thinking and feeling are illustrated in the following diagram.

Perception—Consciousness

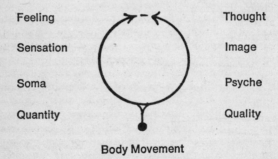

Feeling		Thought
Sensation		Image
Soma		Psyche
Quantity		Quality

Body Movement

Bioenergetic bodily processes

The functional identity of thinking and feeling stems from their common origin in body movement. Every movement of the body that is perceived by the conscious mind gives rise to both a feeling and a thought. The awareness of feeling occurs in a different part of the brain from the formation of a thought.

The centers for feeling, pleasure, or pain and the different emotions are located in the midbrain and hypothalamus. When the nerve impulses, set off by body movements, reach these centers, a person becomes aware of feelings. The impulse doesn't stop at these lower centers, however, but passes on through other nerves to the cerebral hemispheres, where image formation and symbolic thought take place. Because the cerebral hemispheres are the newer and more advanced portions of the brain, we are justified in regarding the thinking process as representing a higher level of consciousness. This may explain why we can think about our feelings but not feel our thoughts. Since, however, perception is a function of consciousness in general, as long as we are conscious and moving we will have both feelings and thoughts.

The concept that body movements give rise to feelings and thoughts runs counter to ordinary thinking. We are accustomed to see movement as a result of thinking and feeling rather than the other way around. This is because we view all personal events through the ego, which occupies a position at the top of the hierarchical pyramid of personality functions. Seen from below, movement not only precedes but also provides the substance for our feelings and thoughts. These informative movements are the involuntary bodily movements. Volitional movements, on the other hand, proceed from feeling and thought.

To place thinking and feeling first in the order of bodily events one has to ignore substantial evidence to the contrary. The fundamental quality of the living organism is its property of spontaneous motility. It is alive because it moves, and we assume it is dead when its body becomes motionless. With a human being we listen for the heartbeat or look for signs of breathing. In making a determination of life or death we do not inquire after feelings and thoughts. We rightly assume that they are absent in a dead man and that they can be present only in a living person.

From the point of view of consciousness, they are not always present. When consciousness dims in sleep, conscious feelings and thoughts fade out, too. They may recur in dreams, but it is now known that dreaming is accompanied by increased bodily activity, especially by rapid eye movements. In the absence of movement, feeling disappears. If a person doesn't move his arm for a long time, it becomes numb and he doesn't feel it. We say it has gone to sleep. Even though one can move it consciously, the feeling is missing. Reactivating the circulation, however, restores the feeling. This phenomenon is also observed in schizophrenic conditions, where there may be a loss of feeling in the whole body. The patient may complain that his body is dead. This symptom, known as depersonalization, can be overcome by stimulating respiration and movement and reestablishing the connection beween thinking and fceling.

A connection between thinking and movement has been reported by many writers. Sandor Ferenczi pointed out that muscular activity is an aid to thinking. We pace the floor when we are trying to think through a problem. Silvano Arieti traces the development of thought from the *exocept,* a simple internal representation of motor movements and responses to the complex concepts of philosophy and science. It has been said that every thought is an incipient action and that thinking enables us to test the action in our minds before embarking on its execution. In this respect thinking differs from feeling, which impels a person to immediate action.

If thinking stems from movement, it follows that man's greater thinking capacity derives ultimately from the greater range of movements that he is capable of performing. A more extensive range of movements requires for its coordination a more elaborate neural mechanism. It is significant in this connection that in the motor area of the brain more space and more neurons are devoted to the movements of the hand than to any other part of the body. This reflects the intricate and complex movements that the human hand is capable of making.

This relation between movement and thinking may explain the observation that mentally retarded persons are clumsy and awkward in their movements. It can be explained by the fact that brain-damaged children cannot develop the motor coordination and skills of a healthy person. But it has been clearly demonstrated that even in the presence of brain damage, any significant improvement in motor coordination that can be produced by exercise improves the overall thinking of the child. In the absence of proven brain damage, it is not always clear which is cause and which is effect. It is logical to assume that a child whose motor expression is severely inhibited will become dull and may even appear retarded. I shall discuss such a case in the next chapter.

The superior thinking capacity of man in comparison with other animals is also a function of his heightened consciousness. Man is more aware of himself and more aware of his environment than is any other animal. While the whole phenomenon of consciousness is still a mystery, man's heightened consciousness cannot be an isolated development. It is paralleled at the other end of the body by a heightened sexuality. Man has more frequent sexual desire, stronger sexual feelings, and a greater sexual responsiveness than any other animal. He has, in other words, more sexual energy, but since there is no specific sexual energy, what this amounts to is that he has more energy for both his sexuality and his consciousness.

Subjectivity and Objectivity

We think subjectively when our point of reference is within ourselves and our thinking is oriented toward the expression of our feelings and the satisfaction of our needs. To think objectively the point of reference must be outside the self, and the understanding of causal relationships must not be influenced by personal feelings and desires. Objective thinking seeks to define causal relationships in terms of actions rather than feelings, for actions are visible, public events, while feelings are internal and private events. Feelings cannot be verified objectively and so have no place in objective thinking.

The question that arises is: Can thinking ever be completely divorced from feeling? In fact, when one ponders the nature of objective thought, that is, unemotional thinking, it seems more of a contradiction than does emotional thought, or subjective thinking. If the mind is completely divorced from the sentient aspects of being, it becomes transformed into a computer that operates only on the basis of information that is fed into it. This is programmed thinking. In limited situations the human mind can function in this way. The thinking of a student doing a geometry problem resembles the operations of a computer. The student attempts to bring all the information he has learned about geometry to the solution of the problem at hand. If this information is inadequate, he cannot solve the problem, since neither his feelings nor his personal experience are of much help.

As long as a person is alive, his body will send impulses to his brain, informing that organ of its activities and producing sensations, feelings, and thoughts. In the midst of even our most abstract deliberations our minds are not free from the intrusion of personal considerations. We are aware of feeling irritated, frustrated, excited, or relaxed. These intrusions make the task of objective thinking difficult, and it often requires a considerable effort of will to keep one's attention focused on the impersonal problem. The intrusions are minimal when the body is in a state of pleasure and the problem provides a creative challenge. Under these conditions the mind has less tendency to wander. But such conditions are rare in a culture or educational system that denies the role of pleasure in the creative process.

When the individual has to struggle with painful feelings that intrude into his consciousness, objective thinking becomes a matter of self-discipline. Painful feelings always produce a greater disturbance than pleasurable ones, since pain is interpreted as a danger signal. To think objectively when the body is in a state of pain, or lack of pleasure, one has to deaden the body to reduce the feeling of pain. This "deadening" dissociates the mind from the body and makes the quality of one's thinking mechanical or computerized. Creative thinking, which depends on the free flow of unconscious ideas, occurs only when the body is most alive and unburdened. We cannot escape the conclusion that the quality of one's thinking, and probably its content, too, cannot be fully divorced from the emotional tone of the body.

Objective thinking becomes even more difficult when a person attempts to be objective about his own behavior. Since behavior is largely determined by feelings, a person has to be cognizant of his feelings to evaluate his behavior objectively. For example, if a person is unaware of his hostility, he will explain his negative reaction by other people's ill feelings toward him. He does not see his actions as others see them, and so he is unable to assess his role in provoking a negative response. Without an awareness of one's emotions and motives, one cannot be fully objective about himself. The eye of the intellect can only evaluate the logic of one's reasoning on the basis of perceived feelings. But if a person is conscious of his feelings and can express them subjectively, he can take a truly objective position: He can say, for example, "I sense that I am hostile, and I understand why people are reacting negatively to me." True objectivity requires a proper subjectivity.

We are much more objective about other people's behavior than about our own. I have found in counseling married couples that each spouse sees the other's faults clearly but is ignorant of his own. An old French proverb says that people are like the postman who carried a double mail pouch slung over his shoulder. In the front pouch were all the faults of other people; the back pouch contained his own weaknesses. The implication is that each of us is blind to his own shortcomings. We literally cannot see ourselves; we only feel what goes on in our bodies. For this reason, I have made it a personal practice not to argue with anyone who criticizes my behavior. I realize that there is always some merit to the criticism.

To be truly objective one must recognize and declare one's personal attitude or feeling. Without this subjective basis the attempt to be objective ends in pseudo-objectivity. The psychological term for pseudo-objectivity is rationalizing. The mechanism of rationalization is to deny the subjective feeling that motivates a thought or action and to justify one's attitude or behavior by causal reasoning. When a person says, "I did it because . . . ," he is placing the responsibility for his behavior on some outside force. Sometimes this may be valid, but more often it is an excuse for one's failure or inadequacy. Only rarely do such self-justifications satisfy the other person. Rather than give reasons, it is much better to express one's feelings and desires. Will Durant remarks that "reason as every schoolgirl now informs us may be only the technique of rationalizing desire." *

Objective thought offers little help in the multitude of problems and conflicts we meet each day. No mother could respond

* Will Durant, *Pleasures of Philosophy*. New York, Simon & Schuster, Inc., 1966, p. 30.

to her child on the basis of objective thinking. If she interprets her baby's cry correctly, it will be because she senses the feeling behind the cry and responds with feeling to the baby's need. The mother who tries to be objective about her children rejects her natural function and in effect abandons her children. She is no longer a mother but an impersonal force. One cannot relate to any other person objectively, because an objective relationship reduces people to objects.

Thinking can never be divorced from feeling. Since everything a person does is determined by his desire for pleasure or his fear of pain, no act can be entirely unbiased, no action without some personal interest. Every thought is related to a feeling, and it will either support the feeling or oppose it according to the character structure of the individual. In a healthy individual thinking and feeling follow parallel lines, reflecting the unity of the personality. In a neurotic individual thinking often opposes feeling, especially in those areas where conflict exists. The schizophrenic state is characterized by the dissociation of thinking from feeling, which is one of the typical symptoms of the illness.

The one fact that stands out in all psychiatric work is the impotence of purely objective thinking to solve the emotional problems of an individual. Such thinking is actually a form of resistance to the therapeutic endeavor, since it maintains the state of dissociation that underlies the emotional disturbance. Every analytic procedure, from psychoanalysis to bioenergetic analysis, aims at getting through the pseudo-objectivity of the patient to his feelings. Until this is accomplished the communication between patient and doctor remains an intellectual exercise that has no effect on the patient's behavior. The most difficult patient to treat is generally the one who maintains an intellectual detachment from the therapeutic effort.

In view of this fact one wonders why objective thinking is held in such high regard and why the ability to think abstractly is considered the highest achievement of the human mind. The major emphasis in our educational effort is directed at developing this ability. But even as one wonders, reasons emerge to explain this popular attitude. Objective thinking, especially abstract thinking, is the prime source of knowledge, and knowledge is power. Civilized societies are power hierarchies. The person who has power or can provide power occupies a superior position in such societies. The power of knowledge is also a most important asset to the security of a community. It has little value, however, in determining the emotional well-being of the individual.

Creative thinking, on the other hand, is deeply rooted in the subjective attitude. All great philosophic thinking contains a strong subjective bias, which is apparent to the sensitive reader. This personal or subjective orientation not only adds flavor to philosophic writing but transforms the intellectual work into a human document. Writing that lacks this quality is dry and unappealing. All other forms of creative thinking, whether in science, the arts, or simple living, start from a subjective basis. The creative person is not incapable of thinking abstractly; quite the contrary. His abstractions, however, grow out of and reflect his feelings. The subjective basis and the abstract development of creative thinking are an organic unity that is not present in so-called purely objective thinking.

People do not think creatively because their subjective thinking is disturbed. They have been taught 1) to regard such thinking as inferior, 2) to distrust their feelings and justify their actions by reasons, and 3) that pleasure is not a sufficient aim in life. Because of this disturbance, their intellectual capacities are either used to rationalize their behavior or diverted to impersonal matters. It is not uncommon to see a good abstract thinker who lacks what is called common sense.

Thinking starts with feeling and develops from the need to adapt our actions to the reality of our situation. It ends with wisdom, which is the appreciation of man's relation to the universe of which he is a part. The essence of wisdom, as the great Socrates pointed out, is to "know thyself." The person who doesn't know himself cannot think for himself, and he cannot think creatively.

Beauty and Grace

People have a feeling that the truth is beautiful and that falsehood and dishonesty are ugly. There is also some belief that the beautiful is true. In this section I shall discuss the relationship between beauty and health, for health may be regarded as the truth of the body.

Beauty is not generally considered to be within the purview of psychiatry. The idea that beauty is in any way connected to mental health seems an odd thought. Any number of psychiatrists have stated that seemingly beautiful women and good-looking men are found among the insane. My experience is to the contrary. Not one schizoid patient that I have treated felt that her body was beautiful, and I would concur in that self-perception. It would be strange indeed if no relationship existed between the beautiful and the healthy. It may be that our ideas of beauty and health need revision.

Healthy children strike us as beautiful; we admire their bright eyes, their clear complexions, and their shapely, lithe young bodies. Our response to an animal is based on the same qualities: its vitality, its grace, and its exuberance. We see a healthy animal as a thing of beauty whether it is a cat, a dog, a horse, or a bird. Conversely, illness or disease has a repelling effect upon us. It is difficult to see beauty in illness. In Samuel Butler's picture of utopia, described in his book *Erewhon*, illness was the only crime for which people were jailed. This is an extreme view of illness, which offends our sensibilities. We are reluctant to think of a sick person as being ugly. We sympathize with his misfortune, especially if he is close to us, and consequently we disavow any repugnance the illness may evoke in us. Such sentiments are particularly human; wild animals destroy their sick ones.

If beauty is dissociated from health, it will be divorced from the most meaningful aspect of existence. It will create a world of split values, one of which promotes the physical well-being of individuals, while the other deals with abstract concepts of beauty that have nothing in common with health. The Greeks, whose culture is one of the foundations of our own, did not make this distinction. Bodily beauty was admired as an expression of mental and physical health. Their philosophers identified the beautiful with the good. In their sculpture and architecture they show the reverence which they felt for the beautiful as an attribute of godliness.

The Greek tradition of beauty, which passed into Roman culture, can be contrasted with the religious attitude of the ancient Jews, which precluded any worship of form or image. The Hebrew God was an abstraction that could not be approached physically. His commandments were a moral law that could only be apprehended mentally or psychologically. The good life for the Hebrew lay in following the Law, which, to the degree that it promoted the well-being of the members of the Hebrew community, added an element of beauty to their lives. But beauty was secondary to morality.

The two cultures eventually came into conflict during the Christian era. Christianity incorporated elements from both cultures and attempted a synthesis in the figure of the Christ, who embodied in his person the concept of beauty together with the ideas of justice and morality derived from the Hebrews. This synthesis, however, was never fully worked through, since the body was regarded as inferior to the spirit. Roman oppression precluded a life of pleasure on earth for the early Christians. Their salvation lay in the Kingdom of Heaven, which could be attained through devotion and belief. As the Christian church grew and gained power, it turned against the body and bodily pleasure. Beauty became a spiritual concept.

This split between body and spirit, or body and mind, has become part of our Western culture. It is responsible for the dichotomy that exists in modern medicine, which views physical illness and mental illness as two unrelated phenomena. The medical mind is trained to think of illness as an adventitious phenomenon that has no relation to the personality. This attitude developed as a reaction against the mysticism of medieval Christianity, which viewed illness as a punishment for sin. It leads, however, to a mechanistic view of the body in which physical beauty is also an adventitious quality that bears no relation to health.

The medical profession sees health as the absence of illness, just as pleasure is viewed as the absence of pain. And because they are suspicious of malingering, doctors are reluctant to describe a disturbance as an illness unless a demonstrable lesion exists to justify this designation. In their desire to avoid subjectivity they ignore their senses and rely on instruments. Instruments are of help in physiological measurements and can be used to determine the mechanical efficiency of an organ or system. But no instrument can gauge the state of function of an organism. For this we need a positive concept of health. In formulating this concept we cannot ignore the significance of pleasure, beauty, and grace.

When we look at a healthy child, we do not see its state of health. What we see is a child who impresses our senses as being energetic, graceful, and attractive. We interpret these physical signs as manifestations of a healthy body. The determination of health or illness is a judgment. The average person makes this judgment on the basis of his sense impressions. Is there any validity to such a judgment?

One of the theses of this study is that pleasure denotes a state of healthy functioning in an organism. If this is so, then beauty, too, is a manifestation of health—provided that the connection between the beautiful and the pleasurable is established. We think of beauty as something pleasing to the eyes—a beautiful woman, for example, or a beautiful picture. Beauty, in its simplest meaning, represents a harmony of the elements in a scene or an object. It is destroyed by the presence of manifest disproportion or disorder. But a static picture is not beautiful. The harmony or order must stem from an inner excitement that irradiates the object and unifies its various elements. This quality which makes an object appear beautiful to our eyes is also found in music when it is pleasing to our ears. Cacophony, or even a discordant note, may make us wince in pain.

The pleasure of the beautiful rests upon its capacity to excite our own bodily rhythms and stimulate the flow of feeling in our bodies. If we respond pleasurably to a thing of beauty, it is because the excitement in the object communicates itself to us. We too become excited. If this response is lacking, we feel no pleasure. It is valid to say that we do not sense any beauty in the object. This may be due to a deficiency in our sensing, or it may be that the object is unexciting. It is difficult to see how an unexciting object can be regarded as a thing of beauty or how an unexcited person can experience beauty.

Our response to people parallels our reactions to all objects in our environment. We are excited by a beautiful person because he is exciting. We feel pleasure in the company of a beautiful person because he feels good about himself. We are therefore justified in regarding him as healthy.

A sick person could not impress us the same way. He would lack the inner excitement to stimulate us and the feeling of pleasure to make us feel good. If anything, he would exert a depressing influence. Only by the wildest stretch of the imagination could he be considered beautiful.

The excitement and the flow of feeling associated with pleasure are manifested physically as grace. Grace is beauty of motion and complements beauty of form in a healthy organism. Like beauty, it is a manifestation of pleasure. In a state of pleasure one moves gracefully. Pain has a disturbing effect on one's movements.

The word "grace" has connotations that suggest superior personal qualities. It is used as a term of reverence. The salutation "Your Grace," addressed to those who command respect, is equivalent to the term "Your Exellency." It suggests that the person so addressed has a special personal power, a grace, that derives ultimately from his kinship with a deity. In earlier times kings were believed to exercise authority by divine right, which conferred on their persons the special attribute of grace.

The Bible tells us that man was created in the image of God, and presumably each man possessed a share of grace; that is, he was Godlike. Freud tried to show that man created God in the image of his father. But to each young child his father is a person of superior virtue, a man of grace, and in the child's eyes Godlike. According to the Bible, man fell from God's grace when he ate the fruit of the tree of knowledge and learned about good and evil. When man began to think about right and wrong, he must have felt like the centipede who became paralyzed when he tried to figure out which leg to move first. The moment one has to think about moving, the spontaneous flow of feeling through the body is interrupted. The break in rhythmic movement produces a condition of gracelessness.

All animals are graceful in their movements. When one watches a bird fly, it impresses us as a thing of beauty in motion. The leap of a deer and the spring of a tiger have an awe-inspiring quality. Primitive people retain much of this animal grace, which is progressively lost in the civilizing process. It is lost when a person is not free to follow his instincts and feelings.

With the loss of grace there is a loss of graciousness. The person endowed with grace is gracious. He is open, warm, and giving. He is open because no tensions restrict the flow of feeling. He has not developed any neurotic or schizoid defenses against life. He is warm because his energy is not bound in emotional conflicts. He has more energy and therefore more feeling. He gives pleasure to others without effort, for every movement of his body is a source of pleasure to himself and others.

In a human being the lack of physical grace is due to chronic muscular tensions that block the involuntary rhythmic movements of the body. Each tension pattern represents an emotional conflict that was resolved by the inhibition of certain impulses. This is no true resolution, for the suppressed impulses find their way to the surface in distorted forms. Muscular tension, inhibition, and distorted behavior are signs that the conflict is still active on the unconscious level. The person who suffers from such conflicts is neither graceful nor gracious. He is not mentally healthy, and in view of the physical stresses which muscular tensions create, he cannot be considered physically healthy.

The argument that is raised against this concept is that many seemingly graceful people are emotionally disturbed. The reference is to dancers and athletes, whose movements are considered graceful. But the gracefulness of these performers is a learned reaction and not at all like the gracefulness of a wild animal. Performers appear graceful only when engaged in the special activity they have mastered. Even then, their performance is not effortless. It only appears that way from a distance. Offstage, these performers are often quite awkward in their behavior. The true test of gracefulness is in the normal everyday movements of life: walking, talking, cooking a meal, or playing with a child.

Beauty of bodily form and grace of bodily movement are the outer or objective manifestations of health. Pleasure is the inner or subjective experience of health. Health is indivisible; it includes the ideas of both mental and physical well-being. A person cannot be mentally healthy and physically ill or physically well and mentally unhealthy. One can arrive at such split judgments only by ignoring the totality of the personality. The average doctor doing a routine physical examination fails to see

the empty eyes, the grim jaw, and the frozen body that characterize a schizoid personality. Or if he does see these expressions
of emotional disturbance, he does not relate them to physical
health. His examination is often confined to a check of the different organ systems, which would reveal an organic lesion but
not a functional disturbance of the total personality. The average psychiatrist, on the other hand, doesn't look at the bodies of
his patients. He doesn't see their restricted breathing, their immobilized bodies, and their frightened eyes. Or if he does see
these signs of emotional disturbance, he does not relate them
to the problems the patients present. Without positive criteria
of health one cannot judge the condition of an individual's total
function. The criteria which I regard as most valid for this purpose are bodily beauty and bodily grace.

A sense of beauty and grace is innate in people. Young children are particularly sensitive to these qualities. When a child
sees a beautiful woman, he exclaims, "You're beautiful." Too
many people, however, are like the crowd in the story of the
emperor's new clothes, who denied their senses and applauded
the emperor's invisible garments until a child remarked that
he was naked. People have been brainwashed into accepting the
dictates of fashion even when these contradict the subjective
truth of their senses. The individual who is a slave to fashion
has surrendered his personal taste to conformity. This situation
has become so bad that the thin, gaunt, schizoid body has become a model of feminine pulchritude. I can only attribute this
state of affairs to the fact that most people have abandoned their
senses.

Beauty and grace are the goals to which much of our conscious effort is directed. We want to be more beautiful and more
graceful, for we sense that these qualities lead to joy. Beauty
is the aim of all creative action, on the personal level in our
homes and surroundings and artistically in our work. Despite
this interest in beauty, the world grows uglier all the time. I
believe this is because beauty has become an adornment rather
than a virtue, an ego symbol rather than a way of life. We are
committed to power, not to pleasure, as a way of life, and as a
result, beauty has lost its true meaning as an image of pleasure.

7 · Self-Awareness and
   Self-Assertion

Knowing and No-ing

A person cannot be aware of his individuality unless he has the right and the ability to assert his individuality. Simply stated, self-awareness depends on self-assertion. Asserting oneself implies the idea of opposition, and it differs in this respect from expressing oneself, which doesn't have this implication. Self-assertion is a declaration of one's individuality in the face of forces which deny it. Such forces exist in society and in the home. To safeguard a person's individuality the United States Constitution contains a guarantee of free speech the essential element of which is the right of dissent. Without the right to express one's opposition, individuality is weakened and creativity is undermined.

I have often been impressed by the observation that the inability of a patient to know himself parallels his inability to say no. To such questions as "Did you have any temper tantrums as a child?" or "Were you breast-fed?" he invariably answers, "I don't know." The lack of knowledge about one's early life is somewhat understandable in view of Freud's demonstration that the earliest memories of childhood are repressed. However, even questions relating to the present—"Why are you smiling?" "What do you feel?" "What do you want?"—often elicit the same reply: "I don't know."

The inability to say no is manifested by the patient's behavior under the stress of life situations. He cannot say no to authority figures, he cannot graciously reject demands that he feels are excessive, and he cannot resist the pressures of his social environment. The same difficulty is made evident in therapy when the

patient attempts to shout or scream "No" and "I won't" while
beating his fists or kicking his legs into the bed. His voice lacks
conviction and resonance. His movements are uncoordinated
and weak. A note of fear is often detected in the voice by the
presence of a rising inflection, or the sound is shortened and
gives the impression of an ineffectual protest. Even an observer
watching the patient's actions on film is struck by the lack of
self-assertiveness.

The parallel between a lack of knowledge of the self and a
characterological weakness in the ability to say no made me
think that there must be a logical connection between the two.
When the patient says "I don't know," is he also saying "I don't
No," meaning "I don't say 'No' "? The similarity of sound between the words "know" and "no" may be simply fortuitous,
but it raises the quesion: To what extent is the negative an essential ingredient of knowledge?

Knowledge is a function of discrimination. To know what A
is, it must be distinguished from all that is not-A. Knowledge
arises from the recognition of differences. The first difference
that an organism can recognize is that between what feels good
to the body or pleasurable and what feels painful. Even such
elementary distinctions as day and night, light and dark, up and
down are beyond the grasp of a newborn human being. Until a
baby's eyes are opened he lives in a world in which the bodily
self is the universe and the other, or non-self, does not exist in
awareness. As the different aspects of the external world become
distinguished from one another, they are identified in the baby's
mind with bodily sensations. The mother becomes a person who
transforms distress into contentment, hunger into satisfaction.
At this early level, however, the baby's behavior is purely impulsive. His reactions have an involuntary quality. He has not
learned to think, and he has not gained any knowledge.

The step from impulsive response to thinking requires the
introduction of a frustration and a negation. If the impulsive
actions of an organism were capable of fulfilling all its needs
and desires, conscious thought would be unnecessary. It is only
when automatic patterns of behavior fail to satisfy the organism
that the need for conscious thought arises. In all the learning
experiments with animals, frustration is the lever that forces

the animal to learn new behavior to achieve a desired end. In one of the most famous of these experiments a banana was placed outside the cage of an ape and just beyond his reach. After a number of unsuccessful attempts to reach the banana with his arm, the ape finally noticed a stick that had been left in his cage. Using the stick as an extension of his arm, he was able to retrieve the banana. On subsequent occasions recourse to the stick occurred after fewer unsuccessful efforts to reach the banana with his hand. It could be said that the ape learned a new skill, that the learning involved thinking, and that in the process he acquired the knowledge of how to use the stick in a new way.

The role of frustration in thinking is obvious; that of negation is obscure. Frustration does not necessarily lead to thinking; it may just as easily turn into anger and rage. These, in fact, are the more natural responses to frustration. Thinking can only happen when the energy of the frustrated desire is shunted away from this avenue of release. Sometime before the frustration becomes overwhelming, the animal must stop its useless effort. "Stop to think" is an old maxim. The "stop" that is so essential to thinking is an unspoken no, a negative command from a higher center that holds back the emotional reaction and allows a higher faculty to take control.

This command that stops an unavailing effort and redirects the energy of the impulse into a new channel is the voice of the ego in its creative function. Three elements enter into a creative impulse: The first is a strong impulse seeking fulfillment in pleasure, the second is a frustration which prevents fulfillment through accustomed actions, and the third is a measure of self-control or self-discipline which prevents the frustrated impulse from spilling over into destructive behavior. If the motivation for pleasure is weak, the effort may collapse in a sense of resignation. If self-discipline is weak, it will change into rage.

A healthy ego holds the reins of the involuntary responses of the body. It doesn't substitute its illusions for the desires of the body. Its influence is a restraining one and is the foundation of self-possession. This is illustrated in the following incident. A young man I knew was caught in a dangerous undertow and found that despite his best efforts to swim, he could not extricate himself from it. Realizing that he was becoming frightened and desperate, he said to himself, "Don't panic." A moment's thought then told him that he should save his strength and call for help. He did this and was rescued. This example could be multiplied many times.

It is my contention that the ability to say no to oneself and the ability to say no to others are merely opposite sides of the same coin. If the right and the ability to assert one's opposition are denied, self-discipline and self-possession necessarily suffer.

Let us now pursue this question a little differently. As our infant grows older, he will inevitably come into conflict with his parents. But let us assume that he has an unusual nature, that he listens to everything his mother says and follows her commands to the letter. "Eat this purée," the mother commands, and the child obeys faithfully. If this program were continued on every level, how would the child ever learn to think? He would have no need to think, since mother knows best. He would have no need to learn, since mother would foresee all problems and handle all contingencies. He would gain no knowledge, since he would have no need of knowledge. Fortunately, no normal child is born with such a disposition, for he would end up a helpless idiot.

When a child obeys a command, he is deprived of an opportunity to learn and to acquire knowledge. This is not to say that one must never command a child. Commands are necessary in emergencies, but not in learning situations. The latter requires a free play of wills if thinking is to occur.

The "I don't 'no' " begins in the home. It begins when a parent overrides a child's opposition and enforces his will over the child's objections. This is so common that it often passes unnoticed. After all, what does a child know? A parent knows more, and certainly he "no's" best. But the issues over which conflicts arise between parents and children are rarely resolvable by superior knowledge. A child wanders off a few paces in a supermarket, and the watchful mother orders him back. If the child doesn't respond quickly enough, he is liable to be jerked off his feet by the irate mother. I have seen this happen many times. The harshness with which commands are frequently voiced is appalling. "Stop that," "Sit still," "Don't run," "Don't touch the candy" are expressed in such tones of authority that one is amazed when some children have the temerity to resist.

The observer who watches parents and children can only conclude that it is seldom a question of "mother knows best" but of authority and obedience. A child must be taught to obey his parents; otherwise, they fear, they would have no control over him, and he would turn out bad. This fear overlooks the fact that a child is a social being whose spontaneous actions are self-expressive and not self-destructive. From the moment of birth his responses are directed by impulses that are rooted in the wisdom of the body. If one starts from the premise that discipline must be imposed from without, a true self-discipline cannot develop. The child becomes submissive out of fear; this is not the same thing as self-controlled. The "good" obedient child in sacrificing his right to say no loses the ability to think for himself.

The belief that children will "go wrong" if discipline is not imposed upon them denotes a lack of faith in human nature. Children are not inherently monsters, but they can become so when parents are hostile and suppress their independence. In the eyes of a child such a parent is a monster who can only be opposed with his own methods. Thus a child becomes like his parent. It is astonishing how easily people forget the fundamental law of reproduction, that like begets like. The monstrous quality in a parent is his lack of respect for the individuality of his child. It is inhuman for a parent not to accept his child as he is but to try to mold him into some image the parent has in his own mind of what his child should be.

All children go through a negative phase in the course of their development. Between eighteen months and two years of age they will say no to many parental demands and offerings. This "no" expresses the child's growing consciousness that he can think for himself. It is often so spontaneous that the child may actually say no to something he likes. I recall offering my young son one of his favorite cookies. Before he even recognized it, he turned his head away in a gesture of rejection. A quick look, however, convinced him that it was a desired object, and he reached for it. Any insistence on my part, however, would have firmed his initial refusal.

Whether we permit a child to make his own choice in any situation depends on the circumstances of the situation. In principle we must always respect a child's right to say no. In practice it is advisable to let the child have his own way whenever possible. This allows a child to develop a sense of responsibility for his own behavior, which is a natural tendency in all organisms. When the early efforts of a child to establish a self-regulatory pattern are rebuffed by parents, conflicts arise that are most difficult to overcome. The child who has the right to say no to his parents grows into an adult who knows what he wants and who he is.

The imposition of patterns of thinking is popularly called brainwashing. A person can be brainwashed only when his resistance and will are overcome. He must be deprived of the right to say no. As long as he has that right, he will attempt to find things out for himself. He may make mistakes, but he will learn. Patients who are incapable of voicing their opposition cannot find out anything for themselves. They look to the therapist for answers he doesn't have. They do not know what they really want or who they are. Fortunately, very few patients are completely brainwashed. Most patients suffer from a relative limitation in their ability to assert themselves, but it is this limitation that is responsible for their difficulties and their lack of self-knowledge.

Self-Possession and "No"

Every organism is surrounded by a membrane that separates it from its environment and determines its individual existence. This means that it is a self-contained energy system and that all its exchanges with the environment take place through this membrane. The health of an organism obviously depends on the normal functioning of this membrane. If it is too porous, the organism will spill out into its surroundings; if it is impermeable, nothing will enter. Every living membrane has a selective permeability which, for example, allows food to enter and waste products to flow out.

In a human being the functional membrane of the body is

composed of the skin, the underlying fatty and connective tissue, and the striated or voluntary muscles. These muscles are included in this membrane because they form a sheath around the whole body just under the skin and, like the skin, play a role in the function of perception. The skin and the special sense organs at the surface of the body receive all incoming stimuli. The voluntary muscles together with their proprioceptive nerves are involved in the perception of outgoing impulses. There are other surface membranes in the human body, such as the linings of the digestive tract and of the respiratory system, but these are not directly associated with the personality.

The relation of this functional membrane to consciousness can best be understood by viewing the body as a single cell. Stimuli which act on the surface from without give rise to sensations if their intensity is sufficient to produce an effect on the surface. Similarly, impulses from within the body are perceived when they reach the surface. Consciousness is a surface phenomenon; it involves both the surface of the mind and the surface of the body. Freud described the ego, which embraces the functions of perception and consciousness, as "the projection of a surface upon a surface." The events which take place at the surface of the body are projected on the surface of the mind where perception occurs.

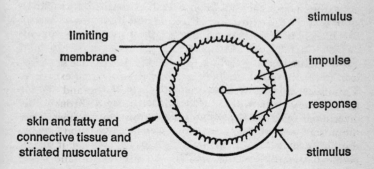

Many events or movements occur within the body which do not reach consciousness. We are not ordinarily aware of the heart's action, we do not perceive our intestinal movements, and we do not sense the production and internal flow of urine. Generally, sensation arises and perception occurs when an internal activity affects the surface of the body. For example, when the heart beats with such force that it causes a thumping of the chest, one feels the heart pounding. Theoretically, impulses arise at the center of an organism and are directed outward toward objects in the external world. We are not, however, conscious of these impulses until they reach the muscular system, where an action can take place which will satisfy the aim of the impulse. Perception does not depend on the actual contraction of the muscles. An impulse is perceived when the muscles become "set" to act or "ready" to respond.

A muscular system that is too flexible or lacks cohesion allows impulses to pass through without adequate ego control and before these impulses have been fully registered in consciousness. The behavior of people with this defect will be either impulsive or hysterical. Despite their hyperactivity or violent outbursts, feeling is reduced in these persons. They show a deficiency of self-containment or self-possession, and their egos can be described as weak. Impulsiveness and hysterical behavior are common in certain schizoid personalities. On the other hand, an inflexible membrane due to an overall pattern of muscular rigidity blocks the expression of feeling and limits the release of impulses. The rigid person shows a lack of spontaneity, and his behavior tends to be compulsive and mechanical. Muscular rigidity also decreases feeling, because the muscular system cannot react or respond freely.

The limiting membrane, especially the skin, also serves a protective function with regard to incoming forces. It allows the individual to screen stimuli and distinguish those which necessitate a response from those which can be ignored. When the skin is undercharged, as in the schizophrenic condition, the individual is easily overwhelmed by the stimuli which proceed from his environment. Our ordinary speech equates hypersensity with being thin-skinned and insensitivity with having a thick skin. Any part of the body that is temporarily denuded of skin is so sensitive that even blowing on the area lightly is extremely painful.

The "no" functions as a psychological membrane that parallels in many ways the function of the physiological membrane described above. It prevents the individual from being overwhelmed by outside pressures and allows him to discriminate among the demands and inducements to which he is constantly subject. It guards against an exaggerated impulsiveness, for the person who can say no to others can also say no to his own desires when necessary. It defines the ego boundaries of an individual, just as the physical membrane defines the body's boundaries.

Saying no is an expression of opposition which is the cornerstone of the feeling of identity. By opposing another, one is in effect saying, "I am me, I am not you, I have a mind of my own." But what about the person who seems to say no all the time and can't say yes? This question always arises when I discuss this subject in lectures. The person who can't say yes is afraid that his assent will commit him irrevocably to a course of action. He doesn't believe that he has the right to change his mind, and his negative position is a defense against his *fear* of being controlled. His no is not a statement of opposition but a declaration of withdrawal or non-participation. It is a passive holding back, not an act of countering the other. When his no is tested on the couch, it is weak in vocal power and uncoordinated in physical movement. It often collapses in the face of a challenge.

The no as an expression of self-assertion derives its strength from the knowledge of the self. To be able to say no effectively one has to know who one is and what one wants. Desires and impulse can only be known when they reach the surface or limiting membrane of the organism. The strength of this membrane depends, therefore, on the inner charge of the organism. At the same time, however, it protects the integrity of the organism. The right to say no ensures the right to know. There is a two-way relationship between the striving for pleasure and the ability to say no, between self-expression and self-assertion.

Self-assertion means that one has a mind of one's own. Implied in the concept of having a mind of one's own is the right and the ability to change one's mind. Having expressed one's mind or asserted one's individuality, one is then more willing to listen to another's point of view. Changing from a no to a yes is relatively easy; it is much more difficult to reverse the procedure. Further, the no gives a person time to think and to make up his mind, and his final assent may be taken therefore as the result of mature deliberation. To know your mind, you should mind your no.

Without the ability to say no, one's assent is merely a form of submission and not the free expression of one's will. "Yesman" is a familiar term of contempt for a person who is afraid to assert himself. We can suspect that there is a layer of repressed negativity underlying this attitude of submission, and we instinctively distrust the person who can't say no. In my therapeutic work I have repeatedly seen how patients who develop the ability to say no become more positive in their attitudes and more certain of their identities. They gain self-possession. This improvement is illustrated in the following case.

Some years ago I treated a young woman, Lucy, about eighteen years of age, who was markedly retarded in both her emotional and intellectual development. In addition her muscular coordination was severely impaired, a condition that is typical of retarded people. Superficially, Lucy was a very agreeable and pleasant person who made a slight effort to do the exercises and movements I suggested. Her movements, however, were very limited in duration and represented a gesture of cooperation rather than a serious commitment to the activity. She would, for example, kick her legs against the couch several times while saying "No" in a quiet voice that carried no conviction. Then she would stop, after only a few moments of activity, and look at me to see if I approved or disapproved of her. It was obvious that Lucy needed my approval, and I gave it to her at the same time that I encouraged her to let go more fully to these expressions.

Kicking is an infantile pattern of body movement, and Lucy enjoyed being allowed to regress. It is also a form of opposition; to kick about something is to protest. She liked to kick her legs, but she did not associate this with self-assertion. At first she would not say no in a loud tone. It was almost impossible to get her to shout or scream. She appeared very frightened of any strong self-assertion.

During the treatment I would catch an occasional glimpse of an alert intelligence behind her mask of retardation. There were moments when Lucy's eyes would meet mine with a look of understanding. When this happened, her eyes temporarily lost their dullness and became bright and sensitive. I had the impression that she was studying me to see how far she could trust me. On other occasions, when I asked her to open her eyes wide in an expression of fear, she froze and became completely immobile. Once when I pressed with my thumbs on the muscles alongside the nose that activate the smiling reflex in order to block the smile, her eyeballs rolled up into their sockets and her face became twisted in a gargoylelike expression. She looked like a complete idiot, and I realized that she had cut off her contact with me and had withdrawn into uncomprehension because of some deep inner fear. It was an unusual defense but also a very effective one. In the face of this apparent idiocy, a parent would feel powerless to enforce his will against a child.

Terror is the etiological factor on the psychological level in predisposing an individual to schizophrenia. Terror is a paralyzing emotion that freezes the body and dissociates the personality. In the dissociated personality the connection between mind and body is severed, resulting in a loss of the sense of reality. Insanity operates as a defense against and denial of terror. Terror loses its force when reality loses its meaning. In the same way idiocy can be a defense against the threat of destruction which a child may sense if it opposes a dominating parent. The child's resistance is no longer a challenge to the ego of the parent. If anything, a mentally retarded child can act out his resistance without fear that it will be seen as opposition.

Pursuant to these ideas, my treatment of Lucy aimed at strengthening her ego through her asserting opposition and at the development of better muscular coordination. Her kicking became more forceful and sustained, and her nos became louder and stronger. She also hit the bed with a tennis racket repeatedly, saying, "I won't." Bioenergetic exercises were also used to deepen her breathing and loosen her body. I was pleased to observe that at the end of each session there was a noticeable improvement in the patient. She spoke up more easily, and her ideas began to flow more freely. Above all, the dullness in her eyes and manner decreased.

It could be expected that her developing ego would bring her into some opposition with her parents. I advised them of this possibility, and they agreed to allow her more freedom. The result was a gradual unfolding of the patient's personality that was apparent to all. This positive response to the therapy was largely based on the rapport that developed between Lucy and myself. She felt that I would support her if she exposed her feelings and asserted her opposition, even against me. She also felt, I believe, that I regarded her as an intelligent person although her range of interest was narrow and her ideas were limited. She understood the significance of what we were trying to accomplish and participated in the work to the best of her ability.

Her ability to express her feelings was blocked by the extreme physical tensions in her body. The muscles at the back of her neck were contracted into hard lumps. The attempt to loosen them by massage was painful, and I always stopped when she became frightened. At each session, however, I could work a little more strongly with her. At first Lucy could not tolerate any stress for more than a few moments. Her tolerance slowly increased as her tensions eased and her breathing became freer and deeper. Initially she moved her arms and legs like a puppet, without rhythm or feeling. As she gained a sense of freedom in expressing herself, her movements became more charged with feeling. She hit and kicked with more vigor, and her voice rose in pitch and intensity as she voiced her nos and "I won'ts." The result was a consistent improvement in her coordination.

One of the most effective procedures was a game. Each time she said "No," I said "Yes"; if she said "I won't," I countered with "You will." It didn't take too long before her voice rose louder than mine and she persisted when I was ready to quit. Most children enjoy this game. If physical force is eliminated and no threats are used, they feel equal to their opponent. Occasionally I engaged in a pulling contest with Lucy, using a towel. I was amazed at the fear she showed of exerting her strength against me. But even this fear diminished as we continued the game.

Lucy's therapy ended when her family moved to another part of the country. We had worked together once a week for about two years. At the end there were times when a casual observer would have taken Lucy for a normal person. She had made considerable progress, and I hoped that with encouragement and support it would continue. She was fortunate in having this kind of support in one member of her family.

Mental retardation is often caused by brain damage, and the more severe cases are probably of this origin, but in this case the medical history did not reveal any trauma or illness that could account for Lucy's condition. Outside my medical practice I have seen two other cases where emotional and intellectual dullness developed in normal children when they were overwhelmed by a parent and became submissive through fear. There can be little question that fear, especially a constant fear, has a stultifying effect on the personality. A person can be brainwashed only when fear has deprived him of his wits.

A child's no can be suppressed, but it cannot be eliminated. It remains operative in the unconscious and becomes structured in chronic muscular tensions, primarily in the region of the neck and head. The muscles that rotate the head from side to side in a gesture of negation become tight and spastic to inhibit this gesture. The person becomes stiff-necked, and his unspoken no changes into an unconscious stubbornness. The jaw muscles contract to set the jaw in either a rigid, defiant expression or in an attitude of holding on to one's self. Muscular tensions develop in the throat to suppress the scream of defiance.

These chronic muscular tensions represent an unconscious negation. Since the motility of an individual is reduced by these tensions, he is in effect saying "I won't move." His bodily rigidity constitutes an unconscious resistance that takes the place of the opposition he could not express. Unfortunately, it becomes a generalized attitude against any demand from the environment and is, therefore, self-defeating.

If the no is not suppressed but only blocked from normal expression, it leads to irrational, negative behavior. This is a problem that confronts many teachers in their efforts to maintain class order. It was handled in an ingenious way by one of my patients, who taught a first-grade class in the New York City school system. Most of her pupils came from disadvantaged homes, and many of them suffered from emotional disturbances. Her class program was often disrupted by a constant restlessness that occasionally erupted into active disobedience. Rather than attempt to fight this restlessness with a stricter discipline, which might not have worked, she organized the children's blocked negativity. In the middle of each morning and afternoon session, she had her pupils form a line and march about the classroom stamping their feet and shouting, "No, I won't. No, I won't." This procedure was followed by some breathing exercises. My patient made no attempt to evaluate the results of her experiment objectively, but she told me how surprised she was at the effectiveness of this procedure. Following the expression of their negative feelings, her pupils were much more receptive to her and to the schoolwork.

The Critical Faculty

In his delightful series of essays *Portraits from Memory*, Bertrand Russell makes the following observation about himself: "Always the skeptical intellect, when I have most wished it silent, has whispered doubts to me, has cut me off from the facile enthusiasms of others, and has transported me into a desolate solitude." Although aware of the pain he suffered because of his skeptical intellect, Russell could not silence it. It was an integral part of the man, and it became an integral part of his work. This statement raises two important questions: Would Russell be the thinker that he is without a skeptical intellect? And second, could anyone have a real intellect if it did not include a screen of skepticism? My answer to both questions is "No."

The skepticism of Russell is an expression of his individuality and independence. It is the attribute of a free thinker who forms his own judgments on the basis of his own experience. It is the mind of a man who can say no. No one can doubt Russell's ability to assert an opposing view. He was arrested in 1915 for expressing his opposition to Britain's entry into World War I. He was ostracized by his liberal colleagues for opposing Russian Communism in the twenties. He was condemned for organizing the opposition to the Vietnam war in 1965. Whatever one may think of his actions, no one can question the courage and integrity that prompted those actions. This integrity is evident in all of Russell's writings, because it is the quality of the man.

It would be a big mistake to believe that Russell lacks enthusiasm. Everything about the man and every line of his writing shows him to be in love with life, positive in his outlook, and constructive in his point of view. His intellectual skepticism is the moderating restraint that a secure ego exercises over an enthusiastic nature. By contrast, the facile enthusiasms of the average individual are a desperate search for meaning and security. Lacking an inner core of conviction, the mass individual attaches himself to any new idea that can serve for the moment to support his faltering ego. A facile enthusiasm is the sign of a fickle lover.

The critical faculty or the skeptical intellect is not the same thing as being negative or distrusting. True criticism requires a point of view that is grounded in experience and supported by clear objective reasoning. The experience on which the critical faculty depends must be personal, not a dogma that one has been taught. Criticizing from the point of view of a dogma is the sign of a closed mind. Russell is not a skeptic or a doubter. He is a believer in mankind. He believes that human beings have an inherent capacity to live in harmony with their world and to be joyful. But he is not naïve and has no illusion that there is a simple answer to the human dilemma. He is a scholar who has studied other people's thinking and who is, therefore, knowledgeable. His creativity arises from his persistent effort to integrate these two worlds, the subjective and the objective.

Criticism is essential to creative thinking. Each advance in the acquisition of knowledge grows out of the questioning and denial of established concepts. No forward movement in thinking can be made without transcending and, therefore, changing a previous understanding or formulation. Copernicus rejected the Ptolemaic concept that the earth was the center of the universe and showed that it was a planet orbiting the sun. Darwin denied the Scholastic view that God had created each species of animal. The theory of evolution resulted. Einstein disclaimed the applicability of Newtonian physics to astronomical phenomena and introduced the theory of relativity. Psychoanalysis would not have uncovered the secrets of the unconscious if Freud had not challenged the accepted ideas of hysteria. These achievements were possible because each of these men had a mind of his own and the courage to say no. The inquiring mind is a skeptical intellect in an eager and curious nature.

Every individual has something to add to the store of knowledge based on the uniqueness of his personal experiences. No two people ever see the world through the same eyes. Each person has a unique body and lives a unique existence. We can all be creative thinkers, therefore, if we accept our individuality. We reject our individuality, however, when we subordinate our own thinking to the voice of authority. We must learn what authority knows, but we will only learn when we listen to authority with our critical faculties in operation.

One gains knowledge when information is broken down and assimilated into the personality. Until this is done, information is like a tool which is useless because the person doesn't know how to handle it. Learning is not simply a matter of acquiring information. The learned person knows how to apply this information to life, especially to his own life. He has related it to his feelings and has integrated it with his experience. It has become a second sense, which is the true nature of knowledge. This is what we mean when we say, for example, that a carpenter knows how to build a cabinet. Obviously he has the necessary information, but he also has a skill which enables him to use his information without thinking too much about it. His information is part of his skill, which is true knowledge. His know-how bears the stamp of his experience, and in the area of his work it identifies his individuality.

A carpenter learns his trade by doing it, and a child learns about life by living it. We cannot teach a child how to live. Teaching imparts information which must be transmuted into knowledge to be useful. The catalyst for this transformation is personal experience. Information that dovetails with one's experience becomes knowledge; the rest passes unassimilated through the mind and is soon forgotten. How many of us remember our high-school mathematics or history? How much of what we were taught in college by our teachers is retained in later life? Much of the real learning that goes on in college is extracurricular, from one's classmates, in social gatherings, and through outside activities. This, however, is often worth the price of a college education.

The emphasis in our educational systems on teaching rather than learning reflects the unconscious belief that information is more valuable than thought. Consciously, every educator wants his pupils to learn, but it is even more important for him to pass on the information that he is charged to impart. Why this great stress on information? Is it a device to prevent young minds from questioning the values that underlie a culture? Certainly the amount of information that students are asked to learn allows no time for creative thinking. It is assumed that creativity will occur after the information has somehow been acquired, but by that time the pleasure of learning has been lost and the creative impulse stifled. The postgraduate doctoral dissertation, the final step in the educational process, reveals the bias of our educational system toward information rather than knowledge. Creative thinking is discouraged in favor of research. That the research has no personal meaning to the student and the information it yields has no value to society is irrelevant. It is information, and in our computerized age we naïvely assume that with enough information we can solve all the problems of mankind.

What place can creative thinking occupy in a computerized world? If information is all we need, are we not abandoning the creative function in the human personality? Without a creative spark, the pleasure of life disappears. We become robots whose behavior is electronically determined because our actions can be electronically calculated. This is not a pleasant prospect, but it can happen unless we assert our individuality. We must retain the right to think for ourselves and not become statistics. But we cannot do this if our thinking is based on statistics.

Suppose four out of five people prefer a certain product; is this a reason for you to prefer that product? If it is, it means that you have no taste and cannot judge for yourself. But you might argue that such a marked preference indicates that the product is superior. Your skeptical intellect should inform you, however, that in a mass market preferences are created by advertising. Although the value of a product can generally be personally tested, advertisers know that the general public has little taste and no critical faculty. If they thought otherwise, they would not base their advertising on preference polls.

Taste is the foundation of the critical function. Without a sense of taste, one has no basis for criticism. A judgment that does not express a personal feeling is moralizing. A critic, for example, who approves or disapproves of a play because of its ideas without stating whether he enjoyed it or not is making a moral judgment, not a critical review. If the personal taste of a critic is not the criterion for his judgment, then he is acting as an authority who believes he has a superior knowledge of what is good or bad. My skeptical intellect questions his right to make such judgments. A person's taste may agree with mine or not, but if it is honestly expressed, I can respect his judgment.

If a person has taste, he can state on the basis of his feeling whether he likes a thing or not. To know what one likes and what one dislikes is subjective knowledge. It can be said of such a person that he knows his mind. If, in addition, a person can say why he likes or dislikes something, that is, if he can support his taste with sensible reasons, he has a critical faculty.

Although we want our children to be creative thinkers and develop a critical faculty, we deny their taste and impose our own on them. At home and in schools we try to improve their taste by telling them what they should like. We fail to realize that a sense of taste is born in a person and that while it can be refined, it cannot be created. Taste can be broadened by exposure to new experiences, but the person who doesn't know what he likes or dislikes gains nothing from such exposure. We are born with a sense of taste, because from the moment of birth we are capable of distinguishing pleasure from pain. We lose the sense of taste when our choices are disregarded and we are deprived of the right to say "No."

All the art appreciation courses, the music appreciation programs, the literature taught in schools often add up to just so much information. Rarely do they help develop one's taste. If one asks why, the answer is that they are presented authoritatively. One is told in advance that this is great art, beautiful music, or fine literature and that one should like it. One is in the same position as the child whose mother tells him what to like, since she knows best. Who can respond with pleasure to this inducement? And if the response is not one of pleasure, how can one regard the offering as a thing of beauty? What one gains from an authoritative presentation is information, not knowledge, and certainly not an appreciation of the beautiful.

A concomitant result of a mass society is the production of a mass culture. It may seem like a great boon to humanity to reproduce the achievements of the masters at prices that everyone can afford, but the net effect of this merchandising effort is to reduce the value of these achievements to information. Too much information can obfuscate one's mind, and too great an exposure can dull one's taste. When culture becomes a mass phenomenon, discrimination is lost. The distinctions between high and low, good and bad, fade out when taste disappears.

I am not against the idea that all people have a right to know the culture in which they live. I do not believe, however, that culture can be brought to the masses. It is the role of culture to transform the mass individual into a true individual, but to do this the individuality of each person must be recognized, his striving for pleasure supported, and his right to say no accorded full respect. We should not mistake information for knowledge. The latter is acquired by subjecting information to the judgment of one's senses. An individual doesn't learn with his head alone, but with his heart and his whole being. What is learned in this way is truly known. What is known only with the head is information.

Learning is a creative activity. We are inspired to learn by the promise of pleasure, and this promise is fulfilled when we do learn something. We seek information to deepen our knowledge and broaden our pleasure. We do not need to have it forced on us, as is done in so many educational systems. When education is geared to pleasure, school becomes a joyful adventure in self-discovery.

8 · The Emotional Responses

Love

In his quest for knowledge man differentiates and isolates the various phenomena of nature. As a consequence of this process, each aspect tends to lose its connections with the whole and is seen as an independent variable. When this analytic procedure is applied to the emotions, they become defined either as physiological responses of the body or as patterns of behavior which can be adopted or discarded by the will. Fear, for example, is a bodily reaction produced physiologically by the secretion of adrenalin in response to a situation of danger. Although neither the secretion nor our bodily reaction to it is subject to conscious control, we are constantly advising children not to be afraid, thereby implying that they can control this emotional response.

This confusion about the nature of emotions is most clearly evident in our attitudes to love. Our sermons and our literature are full of entreaties and admonishments to love. Despite such warnings as Smiley Blanton's *Love or Perish*, all these appeals to the conscious mind are relatively ineffective to create more feelings of love. Then, on the other hand, we also assume that love is a natural feeling in certain relationships, that every mother naturally loves her child and that each child loves his mother. We are often shocked and astonished to find that this is not always so. Seen from the conscious mind there is some validity to both attitudes. We recognize the importance of love, and it helps to be reminded of this importance. The appeal for love is designed to reduce a person's focus on his ego and to restore his awareness, momentarily at least, of his relationship to others and to his community. At the same time we recognize that love should be present in every intimate relationship. What we fail to see, however, is that our emotional responses are not isolated phenomena. They are not voluntary reactions or purely conditioned reflexes. Love, for example, cannot be divorced from pleasure. It arises out of the experience of pleasure and depends for its being on the anticipation of pleasure.

The word "emotion" means a movement "out, out of, or from." An emotion may be defined, therefore, as a movement arising out of an excited state of pleasure or pain. Sandor Rado divides emotions into two groups, welfare emotions and emergency emotions. According to Rado, the welfare emotions, which include love, sympathy, and affection, are "differentiated elaborations of the experiencing and anticipation of pleasure." *
Simply stated, we love that which promises us pleasure. Similarly, our sympathy extends to those people with whom we have a pleasurable rapport. One is not normally sympathetic to people who pose a threat of pain. The emergency emotions, such as fear, anger, and hate, grow out of the experiencing and anticipation of pain.

Memory and anticipation play important roles in differentiating the emotional response from the basic pleasure-pain reactions. If we have been hurt in a situation, we will anticipate a similar pain if the situation repeats itself. Anticipating pain, we will respond with either fear or anger, depending on the direction of our movement. If we flee from the situation, we will experience fear; if we confront the situation in an attempt to remove the threat of pain, we will experience anger. In the absence of memory and anticipation to guide our behavior, our response will be determined by the effect of a direct contact with the object. A pleasurable effect will induce us to reach out to the object, a painful one will cause us to withdraw.

A newborn infant neither feels nor manifests love for his mother. His reactions are based on sensations of pleasure and pain. It can be assumed, however, that the capacity for love is present at birth but that its flowering requires a maturation of consciousness and the experience of pleasure in the infant's contact with his mother. This experience is soon forthcoming, since the infant, if he is to survive at all, must have his essential needs

* Sandor Rado, "Hedonic Self-Regulation" in *The Role of Pleasure in Behavior*, ed. Robert G. Heath. New York, Harper & Row Publishers, Inc., 1964, p. 261.

satisfied by his mother or a mother substitute. When the growing consciousness of the child enables him to identify these pleasurable experiences with the person of the mother, feelings of affection for the mother arise. He brightens at her approach, and waves of pleasurable excitation can be seen to pass through his body.

Unfortunately, in our culture at least, an infant's contact with his mother is not uniformly productive of pleasure. While a mother must satisfy the basic needs of an infant, she can do so in a manner that is disturbing to the well-being of the infant. We hear too many crying babies and see too many unhappy children to have any illusion that in infancy all one's desires are fulfilled. Young infants need an almost unlimited contact with the mother's body, and very few women are prepared to give an infant their full time and attention. Their personal needs often conflict with those of the child. If they yield to the demands of the child, they are irritated and feel resentful. If they don't, the child suffers some distress. In either event, a painful situation often develops for the child, which limits his love for his mother.

Too frequently a mother's attitude to the child is ambivalent. The baby is not an unmixed blessing. He is wanted and not wanted. As a result the infant becomes the object of some hostility, mostly unconscious but expressed in gestures of annoyance, angry looks, rough handling, and so on. Acts of violence against infants are not unknown. The syndrome of the battered child is recognized to be more common than was originally thought. In his book *The Fear of Being a Woman,* Joseph Rheingold documents and shows the prevalence of maternal hostility among women. He relates it to the woman's experience at the hands of her own mother and to the conflict between them. My own clinical experience supports his observations. I have not treated a single patient in all the years of my practice who did not have some negative feelings toward his mother which were fully justified by the experiences of his childhood.

Painful experiences do not give rise to feelings of affection and love. To the degree that pain is anticipated, one's response is guarded or negative. A person cannot love that which hurts unless he has developed a masochistic character. If love arises from the anticipation of pleasure, then its opposite, hate, must arise from the anticipation of pain. I shall explore the spectrum of these two emotions, love and hate, in the next section. Here it is important to understand their connection with pleasure and pain.

The connection between love and pleasure, which seems clear above, becomes confused when we realize that mother love is also an instinctive reaction to one's offspring. It is inbred in those species in which maternal care is essential to the survival of the young. And it is so deeply rooted that from the moment of giving birth a mother animal will defend her young with her life, if necessary. Yet even in the animal kingdom the instinct is not strong enough to prevent maternal destruction of the young under certain conditions. Animal mothers in captivity have been known to abandon their offspring, and the same thing occasionally happens with pets. It can be presumed that the rejection of the young animal occurs under conditions which operate to deny the mother's anticipation of pleasure in the fulfillment of her function. In higher animals the instinct of mother love seems dependent for its full function on the pleasure which instinctual fulfillment normally provides. If this pleasure is lacking, the instinct becomes weaker. Pleasure, on the other hand, reinforces instinctual actions and transforms them into conscious behavior.

Since an instinct cannot fully disappear, there is never a complete absence of mother love even in the most hardened woman. Despite the fear of being a woman, every woman knows in her body that only through the fulfillment of her feminine nature can she experience the joy of life. If this deep awareness is contradicted by the experiences of her life, the memory of which guides her present behavior, she is a woman in conflict, whose desire to love her child is as valid as her hostility. We cannot, however, overlook the fact that in the absence of pleasure a destructive rather than creative attitude toward the child is inevitable.

Underlying the emotion of love is a biological need for contact and closeness with another person. Through this contact our bodies are stimulated and excited; without it they tend to become cold and hard. The need itself is perceived as a feeling of longing, which bioenergetically resembles the feeling of hunger when we need food. Longing, like hunger, becomes more intense when one is deprived. It is also stronger in young children, whose need for contact is greatest. It subsides somewhat during the latency period and surges again during adolescence, when the sexual function becomes operative.

Realization of the difference between the feeling of longing and the emotion of love is important to an understanding of love. Longing bears the same relation to love that hunger does to appetite. Both hunger and longing are non-discriminating biological needs. A hungry person will eat anything; a lonely person will accept anyone as a friend. By contrast, appetite and love are directed toward specific sources of pleasure. One has an appetite for certain foods; one loves a particular person as a friend or mate. The person in love is conscious of the love object as a source of pleasure. If the anticipation of pleasure is added to the biological longing for contact and closeness, the need is transformed into a true emotion. The difference between love and longing is manifest in the manner and behavior of the person. The lover anticipates pleasure, his body is pleasurably excited, warm, and outgoing. The person who longs is sad and withdrawn.

The feeling of longing is also known as dependent love, which is often confused with true love. If a person is dependent on another, he will phrase his feeling as one of love. He will say, "I love you," when what he means is: "I need you." Needing and loving are not the same thing. Need denotes a lack; love is fulfillment. Needing can be painful; loving is pleasurable. Dependent love ties one person to another; true love encourages freedom and spontaneity, the essential elements of pleasure. A dependent attitude decreases the possibility of pleasure and so makes true love difficult, if not impossible. Dependent love is marked by the demand for love or pleasure; true love is a giving of pleasure. The demand for love is rationalized as follows: I need you. I want you. I love you; therefore, you should love me.

The person whose love has a dependent quality believes he is justified in his demand for love. Without his realizing it, he has transferred to another person the unfulfilled longing of his infancy. His dependence reflects his infantile experience, in which he was truly dependent on his mother. His fulfillment then depended on her love, and he was justified in feeling entitled to that love by virtue of need. His unconscious mind refuses to accept the present-day reality—1) that he is no longer a child and 2) that adult love is based on a sharing of pleasure.

In view of the relationship between love and pleasure, how can one demand love? Yet this is done all the time. Parents demand it from children and even regard it as an obligation on the part of the child in return for the effort they make to bring him up. They may get a show of love if they can make the child feel guilty, but the true emotion is not subject to command. Nor can it be earned, as some people think, by acts of self-denial. The self-sacrificing wife is often dismayed to find that her husband has fallen in love with another woman. The self-sacrificing mother is frequently shocked to learn that her children do not appreciate her martyrdom. In general, we are repelled by an attitude of self-denial and drawn to people who enjoy living. I have heard many patients say, "I wish my mother had given herself more pleasure."

But if pleasure is essential to love, love is also necessary for pleasure. For love represents the commitment that makes pleasure possible. We have seen that without a commitment to work, there is no pleasure in work. It is equally important that a person commit himself to a relationship if he is to enjoy that relationship. The commitment arises from the anticipation of pleasure, just as love does. It is, therefore, valid to say that the amount of pleasure bears a direct relation to the degree of commitment or the amount of feeling one invests in an activity or a person.

Love has another important function in those intimate relationships between people on which the cycle of life depends. It adds a degree of security that enables the other person to make a similar commitment to the relationship. This need for security is particularly evident in the relationship of mother and child. Because of his complete helplessness, the human infant requires a feeling of security such that only the total commitment of his mother to his welfare can provide. Any break in his sense of security immediately throws an infant into distress and anxiety, the effects of which are not easily overcome. When we realize that the newborn infant has left a situation in which all his needs were automatically provided for to begin an independent existence, we can see how important to his welfare is the surge of mother love that greets his arrival.

Adults are not helpless, like infants, but in their intimate relationships with one another they too need a feeling of security. They need the assurance that today's pleasure will not become tomorrow's pain through the loss of the person who gave that pleasure. The human being is sharply aware that the greater the pleasure he enjoys today, the greater must be the pain he will feel when the longing for closeness and intimacy reasserts itself and cannot be satisfied. For it is the nature of the animal to seek the renewal of its pleasure in the situation in which it was first experienced.

Man more than any other animal lives in a present that includes his past and embraces his futre. He is keenly aware from his early experiences that in opening himself to pleasure he is exposed to the possibility of pain. If he has suffered numerous disappointments he will be extremely guarded in his anticipation of pleasure. His ability to love will be reduced, and his capacity for pleasure will be decreased. But even with the best of backgrounds, a person is reluctant to commit himself to an intimate relationship that has no possibility of enduring.

Love is a promise that today's pleasure will be available tomorrow. It is no guarantee, nor is it an obligation. The words "I love you" are a commitment that encompasses the future in the present statement of feeling. They are not a promise to love tomorrow, for this emotion like any other arises spontaneously from the depth of one's being and is not subject to the will. More than this, however, is not demanded, and less than this is insufficient. Only with the security that love provides can one surrender fully to the pleasure of love.

Talking of love but dissociating it from its relation to pleasure is moralizing. Morality has never solved the emotional difficulties of man. On the other hand, stressing the importance of pleasure in disregard of the basic need of people for some security, stability, and order in their lives is irresponsible. This can only lead to chaos and misery. The human condition requires a creative approach to its opposing needs. We must recognize that the more pleasure one has, the greater is one's ability to love. We must know that in offering our love, we increase our pleasure.

In this section I used the word "love" as though it had a uniform quality. Actually love, like pleasure, embraces a spectrum of feelings, all of which relate to the experience or anticipation of pleasure. The broad term for these feelings is affection. Affectionate feelings range from friendliness to love. They will be described in the following section.

Affection and Hostility

Emotions may be classified according to whether they are simple or compound. A simple emotion has only one feeling tone, either pleasure or pain. Compound emotions contain elements of both pleasure and pain. Sadness and compassion are compound emotions, as we shall see. Two or more emotions may also combine to produce a more complicated response. In the feeling of resentment, for example, there is anger plus fear. Value judgments are often superimposed on one's feelings, producing what I call a conceptual emotion. Guilt, shame and vanity fall into this category.

The subtle emotional responses of people sometimes defy description. Words are inadequate to portray all the shades of feeling that a human being is capable of experiencing. It is not my intention to analyze each emotional response. Some, however, are important to an understanding of the human personality. These, which include the simple emotions, will receive our full attention.

There are two pairs of simple emotions, the members of which are in a polar relationship to each other. Fear and anger form one pair; love and hate form the other. The second pair includes all the feelings that may be grouped under the headings of affection and hostility. Generally they define our feelings toward other people, although we may speak of love and hate of objects and situations.

Affection is a reaching out to others and the world from an excited state of pleasurable anticipation. It represents an expansive reaction in the body. It is based on a flow of blood to the surface of the body resulting from the dilation of the peripheral blood system. This flow of blood to the surface creates a sensation of physical warmth. Affectionate feelings are characterized by their warmth. We speak of an affectionate person as being a warm person. The other physical manifestations of pleasure are also present. The musculature is soft and relaxed, the heartbeat is slow, the pupils are contracted, and so on.

The warmth of affection is mainly in the skin, which is strongly suffused with blood. This produces a desire for some physical contact with the person who is the object of these feelings—a clasp of the hands, an embrace, or a kiss. All affectionate feelings have an erotic quality and are an expression of the erotic impulse, or Eros. The erotic elements in affection may be either recessive or dominant. They are recessive in friendship and dominant in sexual love. A strong erotic element is produced by a high degree of excitation, with its focus on the erotic zones. These areas then become surcharged with blood.

The opposite feelings, namely, those which can be designated as hostile, are also determined by the flow of blood, but in an opposite direction. The blood leaves the skin and the surface of the body, producing a sensation of coldness. All hostile feelings are cold. The hostile person withdraws his affection and turns cold toward another individual. He loses any erotic desire he may have had and is repelled by any idea of physical contact. All hostile feelings represent, therefore, the withdrawal of feeling.

Neither affection nor hostility represents an aggressive attitude. Aggression is a function of the muscular system, which is not actively involved in the feelings we are discussing. An aggressive component is often added to these feelings, transforming them into specific actions. The sexual act requires this addition for copulation to occur. When an aggressive element is joined to a hostile feeling, it results in an attack or an assault, which differs from the purely hostile reaction of turning cold.

The word "aggressive" is used psychologically as the opposite of passive. Aggressive means to move toward a person or object, whereas the word "passive" denotes an inhibition of this movement. A person can be aggressively hostile or aggressively affectionate, just as he can be passive in the expression of hostility or affection. It is obvious that the word "active" cannot be used in this context as the opposite of passive, since it lacks the connotation of a direction or aim. An aggressive tennis player is out to win; an active player does not necessarily have this goal.

To show the polarity of affectionate and hostile feelings, I shall discuss and contrast friendliness with unfriendliness and love with hate.

Friendliness differentiates our feelings for the person who has tastes and attitudes similar to our own from the feelings we have toward a stranger. Pleasures are shared with a friend. One hesitates to share them with strangers. But by the very act of sharing a pleasure with a stranger, he is changed into a friend.

The reserve that is manifested toward the stranger is very evident among most older children. A very young child, who has an undeveloped sense of self, makes no distinction among children his own age. On the other hand, not only is the newcomer to an established group of children viewed with reserve, but he too approaches the group cautiously. For some time he watches their activities from a distance, then gradually he moves closer. As he becomes more familiar, he may be invited by one of the children to join their play. When he does, his acceptance is assured.

The stranger represents a disturbing element in the feeling of ease and harmony that pervades an established group. His presence may inhibit the flow of pleasurable sensations that takes place between intimates and may evoke, therefore, some degree of hostility or coldness. On the other hand, the stranger introduces novelty and excitement, with their promise of pleasure. He will therefore evoke some curiosity, which will lead to contact. Which of the two factors is most operative in determining the response to a stranger depends on the personality of the group members. A secure person will accept a stranger more readily than will an insecure one.

Friendliness to the stranger is more manifest in people who are enjoying themselves than in people who are involved in a power situation. Generally speaking, when people are having a good time, they tend to be receptive to the stranger. This pleasure makes them expansive and opens them to new experiences. A stranger is often welcomed to a party; he is generally *persona non grata* at a power enclave. In a struggle for power people distrust and fear the stranger. When pleasure is absent, the stranger is often met with hostility or even enmity. Many years ago I saw a cartoon which depicted this situation vividly. Two dour Welshmen were standing in a field watching a stranger approach.

> "D'ye know 'im, Bill?" asked the first.
> "No," replied the second Welshman.
> "'Eave a rock at 'im," said the first one.

Hospitality to the stranger is a concept that is taught as part of either the Judeo-Christian tradition or some other. Modern civilization, with its worldwide facilities for travel and communication, tends to break down the natural barriers between strangers. But this is only a surface phenomenon. Beneath the seeming cordiality that greets the tourist, one can always sense the underlying reserve and coldness that are felt for the stranger by a people whose lives are devoid of joy.

Persecution of the stranger is an expression of hate, rather than of simple unfriendliness. Since he can be a natural object for hostile feelings, he easily becomes a target for the suppressed hatreds that stem from painful childhood experiences. People project on the stranger the intense hostilities that were initially experienced toward parental figures and have become repressed through guilt. The stranger becomes the scapegoat on whom these hostile feelings can be vented. This transference generally meets with social approval and is easily rationalized by the ego. The unfriendliness that greets the stranger can be overcome by increasing familiarity, but it would be a mistake to think that hatred of the stranger can be overcome by education.

Repressed hatreds require a therapeutic situation for their release. First, some form of analytic technique must be used to make them conscious. Second, the guilt which serves to keep these hostile feelings suppressed must be worked through and released. And third, some means must be provided for the physical expression of the hostility in a controlled setting, so that the physical tensions which underlie the feelings are discharged. When this occurs, the capacity of the person to experience pleasure is restored, and "good feelings" become the normal tone of his body.

Love and hate are a familiar polar pair. It is not difficult to understand the polarity if one realizes that hate is frozen love, that is, a love that has turned cold. When love turns into hate, it is not because one is disappointed. Since love is based on the anticipation of pleasure, it fades slowly in the absence of pleasure. A rejected suitor feels hurt, but not hating. Hate is caused by a sense of betrayal. If one has made a commitment of love which the other person has accepted, one's heart is wide open, one's faith is given to the other. A betrayal of this faith is like a knife thrust into the heart. It causes a shock to the personality that immobilizes all movement and arrests all feeling. It is like the quick freezing of food, which preserves the flavor by stopping all biochemical processes.

It is always the feeling of betrayal that changes affectionate feelings into hostility. The betrayal of a friendship turns the positive feeling into enmity. The betrayal of trust turns affection into hostility. The degree of hostility is, therefore, proportionate to the amount of positive feeling invested in a relationship.

Affectionate feelings unite people in a true spirit of community, so that the well-being of one person becomes the concern of the other. Love in particular involves a mutual caring and a mutual dependence. The person in love takes the loved person into his heart and at the same time gives his heart to the other. It is easy to see why a betrayal has such a profound effect. It causes a deep wound that heals very slowly and leaves a scar.

The most important betrayal is that of a child by a parent, especially the mother. Not only is a young child completely dependent on his mother, he is by nature completely open to his mother. A child is betrayed when his mother expresses hostility or shows a destructive attitude toward him. The child can only react with the feeling, "She really doesn't care." A manifestation of anger does not have the same effect. Anger is a positive feeling and expresses a real concern. Hostility toward a child is another matter. It is never biologically justified, since the child is an extension of the mother. It is an expression of self-hatred and a transference of the hostility that developed out of the woman's betrayal by her own mother.

Hostility toward a child generally arises when he fails to conform to the image which the parents have of what their child should be. This image is also their own unconscious, idealized self-image. When the child fails to measure up to this image, the parent feels betrayed. This sense of being betrayed turns the parent's affection into hostility, which then provokes a negative reaction from the child. In this way there is created a vicious circle from which neither parent nor child can escape. Such an unfortunate situation can be prevented by the parents' realization that an infant or child is an animal whose behavior is governed by the pleasure principle. Raising a child to become a member of civilized society requires a creative approach based on an appreciation of this principle if the destructive effects of parental hostility are to be avoided.

Hate contains the possibility of love. If, for example, the betrayal is forgiven, the person thaws and love flows again. This often happens in the late stages of therapy. In the early stages each patient becomes conscious of the repressed hostility or hate which he bears toward his parents because of their betrayal. These negative feelings are then released as described earlier. When his tensions are discharged and his good feelings restored, a patient can accept the fact that his mother's behavior was determined by her own upbringing and can forgive her. He now feels a genuine affection for his mother, instead of the compulsive love with which he was burdened. Hate changes back to love outside therapy, too, when there is an honest exchange of feelings and a true reconciliation.

Situations in which an initial reaction of hate spontaneously changes to love are not unknown. This development can be explained by assuming that a strong attraction always existed but was prevented from flowing by the fear of betrayal. This fear can be expressed as follows: "If I let myself love you, you will turn on me and hurt me, so I hate you." As the fear diminishes with further contact, love blossoms. Fear of betrayal underlies the inordinate jealousy that makes one suspicious of the loved person's every move.

Anger and Fear

The other pair of emotions, anger and fear, is related to the experience or anticipation of pain. Their emergence in consciousness coincides with the growth and coordination of the muscular system. Before the end of the first year of life a child begins to react to pain and distress with volitional movements. His previous purely involuntary response took the form of crying, squirming, wriggling, and random kicking. These movements express a sense of irritation which, as he grows stronger, changes into a feeling of anger. Instead of merely trying to avoid an unpleasant situation, he will push a distasteful object away, strike out with his arms, or even bite when frustrated or hurt. The emotion of anger slowly supersedes crying as a means of releasing tension. A young child's anger, however, is generally impotent to change his situation and usually subsides into crying, the more basic tension-releasing mechanism.

Generally speaking, anger is a more effective response than crying, since it aims to remove the cause of the pain. It requires, therefore, an ability to discriminate a cause and to know the object against which the anger is to be directed. Whereas crying gives one the feeling of being helpless in a situation, anger overcomes the sense of helplessness.

In the feeling of anger, the excitation charges the muscular system along the back of the body, mobilizing the powerful movements of attack. The main organs of assault are located in the upper and front end of the body, because this end is directly connected with the search for and seizure of food. Anger is experienced, therefore, as a surge of feeling upward along the back of the body and into the head and arms. This surge of feeling is associated with a strong flow of blood to these parts, which accounts for the fact that some people literally see red when they become intensely angry. If inhibitions and tensions exist which block this surge of feeling, a tension headache may develop. Crying, on the other hand, is experienced as a letting down. In crying, the charge withdraws from the muscular system, and the tension is released in a series of convulsive sobs. In many respects anger is like a thunder storm. When the angry feeling is discharged through violent movements, the brow clears and good feelings return. Crying is like a soft rain.

Anger and fear belong to the group of emergency emotions; both activate the sympathetic-adrenal system to provide the extra energy for fight or flight. In both emotions the muscular system is charged and mobilized for action. If the feeling is one of anger, the organism attacks the source of the pain. When the feeling is fear, it turns and flees from the danger. These two opposite directions of movement reflect what happens in the body. The upward movement along the back, which raises the hackles in a dog, together with a forward movement of the head and a lowering of the shoulders is the preparation for an assault. The downward movement along the back results in a pulling in of the tail section and the charging of the legs for flight. In a state of fear one turns tail and runs. If flight is impossible, the excitation is caught in the neck and back, the shoulders are raised, the eyes are wide open, the head is pulled back, and the tail is tucked in. Since this is the typical expression of fear, this bodily attitude denotes that a person is in a constant state of fear whether he is conscious of it or not.

The pathway for the flow of excitation in anger along the back and over the head can be explained by the fact that in man, as in most mammals, the primary organs of attack are the mouth and teeth. The impulse to bite is the primordial form for the expression of anger. Biting occurs in almost all children, and it is sometimes seen in adults, too, particularly in women. It is a very effective form of attack, since it causes severe pain, but it suffers from the disadvantage of requiring very close contact. Hitting, which has a greater range and allows more maneuverability, has therefore superseded biting as the main physical expression of anger. But when a person is very angry, his face often assumes a snarling expression, which is associated with biting.

"Man bites dog" is said to be news, obviously because of its rarity. I have never seen a man bite a dog, but I did see my son, when he was about four and a half, bite the family dog. This was no mean feat, since the dog was a full-grown Afghan hound who came up to the boy's shoulders. The dog, in his effort to get close to the food that was being prepared in the kitchen, was pushing the boy, who became so angry that he reached over and bit the dog on the back. The dog howled and took off out of the kitchen.

I mention this incident because I believe that inhibitions about biting are partly responsible for many disturbances in the expression of anger. These disturbances take the form of an inability to get angry, hysterical outbursts, and persistent feelings of irritation. Anger, like all true emotions, is an ego-syntonic expression. Unlike hysterical reactions, it does not erupt against the conscious intention; it is ego-directed and aims at a positive result, namely, to remove a cause of frustration or pain. Anger is not hostility, for it is not a turning away or a turning cold. Inhibitions against biting prevent the flow of excitation into the head and mouth and block the natural experience of this emotion.

The inability of people to "bite into life" or to "sink their teeth into a situation" is one result of the suppression of the biting impulse. I am not advocating that children be encouraged to bite; but they should not be punished for biting or for any other expression of anger. The person who is denied the right to express anger is rendered defenseless. He is reduced to a condition of fear and helplessness which he will try to overcome by manipulating his environment. It has been shown bioenergetically that underlying all chronic feelings of fear and helplessness is suppressed anger.

The correspondence between fear and anger is such that one changes into the other. If a frightened person turns to attack, he will become angry and unafraid. This is because the flow of excitation has changed direction in his body. His new feeling is the perception of this change. When an attacking person starts to retreat, he will become afraid for the same reason. The feeling of anger is discharged in the movements of attack. The feeling of fear is discharged through flight.

Fear develops when the threat of pain is posed by a seemingly superior force. Caution advises that one should retreat to avoid getting hurt, but caution is the voice of reason, and the emotions are not subject to the control of reason. Whether one chooses fight or flight will depend on the individual and the situation. Despite the superior force of the aggressor, one may react with anger to a violation in circumstances where withdrawal is physically or psychologically inadvisable. True anger adds a considerable measure of strength to the individual and is often sufficient to compensate for a handicap in size or weight. The person who feels angry is generally supported by the conviction that his position is justified or right.

In situations, however, where anger cannot be mobilized because the danger is vague, unknown, or impersonal, fear is a natural reaction. Thus children, for example, are afraid when alone in the dark. They feel helpless and will either run or cry. For the same reason adults are afraid of the unknown. To tell a child that he should not be afraid of the dark is absurd. It may be pointed out that there is no real danger, but it must be recognized that his fear is a biological response that cannot be judged. We do irreparable damage to children by calling them cowards and making them feel ashamed of their natural reactions. This irrational attitude on the part of some adults is due in part to their confusion about the nature of emotional responses. In part, too, it represents the acting out on children of the treatment they received when they were young and helpless.

Although the spontaneous impulse when one is afraid is to escape, this impulse can be blocked by an effort of will. The will is an emergency mechanism under the control of the ego which can on occasion override the emotional response. And in some situations it may be lifesaving. The will, however, does not diminish fear. It enables an individual to stand his ground or advance in the face of his fear. It can also be foolhardy, as when the will is used to override the fear for the sake of ego gratification.

When the ego is identified with the body, it will support the body's emotional responses and direct them into effective actions. If a person is afraid, it will function to assure his escape from the danger. Without the ego control that comes from identification with one's feelings, fear can easily degenerate into panic. Similarly, when a person is angry, his ego limits his behavior to what is necessary to stop or prevent his being hurt or injured. The ego adds a rational element to anger and keeps it from getting out of hand. Since anger generally subsides when the violation ceases, anger cannot be considered a destructive action. This is not true of rage. When the ego's identification with the body is diminished and its control is weakened, the surge of anger often erupts as rage, which is frequently destructive to the person and his environment.

Like most personality functions, panic and rage have a polar relationship to each other. Both are based on a feeling of being trapped. When a person is confronted by an overwhelming threat of pain which cannot be countered by either flight or fight, he will develop either a feeling of panic or one of rage. If he flees, his flight will be desperate, a wild desire to get away at any cost. He will run blindly, that is, without a proper appreciation of the reality of his situation—in other words, without ego control or direction. If he cannot flee, he will react with rage.

We are familiar with panic from the behavior of people who feel trapped by fire. In their blind desire to get out of the threatening situation, they often overlook possible avenues of escape and become self-destructive. Panic often occurs in wartime when people flee blindly from an advancing enemy. What we fail to understand is that a child can become panicked when threatened by an irate parent. He is literally trapped since neither fight nor flight is a reasonable possibility. Since there is no escape, his panic may take the form of hysterical screaming.

Children who live under a more or less constant threat of pain develop a chronic state of panic, the feeling of which becomes suppressed as they grow older. This suppression is only relatively effective. The panic breaks through in later life in situations of stress which do not rationally justify such an intense reaction. Some people are so close to panic that they are afraid to go out of their homes alone. I have treated a number of such cases. In others the panic is just under the surface. It is manifested generally in an overinflated chest and difficulty in breathing. The person in a state of panic feels that he cannot get enough air. Conversely, when a person feels unable to get enough air, he goes into a panic. Underlying the respiratory difficulty is a blocked scream. If the scream is released therapeutically, the breathing improves and the feeling of panic diminishes.

When a person feels trapped, he can also react with rage, especially if some object is present on which the rage can be vented. In rage the muscular excitation is excessive, and the person loses control over his actions. Like panic, rage is blind. The raging person strikes out indiscriminately, unaware of the destructive effects of his actions. Unlike anger, rage is not associated with a specific provocation, because it stems from a feeling of being trapped.

How can we understand the rage that some parents occasionally manifest toward their children? It is difficult to imagine how a child can cause an overriding fear in a parent. We must seek the explanation in the parent's feeling of being trapped by the child. For one thing, a mother is bound to her child. She knows she has an obligation to give it the continued care and attention it needs. If her energy is low, she will feel the child to be a burden. If her relation to her husband is painful, she will see the child as a chain that locks her to the pain of this relationship. If her own infantile needs were not fulfilled, she will resent the child's demands for love. Unless her experience of mothering is a pleasure and a joy, she will feel trapped by the obligation she has assumed. And in moments of extreme stress she will turn on the child with rage.

The effect of parental rage on a child is terror. I shall describe this emotion in the next paragraph. Here I would like to state that this effect is produced even if the rage does not take the form of overt violence. The child who senses the latent violence in a parent is equally affected. The expression of rage on a parent's face is something no child can understand or cope with. It is a threat to the child's existence. I have seen parents look at children with rage in their faces. It has happened in my office without the parent's being aware of her expression. The mother's face became dark, as if a black cloud had descended over her brows and eyes. Her jaw was grim. The eyes were cold and hard. It was a look of murder. Confronted with such a look, a child is frozen with terror.

In terror the muscular system is paralyzed, making any form of fight or flight impossible. Terror is a more intense form of fear than panic and develops in situations where any effort to resist or escape appears hopeless. Terror is a form of shock; feeling is withdrawn from the periphery of the body, reducing the organism's sensitivity to its anticipated final agony. It represents a flight inward.

The child who experiences terror in relation to its parents develops a schizoid personality. Its body structure shows all the signs of this emotion; it is tight and contracted or flabby with poor muscle tone. The surface of the body is undercharged. The eyes tend to be blank, and the facial expression is mask-like. Breathing is severely constricted by spasms in the muscles of the throat and bronchi. Inspiration is shallow, and the thorax is held in the expiratory position. The immobilization of movement leads to a depersonalization, that is, a dissociation of the perceiving ego from the body.

When panic is the underlying feeling, the body has a different expression. It is tense, as if poised for flight. The chest is inflated and held in the inspiratory position. Fright causes a person to suck in air to provide the extra oxygen for fight or flight. In panic this air is held, the throat closes, and the person cannot seem to breathe. This inability to expel air fully maintains the state of panic, just as the inability to breathe in fully continues the state of terror.

Fury is the counterpart of terror. It is a remorseless anger that is devastating in its effect. Unlike anger, which is hot, and rage, which is wild, fury is cold and hard. It represents, therefore, the aggressive aspect of hate. A hateful person is inwardly furious and outwardly cold. A loving person is inwardly relaxed and outwardly warm.

This spectrum of the simple emotions is not intended to be definitive. It is a convenient format to show the biological order that prevails on this level of the personality. In the next chapter I shall discuss how we distort our emotional lives.

9 · Guilt, Shame, and Depression

Guilt

Too many people in our culture are plagued by feelings of guilt and shame or suffer from depression. Their emotional lives are confused and full of conflicts. In this state it is very unlikely that they can have a creative approach to life, and in fact, this tendency toward depression denotes an inner awareness of defeat.

How does the feeling of guilt arise? It is not a true emotion stemming from the experience of pleasure or pain. It is not rooted in the biological processes of the body. Apart from man, it is not found in the animal world. We must assume, therefore, that guilt is a product of culture and of the values that characterize the culture. These values become embodied in moral principles and codes of behavior which are indoctrinated into each child by its parents and become part of the child's ego structure. For example, most children are taught that lying is wrong. If they accept this principle and then tell a lie, they will feel guilty. If they rebel against the teaching, they are forced into conflict with their parents, which can also be productive of guilt feelings.

The problem is further complicated by the fact that it does feel wrong to tell a lie in situations of trust. It feels wrong because it feels bad; that is, it produces a state of pain in the deceiver by disturbing the harmony between himself and those who trust him. There is some justification, therefore, for the moral precept that one should not lie, but this biological justification is rarely used in the teaching of ethical principles. Instead, parents and others rely on a doctrinaire attitude, which rigidifies the moral principle and dissociates it from its connection with the emotional life of the individual. A moral principle that has become an authoritative rule will necessarily conflict with the spontaneous behavior of an individual, which is guided by the pleasure-pain principle.

A culture without a value system is meaningless. Culture itself is a positive value. A society without an accepted code of behavior based on moral principles degenerates into anarchy or dictatorship. As man developed culture and transcended the purely animal state, morality became part of his way of life. But this was a natural morality based on the feeling of what was right or wrong, specifically, that which promoted pleasure in contrast to that which led to pain. I shall illustrate this concept of natural morality with another example from the parent-child relationship. A normal parent is pained by his child's lack of respect, and the child is disturbed by his parent's pain. Every child wants to respect his parent—this is natural morality. He will not do so, however, if this leads to a loss of self-respect, to a surrender of his right to self-expression. If the parent respects the child's individuality and above all his striving for pleasure, there will be a mutual respect between parent and child that will increase the pleasure and enjoyment each has with the other. In this situation neither parent nor child will develop feelings of guilt.

A feeling of guilt arises when a negative moral judgment is imposed on a bodily function that is beyond the control of the ego, or conscious mind. To feel guilty about sexual desires, for example, makes no biological sense. Sexual desire is a natural body response to a state of excitation and develops independently of one's will. It has its origin in the pleasure functions of the body. If this desire is judged morally wrong, it means that the conscious mind has turned against the body. When this happens, the unity of the personality is split. In every emotionally disturbed individual there are conscious or unconscious feelings of guilt which disrupt the internal harmony of the personality.

The acceptance of one's feelings does not imply that one has the right to act upon them in any situation. A healthy ego has the power to control behavior so that it is appropriate to the situation. The lack of this power in a weak ego or sick personality may lead to actions that are destructive to individuals and to the social order. Although society has the right and the obligation to protect its members against destructive behavior, it has no right to label feelings themselves as wrong.

This distinction becomes clear if we recognize the difference between guilt as a moral judgment of one's feelings and guilt as a legal judgment of a person's actions. The latter is a determination that certain behavior has contravened an established law. The former gives rise to a feeling that often bears no relation to one's actions or behavior. A person who breaks a law is guilty of a crime whether he feels guilty or not. A child who feels hostile towards his parents may feel guilty, though he hasn't committed a destructive act. The *feeling* of guilt is a form of self-condemnation.

Any feeling or emotion can become a source of guilt feelings if a negative moral judgment is attached to it. Generally, however, it is our pleasure feelings, sexual or erotic desires, and hostility that are colored by such judgments, which stem directly from parental attitudes and ultimately from social mores. A child is made to feel guilty about his pleasure strivings in order to make him into a productive worker, he is made to feel guilty about sexuality to subdue his animal nature, and he is made to feel guilty about hostility to render him obedient and submissive. In the course of such training his creative potential is destroyed.

A major part of all psychotherapeutic efforts is directed toward the removal of guilt feelings in order to restore the integrity of the personality. For it is the feeling of guilt that undermines the ego's power to control behavior in the best interests of the individual and the community. And it is the feeling of guilt that makes people act in a destructive manner by preventing the natural self-regulatory processes of the body. In every obedient child there is a streak of rebellion that may break through at any time. In every sexually suppressed person there are tendencies toward perversion. And every pleasure-deprived individual is tempted by the escapade that promises fun.

To remove a feeling of guilt, the guilt must first be made conscious. It may seem like a contradiction to speak of a feeling that one doesn't feel, but the fact is that there are latent feelings in people, that is, feelings that have been suppressed and exist just under the surface of awareness. The best examples are in the realm of sex. In today's swinging world many people deny that they feel any guilt about their sexual activities. Guided by the morality of fun, they believe that "anything goes" between two "consenting adults," provided nobody gets hurt. Thus they claim that they have no guilt about their sexual promiscuity or their extramarital affairs. Yet when I ask some of these people who consult me about masturbation, their expression is one of disgust. They believe that masturbation is wrong, and they avoid it. They claim that they get no pleasure from masturbation. But how can this be? If they enjoy sex, they should enjoy masturbation when no sexual partner is available. When they admit that they feel bad after masturbating, it can be pointed out that this is a feeling of guilt without its moral overtones. It soon becomes apparent that their other sexual activities leave them with mixed feelings. They have some pleasure but also some pain in the form of self-doubts and self-condemnation.

The feeling of guilt derives its charge from the natural emotion. When an emotion is fully expressed and the excitation of the emotion released, one feels good. One has a feeling of pleasure and satisfaction. However, when an emotion is not fully expressed, the residual undischarged excitation leaves one feeling dissatisfied, unfulfilled, and bad. This bad feeling can be interpreted as guilt, sin, or wickedness, depending on the moral judgment. Avoiding the labels of guilt or sin does nothing to change the underlying bad feeling. An experience of complete satisfaction and pleasure leaves no room for guilt to operate.

Guilt creates a vicious circle. If a person feels guilty about his sexual desires, he will be unable to give in fully to these desires or to commit himself wholeheartedly to the sexual relationship. His sexual activity under this condition cannot be fully satisfactory or enjoyable. The unconscious holding back, enforced by the guilt, introduces a painful element into the experience, and one comes out of it with the feeling that it was somehow "wrong." To *feel* right, an activity must have an enjoyable or pleasurable quality. Then it really feels right. When it lacks this quality, one is justified in assuming that it was not fully right, and one will necessarily feel as guilty as before, if not more so.

The existence of unconscious guilt feelings is evidenced, therefore, by a decreased capacity for pleasure, by an overemphasis on productivity and achievement, and by the frantic pursuit of fun. By denying themselves pleasure, people can mask their guilt, but this maneuver also betrays their guilt. Their diminished ability to enjoy life is originally caused by guilt. The shoulds and shouldn'ts by which children are raised have the insidious effect of inducing guilt, even if such terms as "wrong" and "sinful" are avoided. A common remark is "You shouldn't waste your time." The very notion of wasting time is a reflection of unconscious guilt.

By the time a child grows up, the feeling of guilt and the inhibitions which it produces have become structured in his body in chronic muscular tensions. He may in the meantime have become rebellious, acting out his defiance in ways his parents would not approve, but this procedure does not change the underlying guilt. It may even increase it. He may rationalize away the awareness of guilt, but this only represses the guilt to levels where it is inaccessible. As long as his body is bound by chronic muscular tensions that limit its motility and decrease the individual's self-expression, the existence of unconscious guilt cannot be denied.

Guilt is attached not only to the striving for pleasure but also to feelings of hostility. The two are directly related; a child becomes hostile when his pleasure-seeking is frustrated, and he is then punished and made to feel guilty for his anger. Here again we have a list of shoulds and shouldn'ts. "You shouldn't scream," "You should listen to your parents," "You shouldn't be angry," and so on. Since the resulting hostility *feels* wrong to the child, he becomes convinced that he is bad. He is the guilty one.

The relationship between repressed anger and guilt was demonstrated by one of my patients. She told me that she was feeling terribly guilty, and decided to hit the bed with a tennis racquet. This is one of the therapeutic exercises in bioenergetic therapy. She did so with full vigor, giving herself fully to the activity. When she had finished, the feeling of guilt was completely gone. "Guilt," she said, "is nothing but repressed anger."

I have, however, had patients who were unable to strike the therapeutic couch effectively. They derived no satisfaction from this activity. Many said it was silly. In such cases analysis always reveals a feeling of guilt about expressing hostility, especially toward the mother. As a result, the patient is unable to commit himself to the activity. By analyzing the underlying guilt, and with continued practice, the patient becomes more aggressive. His blows become stronger and are made with more feeling. It may seem surprising, but when all the hostility is thus vented, the patient feels no guilt, and there is a resurgence of affection for the parent.

Since the feeling of guilt is a form of self-condemnation, it can be overcome by self-acceptance. Subjectively, one is what one feels. To deny a feeling or emotion is to reject a part of the self. And when a person rejects himself, he is left with a feeling of guilt. People reject their feelings because they have an idealized self-image which doesn't include feelings of hostility, fear, or rage. The rejection, however, is only mental; the feelings are still there, buried and encrusted with guilt.

The initial rejection is always a parental rejection. "You are a bad boy for not obeying your parents," if repeated enough, can brainwash a child into believing he is bad. No child is born good or bad, obedient or disobedient. He is born an animal, with an animal's instinctive tendency to seek pleasure and avoid pain. If this behavior is unacceptable to his parents, so is the child. The parent who believes he loves his child but cannot accept the child's basic animal nature is guilty of self-deception.

The original feeling of guilt arises from the sense of being unloved. The only explanation a child can formulate for this state of affairs is that he is not deserving of love. He is incapable of thinking that the fault lies with his mother. This concept will develop later, when he has gained more objectivity. At an early age his sanity and survival depend on his seeing his mother in a positive light, as the "good mother," all-powerful and protective. Those aspects of his mother's behavior which belie this image are denied and projected on a "bad mother" who is not really the true mother. This reaction on the part of a child is consistent with nature, that is, with the view that mother love is inbred and instinctive. If mother is "good," then the child must be bad, since these categories only apply to opposites. These distinctions do not arise when mother and child fulfill each other's needs and provide each other with the pleasure of love.

Just as some feelings are judged morally wrong, others are judged morally superior. These feelings are then deliberately cultivated, and one puts on a show of love, compassion, and tolerance which are not genuinely felt. This pseudo-love gives one a feeling of righteousness, but not a feeling of pleasure. The righteous person does not love in anticipation of pleasure but as a moral duty or obligation. Such behavior is designed to hide the opposite feelings. The pseudo-affection of the righteous person covers his repressed hostility, his facade of compassion masks his repressed anger, and his feigned tolerance cloaks his prejudice.

The righteous person has suppressed his striving for pleasure in favor of an ego image of moral superiority. He has also repressed his feeling of guilt about his true emotions. His righteousness, however, betrays his guilt, for righteousness and guilt are like the head and tail of a coin. One does not exist without the other, although only one shows at a time. Each person who feels guilty also carries a hidden feeling of moral superiority.

Shame and Humiliation

The feeling of shame, like that of guilt, has a disintegrating effect on the personality. It destroys an individual's dignity and undermines his sense of self. To be humiliated is often much more traumatic than to be physically injured. The scar it leaves rarely heals spontaneously. It is experienced as a blemish on the personality which generally requires considerable therapeutic effort to remove.

Few people in our culture grow up without experiencing some feelings of shame or humiliation. Most children are shamed into behaving in civilized ways. They are made to feel ashamed if they appear naked in public, if they fail to develop excremental control, and if they do not learn proper table manners. I recall a scene from a family gathering in which my two-and-a-half-year-old son was reaching into his mother's blouse to get some "titty." He was still nursing at that time. Watching this action, his grandfather said, "Aren't you ashamed, a big boy like you still wanting to nurse!" I asked the grandfather, who was born and raised in Greece, how long he had nursed. When he answered, "Four years or more," he realized how irrational his previous remark had been.

There are many irrationalities associated with the feeling of shame. At a time when the female breast is publicly displayed for adult delectation, it is considered shameful for a woman to nurse her child in public. And when a young woman would have been ashamed not long ago to admit that she was not a virgin, she may be ashamed today to admit that she is still virginal. The miniskirt, which is socially acceptable today, would have been a source of shame earlier. By the same token, wearing a knee-length dress would embarrass or shame the modern woman.

It is obvious that the feeling of shame is closely related to socially approved standards of behavior. Just as every culture has its value system, so every society has its code of conduct which embodies these values. If we are to understand the sense of shame, it is important to recognize that the code of conduct is not always the same for each member of society. It may vary considerably with the social position of the individual. This becomes immediately evident when we realize that behavior which would be considered shameful by one class of people may be regarded as acceptable by another. Table manners are a good example. A person raised in an upper-class family would feel ashamed if he ate in the company of his peers with the manners of a peasant. Table manners, like diction and dress, reflect one's breeding and background and are therefore considered signs of one's social position. A person will feel ashamed if his deportment in these areas makes him conscious of social inferiority. Perhaps the extreme example was the shame that attached to an English gentleman of the preceding century who was forced to work. Work was associated with the lower classes and was a mark of social inferiority.

The feeling of shame, however, has deeper roots than class

distinction. There are actions which are viewed as shameful regardless of one's social position. These actions pertain to the bodily functions of excretion and sexuality. Every child in our culture is trained to excremental cleanliness at an early age, and this training necessarily inculcates a sense of shame in respect to this function. All adults carry within their ego structure a sense of shame about soiling or wetting themselves even when these occurrences are unavoidable. It is not the function that is shameful but the way in which it is performed.

If a man urinated on the street, he would receive glances from passersby designed to make him feel ashamed. And if he was in full possession of his faculties, that is, not drunk or psychotic, he would feel ashamed. The shame is not in the act of urinating but stems from the fact that this is not a socially accepted way for a man to behave. A little boy may be permitted to act in this way, and our animal pets are allowed to "do their business" in public, but when a person who should know better behaves like an animal, we find it shameful.

The first class distinction, and the one in which the feeling of shame has its origin, is that between man and the animals. This distinction exists in all cultures and is based on the fact that man regards himself as superior to the animals. It is a derogatory remark to say of a person that he behaves like a beast or has the table manners of an animal. Although the behavior in question may not be typical of an animal, the remark is really intended to signify that it is unworthy of a human being. Man, in contrast with the animal, lives by a set of conscious values. These values vary in different cultures, but whatever they are, they underlie the feeling of shame if one fails to live up to them.

Values are ego judgments about behavior and feeling, and like all ego functions, they can operate to promote pleasure or deny it. Cleanliness is a simple example. We value cleanliness—some people say it is next to godliness—because it gives us the feeling that we control to some extent our immediate environment. A dirty or littered house indicates a lack of control. It degrades the ego to live like a pig. Since cleanliness enhances the ego, it can further one's pleasure in the house. It can also be said that cleanliness is more healthful, but this is only true of a minimal cleanliness. The normal dust, dirt, or litter that would disturb an average housekeeper poses no threat to health. When cleanliness, however, becomes a dissociated value, when it becomes an obsession, it can seriously interfere with the pleasure one has in the home. In too many homes the pleasure of living is sacrificed for a condition of cleanliness that has meaning only in terms of a housekeeper's feeling of shame that her home doesn't measure up to some standard. For many people uncleanliness is a personal reflection that diminishes one's stature and status.

Shame and status are closely related. If one's status in a group depended on having a new automobile, one would be ashamed to drive an old car. Similarly, if status in a group is determined by the degree to which one rejects the established values, then uncleanliness may become a new value, and the individual who dresses too neatly may feel ashamed in the presence of those upholding this new value if he seeks their acceptance. Only on this basis can we understand the appeal of the new adolescent vogues. Whereas previously a person would be ashamed not to wear shoes, now in some circles he would be ashamed not to go barefoot. As long as there are ego values which determine position and status, the feeling of shame can arise.

Status, as we saw earlier, also plays an important role in animal societies. It is determined, however, by different factors from those we use. In most animal groups, a hierarchy develops in which the stronger, more aggressive members are at the top of the order, with the weaker and younger ones at the bottom. This inequality, based on natural endowments, is never questioned. On the other hand, it does not lead to feelings of superiority or inferiority, nor does it produce a sense of shame among the group members. The differences are accepted as facts of nature and are not due to judgments based on ego values.

There are natural differences among people which, because they are accepted as facts, do not produce feelings of shame. These differences will determine an order of prestige and authority. The most valiant fighter will naturally be chosen to lead his group into combat. The older and wiser men are normally the counselors. Each person in a true community finds the proper place for his talents and abilities and is not ashamed if his place is different from or lower than that of others. On the body level each person feels equal to the others; he shares the same functions and has the same needs and desires. This sense of equality exists among young children, who live very much in terms of bodily feeling and have not yet developed a set of ego values. When these values develop and become the basis by which their relative social position with respect to one another is determined, the bodily sense of equality is lost, and individuals are judged to be superior or inferior.

Shame derives from the consciousness of inferiority. Any act that makes a person feel inferior will also make him feel ashamed. Shame and humiliation go hand in hand. Both rob an individual of his dignity, of his self-respect, and of his feeling that he is equal to (as good as) others. It can be said, therefore, that every person who lacks a feeling of dignity and who feels inadequate suffers from a sense of shame and humiliation that may be conscious or unconscious.

The gradual disappearance of class distinctions has lessened the sense of shame in many aspects of life. There is an increasing acceptance of the body and its functions. Exposure of the body that would be considered shameful in the past is socially acceptable today. The same thing is true of public references to sex. It may actually seem to some observers that people have lost all sense of shame. Unfortunately, this is not true. Feelings are frequently denied by going to the opposite extreme.

In rejecting an ego value, we eliminate the shame that attached to that value only. But new values take their place and become the criteria of status, giving rise to feelings of shame when one's behavior fails to reach the new standards. I find that people are still ashamed of their bodies when they fail to conform to current fashion. The new look in bodies is the look of youth. Many people feel ashamed because their bodies show some fat or because their bellies protrude. At other times these were signs of affluence and were valued accordingly. The look of youth is an ego value that may or may not increase one's pleasure. If one looks youthful because one feels vibrant and alive, it is a positive value. But starving the body and tightening one's muscles to fulfill an ego image is not the way to bodily pleasure. Success is another current ego value, and many people feel ashamed because they have not attained the success which others in their group seem to have achieved.

I find that many people are shamed of their feelings. Even in the therapy situation they are embarrassed to admit their weaknesses, ashamed to cry, humiliated to acknowledge their fear and helplessness. "Don't be a crybaby" is a way of shaming a child into suppressing his unhappiness. "Don't be a coward" shames a child into suppressing his fear. The inordinate striving for success that characterizes our culture has its roots in the humiliation children are subjected to when they fail to measure up to their parents' image.

Shame, like guilt, is a barrier to self-acceptance. It makes us self-conscious and so robs us of the spontaneity that is the essence of pleasure. It sets the ego against the body and, like guilt, destroys the unity of the personality. Emotional health is not possible in the individual who struggles with a feeling of shame.

Does this mean, then, that human beings must give up their civilized ways to free themselves from this burden? I don't think so. A civilization requires civilized ways of behaving if it is to function smoothly. I for one am not prepared to give up our civilization, although I believe that many changes should be made in it. We must eliminate the use of shame in our educational methods. It is employed because parents and teachers do not trust a child's natural impulses. They assume that he will resist learning civilized ways unless pressure is put on him. They forget that the human animal wants and needs to be accepted by his community and will make every effort to learn the accepted ways. This effort will be facilitated if these ways are associated with pleasure and not with the pain of shame.

Raising a child with pleasure rather than shame is a creative approach to the problem of teaching him civilized ways. In this approach neither rewards nor punishments are employed. If the pattern of behavior in a home is conducive to pleasure, a child will spontaneously adopt this pattern. He will naturally imitate his parents if he sees that their ways of acting make life more enjoyable. And he will learn the accepted forms of social intercourse when he finds that they facilitate interpersonal relationships.

I have been asked by mothers what to do with a child who

resists toilet training and insists on wearing diapers. Apart from the extra work it may cause his mother, the only person who is truly handicapped is the child. Whatever his fear may be of the toilet, it is unlikely that he will persist in his infantile ways when he sees that other children have freed themselves from this handicap. If the mother could overcome her own feeling of shame, this problem would naturally resolve itself. I have never known a child who continued to wear his diapers to school. An emphatic understanding of the child's feeling would prevent a serious conflict that might have traumatic effects. If a child is not judged, he will learn civilized ways through his natural striving for pleasure without developing a feeling of shame.

By splitting the unity of the personality, the feeling of shame produces its opposite, the feeling of vanity. Like the person with a sense of shame, the vain person is self-conscious, although his judgment of his bodily appearance is positive. Is not his vanity a rebound from a previous state of shame? Having suppressed every aspect of his behavior and appearance that could cause him to feel ashamed of himself, he can now parade himself as a model of his class, which in fact he does. But he is just a model, not a human being.

The normal feelings about the body, which are free from value judgments, are modesty and pride. In his modesty and natural pride a person expresses his identification with his body and his pleasure and joy in its functioning.

Depression and Illusion

The suppression of emotion and feeling by guilt and shame sets a person up for a depressive reaction. Guilt and shame force the person to substitute ego values for bodily ones, images for reality, and approval for love. His energy is invested in trying to realize a dream that will never come true because it is based on an illusion. The illusion is that one's good feelings and pleasure are solely dependent on the response of the environment. Recognition, acceptance, and approval become the overriding goals of one's efforts in complete disregard of the fact that these responses from others are meaningless until one first recognizes, accepts, and approves of himself. This illusion ignores the fact that pleasure is largely an internal state which spontaneously evokes a favorable response from the environment.

The emotions that are suppressed are those deriving from the anticipation of pain, namely, hostility, anger, and fear. These emotions are suppressed when they can be neither expressed nor tolerated. The individual has no choice but to deny them. The situation that produces this state of affairs is a clash of wills between parent and child. Once this happens, the original issue of conflict becomes transformed into a question of right or wrong, and the child's feelings are no longer important. Since it is extremely difficult for a parent to concede or even conceive that he is wrong, the child is forced eventually into submission. This submission, which generally occurs some time prior to puberty, enables the child to develop a *modus vivendi* with his parents that facilitates his movement toward adulthood. Underneath the submission, however, is a latent rebellion which generally flares again when the young person gains more independence as a teen-ager.

Teen-age rebellion does not release the suppressed emotions of childhood. It is based on the newly discovered teen-age prerogatives and thus introduces a new conflict into the relationship between parent and child. Even though the youth may be dominant in the new clash of wills that ensues, the guilt and shame that stemmed from childhood experiences are not resolved. Buried in the unconscious, they feed the fires of a rebellion that doesn't know its true aim. It seems unfortunately true that without some form of therapy the rebellion fails to have a constructive outcome.

It is extremely difficult for a child to function under the pressure of a negative relationship with his parents. A good relationship is so essential to a child's security that any disturbance preoccupies the child's mind, absorbs his energies, and upsets his equilibrium. A disturbed relationship produces a disturbed child, and this disturbance is commonly manifested in restlessness and temper tantrums. The latter are gradually brought under control as the child gains "outside" interests; school, friends, games, and so on. These new associations demand a positive attitude if he is to be accepted by his peers. To make this change on the outside, the child must also make some adjustment to his home situation. He must forgo his hostility towards his parents, curb his anger and control his fear.

Suppression involves a number of steps: First, the expression of the emotion is blocked to avoid a continuing conflict, second, guilt feelings develop which make the emotion feel "wrong"; and third, the ego succeeds in denying the emotion, thereby barring it from consciousness. The suppression of emotional expression is a form of resignation. The child gives up any expectation of pleasure from his parents and settles for a reduction of open conflict. He realizes as he grows older that all parents are somewhat alike; few indulge the wishes of a child, and almost all demand obedience. And he also realizes that parents generally mean well, that their conscious desire is to help him adjust to the conditions of social living.

The ability to be objective, to see that parents too have a difficult time and that their values are grounded in their way of life, marks a further step in the development of the child's consciousness and lays the basis for the feeling of guilt. This development occurs during the latency period, from seven to thirteen years of age, and represents a resolution of the Oedipal situation. The child now accepts his position in the family and judges his feelings and behavior from that point of view. In the pre-Oedipal period, up to six years of age, most children are too subjective to feel guilty about their attitudes and behavior.

The ability to judge one's own attitudes stems from the process of identifying with one's parents and other authority figures. Through these identifications, good and bad, one achieves a vantage point that is outside the self. Only from such a vantage point can the ego turn against the self, condemning its emotions and creating a feeling of guilt. From this position "outside" the self, the condemned emotions *feel* wrong. One is justified, therefore, in dissociating himself from them to reduce the feeling of guilt.

In the last step of this process the ego attempts to reconstruct the split personality by denying the emotion and replacing it with an image of the opposite feeling. The person who represses his hostility will see himself as a loving and dutiful individual. If he represses his anger, he will imagine himself to be good-natured and kind. If he represses his fear, he will conceive of himself as courageous and brave. The ego normally works with images; the body image is one, the self image is another, and the image of the world is a third. When these images are true to experience, the person is in touch with reality. An image that contradicts experience is an illusion; when it contradicts a self-experience, it is a delusion.

How can one tell that these delusions are not the reality of a person's character? Is it not natural for a person to be loving and dutiful? Yes, but no more natural than it is for him to be hostile and defiant. The individual operating under a delusion develops a compulsive pattern of behavior to sustain the delusion. He must always act loving and dutiful, for any break in the pattern may puncture the delusion. Similarly, the person who is always good-natured and kind, who sees both sides of every position, has erected powerful defenses against any feelings of anger. True courage is the ability to act in the face of fear. The person who has repressed his fear is afraid to be afraid. In bioenergetic therapy the measure of a patient's repressed fear is his inability to feel or express fear. Those patients who are the most frightened inwardly deny any feeling of fear, even when their bodily and facial expressions show their fright.

The true emotions arise, as we have seen, from the experience or anticipation of pleasure or pain. A delusion has no connection with these feelings. The person who proclaims his love regardless of circumstances is either deceiving himself or deceiving others. Not to react with anger when one is hurt or with fear when one is threatened is an indication that these emotional responses are blocked. But they are only blocked from conscious perception. Repressed hostility manifests itself in subtle, sadistic ways which are evident to all but the person suffering from delusion.

To maintain a delusion one must distort outer reality into its opposite. This is the essence of the paranoid mechanism. One will distrust the positive and disbelieve the negative. If, for example, one plays the role of a loving and dutiful child, one has to pretend that the parents are loving and beneficent figures. I had a young schizoid patient who was inwardly terrified but completely unconscious of this emotion. Despite the common knowledge that most city parks are dangerous places at night, this young man and a friend strolled through one of these parks at night. He was jumped and beaten up by a gang of hoodlums. We would say that a person in his right mind would not have taken such a chance. My patient could not allow himself to feel afraid, and he had to prove his courage by taking this unnecessary risk. Having disclaimed his own hostility, he could not believe that others would be hostile to him.

Some years ago I treated a man who had a passive-feminine character structure. This personality results from the suppression of aggressive feelings and especially from the suppression of anger. He ran a successful retail business on the principle that he and his employees were one big, happy family. The business was successful as far as the sale of merchandise was concerned. In its best year it failed to yield a profit, and my patient was shocked to find out that his employees had mulcted him of many thousands of dollars. Thus self-delusion goes hand in hand with illusions about life.

I could cite many examples of the naïveté that characterizes suppressed individuals. It is manifested in their social attitudes as much as in their personal lives. They cannot see the hostility about them because they have suppressed their own. They talk about the inherent "goodness" of man without realizing that there is no good without bad, no pleasure without pain. They cannot accept the reality of life because they have denied their own reality. Their specific illusions take different forms, which are determined by the nature of their parents' demands. There is the illusion that self-sacrifice is the way to happiness, that hard work is rewarded by love, that conformity leads to security, and so on. All illusions have in common a rejection of the importance of pleasure, which therefore renders them sterile as creative forces.

Since the delusion-illusion complex is created by the mind, it is supported by the rationalizing power of the mind. It not only affects one's behavior but also determines the quality of one's thinking. It is extremely difficult to counter with logic. The person who suffers from this complex is convinced of the moral "righteousness" of his position and can muster sufficient arguments to defend his position. It is not until the complex collapses into depression that he becomes open to help. And depression is inevitable.

The collapse occurs because the delusion-illusion complex is a constant drain on the energy of the individual. Sooner or later he will exhaust his reserves and find that he can no longer carry on. The depressed person literally doesn't have the energy to sustain his functions. All his vital functions are depressed; his appetite is reduced, his breathing is restricted, and his motility is sharply decreased. The consequence of this reduced vital functioning is a lowered energy metabolism and a loss of feeling in the body.

If one compares depression with disappointment, the relation of the former to illusion is clear. If one fails to realize a valid hope, one is disappointed but not depressed. The depressed person feels that his life is empty. He has neither the interest nor the energy to fight back. Disappointment has no such effect on the personality. It is a painful experience, but it enables the individual to evaluate his situation and take a more constructive approach to his problem. If one is disappointed, one feels sad. The depressed person feels nothing. A depressive reaction is clear evidence that a person has been laboring under an illusion.

To overcome the depressive tendency, the delusion-illusion complex must be uncovered and the suppressed emotions released. The basic illusion that makes one look outside one's self for pleasure and ignores the functioning of the body must first be attacked. This is done by making the patient conscious of the tensions in his body and by releasing some of these tensions by the physical maneuvers and exercises described in Chapter 2. These simple physical techniques are generally quite effective in stimulating a flow of feeling in the patient's body. In many patients they will also produce a strong emotional reaction. Very often this first experience will make a patient aware of the need to revitalize his body. He will feel more alive and also hopeful that through his body he can find a way out of his dilemma. And he will be inspired to explore this possibility.

This initial enthusiasm is soon tempered by the realization that the creative process of getting well involves hard work and a serious commitment to the body. The chronic muscular tensions that block the expression of feeling yield slowly to the therapeutic effort. In most cases the effort to mobilize the tense musculature is painful. Releasing the tension, however, produces such feelings of pleasure and joy in the body that the reward is well worth the pain. The effort, therefore, must be a continuing one, and it must be combined with analysis on the psychological level of the guilt and shame that are the deterrents to self-acceptance. The delusion-illusion complex progressively diminishes as the patient gains increasing contact with reality.

Reality has two faces or aspects. One is the reality of the body and its feelings. This reality is perceived subjectively. The other is the reality of the external world, which is perceived objectively. Any distortion in our internal perceptions causes a corresponding distortion in our external perceptions, since we perceive the world through our bodies. The person who is depressed is out of touch with both aspects of reality, because he is out of touch with his body.

The person who is in touch with his body doesn't get depressed. He knows that pleasure and joy depend on the proper functioning of his body. He is aware of his bodily tensions, and he knows what causes them. Thus he can take appropriate measures to restore his bodily good feelings. He has no delusions about himself and no illusions about life. He accepts his feelings as expressions of his personality, and he has no difficulty in voicing them. When a patient gets fully in touch with his body, the depressive tendency is eliminated. The activation of breathing and the mobilization of motility help the patient get in touch with his body. He will experience its pain and frustration, and it will make him cry. Then as the breathing deepens and becomes more abdominal, his crying will develop into a rhythmic sobbing that expresses his underlying sadness—the sadness of a person who has lived in illusion. He will become angry at the deception that forced him to suppress his feelings, which he will express by beating and kicking the couch. He will vent his resentments and fears, and as he does this, he will strip the mask of delusion from his personality and see himself as an individual who desires nothing more than to enjoy life. His depressive tendency will be gone.

Release of suppressed emotions is the cure for depression. The crying of sadness, for example, is a specific antidote to depression. A sad person is not depressed. Depression leaves an individual lifeless and unresponsive; sadness makes him feel warm and alive. Feeling one's sadness opens the door to feeling all emotions and returns an individual to the human condition, in which pleasure and pain are the guiding principles to behavior. To be able to feel sad is to be able to feel glad. The restoration of a patient's capacity for pleasure is the guarantee of his emotional well-being.

Spontaneous Rhythms

In the third chapter pleasure was defined as the conscious perception of the rhythmic and pulsatory activity of the body. All living tissue is in a constant state of motion produced by its inner charge or excitation. Even in sleep or at rest, a body is not still. The heart beats, blood vessels expand and contract, respiration is continuous, and cellular activity never comes to a stop. These involuntary activities have a rhythmicity which varies according to the degree of excitation in the organism and in its parts. The different rhythms harmonize with each other, and the separate movements flow together to create a spontaneous motility in the whole organism. The flow of feeling in the body is like a river which is formed by the confluence of many streams, each of which in turn arises from numerous small rivulets. Looking at the river, we cannot distinguish the separate streams; looking at a stream, we do not see its original sources in the small trickles that emerge from the earth. But the process of river formation is only one part of a natural cycle that moves the water from the sea to the mountain and back to the sea again.

The roots of pleasure go deep into man's connections with nature. At the deepest level we are part of nature; at the highest we are unique organisms consciously experiencing the pleasure and the pain, the joy and the sorrow of our relationship to nature. For example, we feel pain in a period of drought, when no rain falls and the earth is parched. The coming of the rain ushers in a feeling of joy. We are grieved when the rainfall is torrential and destructive, and we are pleased when the cycle of rain and sun is regular and undisturbed.

The feeling of pleasure that stems from a natural and undis-

turbed rhythm of life embraces all our activities and relationships. There is a time to work and a time to rest, a time to play
and a time to be serious, a time to be together and a time to be
alone. Too much togetherness can be as painful as too much
aloneness, and too much play can be as dull as too much work.
The ryhthms that govern life are inherent in life; they cannot
be imposed from without. Each individual knows what his
rhythms are and knows by the feelings of pain or lack of pleasure when his rhythms are disturbed. However, the biological
rhythms of one individual are not completely different from
those of another. There are unique differences, of course, but
there are many rhythms which are common to the members of
each species. One has only to watch a flock of birds to see how
finely tuned the rhythm of each is to that of the others. Among
human beings, in whom the sense of individuality is more developed, the differences are more apparent.

The concept that each organism contains a biological clock
that regulates its activities is a challenging one. It has been observed that people who travel long distances by jet plane have
their normal rhythmic patterns upset. They become irritable
and feel ill at ease, and their sharpness and acuity are disturbed.
A displacement of five hours or more has been shown to be
critical. The timing devices that regulate the body's activities
become out of phase with environmental or solar time. It may
take several days for an adjustment to occur. We have all experienced the disturbance in our body's equilibrium caused by
a major change in our sleeping patterns. The person who regularly gets eight hours of sleep each night feels out of sorts when
circumstances limit him to six hours of sleep for several nights.
Similarly, the person who is used to six hours of sleep a night
feels listless and tired when he sleeps eight or more hours a
night. It seems that a bodily rhythm, once established, becomes
a force that compels its continuance. In this respect it is relatively unimportant whether we eat three meals a day because
of training or because of the body's need for sustenance. For
the person who is accustomed to three meals a day, skipping a
meal may throw his body out of equilibrium.

The concept of a biological clock emphasizes the importance
of rhythmicity in life, which is a function that the living share to

some degree with inorganic nature. All matter is in constant motion. Theoretically, the point at which all movement in matter stops is minus 273 degrees Fahrenheit, which is absolute zero on the Celsius scale. This motion is a vibratory phenomenon. The molecules of matter move to and fro as they are influenced by the forces of attraction and repulsion within the substance. The movement of molecules in a solid is more restricted than their movement in a liquid, which in turn is more limited than the movement of molecules in a gas. This vibratory movement of molecules may be described as a state of excitation in matter. Whether or not we can discern the pattern, the movements of molecules must, I believe, follow some pattern and manifest some degree of rhythmic periodicity. We have discovered some of the patterns and know some of the periodicities of the heavenly bodies, the macrocosmos. With better techniques we shall, I am sure, find these patterns and periodicities repeated in the microcosmos on a different scale.

Protoplasm is a special case of matter in motion. It is special in its composition, and it is special in that it is enclosed within a membrane to form a cell. The functions of the membrane in terms of perception and the awareness of self were explored in Chapter 7. The protoplasm of the cell exhibits a rhythmic and pulsatory activity which can be viewed as an extension of the vibratory motion inherent in molecules. Alain Reinberg and Jean Ghata have observed pulsatory vacuoles which are found in unicellular organisms. "These pulsatile vacuoles have a thick, mainly lipidic, membrane which contracts according to a rhythm that depends on the environmental conditions and the state of the cell." * Wilhelm Reich, using a Reichert microscope with an optical magnification of 5000x, described the pulsatory activity of human red blood cells.†

On the cellular level periodicity has also been observed in the ciliary action of the mucosal cells that line the respiratory tract and in free-swimming single-celled animals. The movement of the cilia, minute, hairlike structures that extend from the periphery of the cell, has been compared to the waving

* Alain Reinberg and Jean Ghata, *Biological Rhythms*. New York, Walker & Company, 1964, p. 7.

† Wilhelm Reich, *The Cancer Biopathy*. New York, The Orgone Institute Press, 1948.

motion of a wheat field produced by a current of wind. The cilia wave backward and forward, yet their net effect is to move foreign particles upward and outward, away from the lungs. Dust and minute food particles which may inadvertently enter the bronchi are thereby prevented from settling in the lungs. This action may be under nervous control, although the movement is regarded as being independent of nerve impulses. J. L. Cloudsley-Thompson reports: "This beat is often continuous throughout the life of the animal and the stimulus for this arises endogenously in the protoplasm of the cell under the control of the basal granules." *

Nerve tissue shows an inherent periodicity in its functioning. The passage of an impulse along a nerve depolarizes the membrane and produces a refractory period during which no other impulse can pass through the depolarized area. After a short period of rest the membrane is repolarized spontaneously. The nerve cells of the brain are known to "fire" repeated bursts of impulses. These are reflected in the rhythmicity of the brain waves, which are recorded on an electroencephalogram. This apparently spontaneous activity of the brain cells is responsible for the smooth maintenance of muscle tone, posture, and other physiological functions.

Of all body tissues, cardiac muscle shows the greatest spontaneous rhythmicity. While the beat of the heart is coordinated with other bodily activities by the vegetative nervous system, it has its own pacemakers known as the sinoauricular node and the atrioventricular node. But an ordinary piece of cardiac muscle detached from the heart will continue to contract spontaneously while suspended in a physiological saline solution. This evidence of rhythmicity on the cellular and tissue levels supports the thesis that rhythmicity is an inherent quality of life.

Throughout the animal and vegetable worlds the sexual function is a periodic phenomenon, from the flowering of plants to the monthly efflorescence of the woman. The parallel between the menstrual cycle and the lunar cycle is well known. The relationship between the two, however, is a mystery, as are

* J. L. Cloudsley-Thompson, *Rhythmic Activity in Animal Physiology and Behavior*. New York and London, The Academic Press, Inc., 1961, p. 27.

so many of the rhythmic activities of life. However, climatic conditions are known to influence the menstrual cycle. Among Eskimo women menstruation occurs approximately four times a year. The majority of authors on the subject of menstruation state that about two-thirds of the women they interviewed reported increased sexual feelings before and after menstruation. This flood of sexual feeling may be responsible for many of the emotional and physical symptoms that distress women before the onset of their periods. Women who have had satisfactory sexual relations prior to menstruation generally report an absence of pain, cramps, and irritability. Premenstrual tension, the term applied to this condition, is created by an inability to discharge the sexual excitation which develops at this time.

In the ancient cultures of Greece and Rome, the flower festival of Dionysus was celebrated at the time of the spring equinox. This was an occasion for dancing, drinking, and sexual activity. The Dionysian festivals had their origin in earlier rites associated with the return of spring. Spring is proverbially the time for love, the time when the sap begins to flow in trees and the blood becomes excited in young people. Through our rhythmicity we are part of the animal world and allied to the plant world. The rhythms of our activities are strongly influenced by the rhythms of nature: day and night, summer and winter, early morning and high noon, and so on. This harmony between the inner rhythms of a person and the outer rhythms of nature is the basis for one's sense of identification with the cosmos, the deepest root of pleasure and joy.

Rhythms of Natural Functions

Phylogentically, life began in the sea, and for most people a return to the seaside is an occasion for good feelings and pleasure. Close to the ocean we feel liberated and more in contact with the elemental forces of nature. It is not generally appreciated that ontogenetically, each life also begins in a water medium that closely resembles the chemical composition of the ancient seas. For nine months the human embryo develops in a fluid environment in which it is softly rocked by the movements of its mother's body. It passes progressively from the single-cell stage through all the phases of evolutionary development to becoming a human infant. At birth it undergoes a cataclysmic transition, when it becomes an air-breathing mammal in a dry environment.

The transition is softened somewhat by the fact that it does not lose touch with the source of its strength, its mother's body. It is put to her breast to suckle. It is held close to her body, where it feels her warmth and is lulled by the beat of her heart. Nurseries have used the recorded sound of the human heart to lull infants who are deprived of contact with their mothers. It should be recognized, however, that the best bottle, the proper temperature, and recorded heart sounds are only poor substitutes for the real thing. A loving mother's body is the most important root of pleasure and joy to a child.

The rhythmic activities of the body fall into three categories. Some are completely involuntary and beyond any conscious control. The heart beats and the blood circulates without direction or control by the will. Digestion, assimilation, the production of urine, and the secretion of hormones and enzymes are other examples of completely involuntary activities. There are other activities which lie on the border between the involuntary and the voluntary. They are normally not willed activities, yet a certain amount of conscious control can be exercised over them. The functions of eating and swallowing, breathing, and sleeping belong to this category. We can consciously stop ourselves from swallowing, we can inhibit our respiration, and we can prevent ourselves from falling asleep. This second category is strongly influenced by a person's relationship to his mother. There is a third category of activities in which the conscious mind plays a dominant role. No form of self-expression that involves bodily movement, such as dancing, singing, working, or playing, would occur without conscious intent.

The statement that breathing is closely tied to the relationship with the mother is based on the observation that in healthy breathing the air is literally sucked into the lungs. I have found that the patient whose sucking impulse is depressed breathes passively and shallowly. And Margaretha Ribble in her important study *The Rights of Infants*,* showed that any weakening of the sucking impulse depresses the respiratory function. In the typical schizoid patient, whose personality and body dynamics are analyzed in *The Betrayal of the Body*, the chest is constricted and inspiration is markedly reduced. Underlying this disturbance is a feeling of despair commonly expressed as "What's the use? No one was there." The "no one" is always the mother.

It is mistakenly believed that we breathe with our lungs alone, but in fact breathing is done with the whole body. The lungs play a passive role in the respiratory process. Their expansion is produced by an enlargement of the thoracic cavity, and they collapse when that cavity is reduced. Proper breathing involves all the muscles of the head, neck, thorax, and abdomen, in addition to the involuntary musculature of the larynx, trachea, and bronchi. Inspiration is an active reaching out to suck in the gaseous environment, much as a fish opens its mouth to suck in its liquid environment. How well we breathe depends on how well we can execute these sucking movements with our whole bodies.

The importance of breathing need hardly be stressed. It provides the oxygen for the metabolic processes; it literally maintains the fires of life. On a deeper level the breath as *pneuma* is also the spirit or soul. We live in an ocean of air like a fish in a body of water. Through our breathing we are attuned to the atmosphere. In all Oriental and mystic philosophies, the breath holds the secret to the highest bliss.

The respiratory system is closely related to the digestive system, since the lungs develop embryologically as an outgrowth of the primitive alimentary tube and remain connected with it throughout life by their common opening in the mouth and pharynx. Both functions have a common base in sucking movements, and both are associated with the mother.

Food is recognized as a symbol for the mother. Many mothers express their love by giving a child food and regard its acceptance of food as equivalent to love of the mother. Alimentary problems can often be traced analytically to disturbances in the

* Margaretha A. Ribble, *The Rights of Infants*. New York, The Columbia University Press, second edition, 1965.

mother-child relationship. I pointed out in *The Betrayal of the Body* that dieting always produces a good feeling because it represents a symbolic rejection of the mother.

The bodily functions related to food—ingestion, digestion, and elimination—normally follow a rhythmic pattern governed by the energy needs of the organism and its state of development. Very young infants nurse as often as every two hours and have several bowel movements a day. In the adult the pattern tends to become stabilized at three meals and one bowel movement a day. Eating is a pleasure when it conforms to an inner rhythm. Too many people, however, are compulsive eaters. Their food habits bear little relation to their metabolic rhythms. They eat before they are hungry, probably to avoid the feeling of hunger, since this feeling is associated with sensations of emptiness which are frightening to affection-starved individuals.

The alimentary tube from mouth to anus is a rhythmically pulsating organ system which functions on the principle of the worm. Food is moved from one end of this tube to the other by peristaltic waves similiar to the waves which pass through the body of a worm or caterpillar as it moves forward. Along the alimentary canal there are constrictions and enlargements, such as the stomach, which facilitate the digestive process and modify the frequency and form of the wave but do not change its essential character. Since this peristaltic activity is always present, there is a continuing excitation in the digestive tract, higher at mealtimes, lower during sleep. When this excitation is maintained within normal limits, the person has a "good" feeling in his body. A hyperactive state in any part of this system, hyperacidity or colitis for example, produces painful sensations. Hypotonicity, or a loss of tone, in any segment leads to bloating and gas production, with consequent feelings of distress.

A person is generally unaware of the normal functioning of the alimentary canal, which extends from the esophagus to the rectum. The conscious pleasure in eating good food is because of its ability to excite the olfactory receptors, the taste buds, the salivary glands, and the reflex of deglutition, that is, the area from the nose and mouth to the esophagus. This excitation, however, passes through the alimentary canal, quickening its rhythms and stimulating its secretions. Thus, the initial pleasure of taste is transformed into the enjoyment of food. When tensions exist in the tube, the smooth flow of the peristaltic waves is disturbed and one is denied this satisfaction. One may even lose his appetite or feel sick to his stomach.

Few conditions make a person feel as miserable as sensations of nausea. The body seems to revolt at its core as it seeks to disgorge itself of a noxious substance. Nausea induces strong peristaltic waves in a reverse direction, which increases in intensity until the body heaves up the offending substance. Vomiting produces a sense of relief which is often as great as the preceding distress. The procedure, however, is never pleasurable, because the peristaltic waves move counter to their normal direction.

The mechanism of vomiting is a protective reflex against harmful or disturbing substances which have been swallowed in error. But the reflex can also be evoked by tension states, especially by the stress of emotional conflict while one is eating. Almost everyone has had experiences of this kind. The wisdom of the body is revealed in an incident which happened to my son when he was one year old. We had all just finished a hurried lunch and were rushing to leave for an appointment. While my wife was dressing the baby, he suddenly put his finger in his mouth and threw up his meal. I was surprised that a child so young would know how to relieve his distress by gagging himself.

Many patients in bioenergetic therapy develop feelings of nausea in the course of their efforts to breathe more deeply. The deeper breathing activates chronic tensions in the diaphragm and stomach which the body seeks to relieve by throwing up. In this situation I advise the patient to drink a full glass of water and then bring it up, using his thumb to stimulate the gag reflex. Some patients find it difficult to throw up. It often requires considerable work with the gag reflex and breathing before the throat and diaphragmatic tensions are sufficiently released to allow this function to operate normally. It may be necessary for them to follow this procedure every morning before breakfast for a short period to break through this block.

The value of this procedure is illustrated in the following

case. I saw a young homosexual man in consultation who had a tight, rigid body. His jaw was tense, his breathing was restricted, his complexion was sallow, and his breath smelled sour. After working with his breathing for some time, I had him drink some water and throw up. The immediate effect was a sense of release and easier breathing. On my recommendation he used the gag reflex every morning for about a month. When I saw him again, the sour smell was gone, his complexion had improved somewhat, and his body was looser. One result of this procedure is the elimination of chronic heartburn, from which so many people suffer. In most cases the release of these tensions by this maneuver restores the pleasure to the basic activities of eating and digestion and facilitates a deeper respiration.

In part the origin of these tensions lies in childhood feeding experiences: Children are often made to eat food they do not like or in amounts they do not want. Many jokes have been made about mothers who overfeed their children in the name of love. In other homes, as patients have told me, they were forbidden to leave the table until they had finished everything on their plates. Not only is a child often made to eat food in conflict with his desire, but he is shamed and scolded if he throws it up. To hold it down a child must tense his throat and diaphragm to block the impulse to vomit.

Food is not the only thing a person may have to swallow against his wishes. Psychological traumas such as insults and humiliations may also have to be "swallowed" when one is afraid of the insulting person. The expression "I can't stomach it" indicates the effect on this organ of submission to painful situations. In addition, children are often forced to swallow their tears or hold in their crying, which leads to chronic tensions in the throat and diaphragm. Throwing up is a rejection of food and therefore a symbolic rejection of the negative aspects of the mother. It removes the blocks to the full experience of pleasure in the basic function of eating.

Just as the upper end of the alimentary canal is disturbed in its functioning by traumatic experiences in childhood, so is the lower end of the tube. Too early or too severe toilet training leads to chronic tensions in the large colon, the rectum, and the anus. Constipation, diarrhea, and hemorrhoids are common ymptoms that result from such disturbances. It is my opinion that bowel training should not be started before two and a half years of age. Since the nerve to the anal sphincter is not fully myelinized until that time, the normal pattern of anal control is not available, and substitute mechanisms must be employed. These include pulling up the pelvic floor and contracting the gluteal muscles. The effect is to disturb the pleasure functions of the lower end of the body, including sexuality.

Another rhythmic activity that belongs in this category, because it involves the child's relationship to the mother, is sleep. During the day we are conscious and active; at night consciousness is surrendered and activity is reduced. The body renews itself in sleep, but the phenomenon of sleep is still a mystery. In some respects sleep is like a return to an intrauterine existence.

Sleep is a state of diffused and lowered excitation. In sleep many vital functions of the body show a reduced rhythmicity: The heart beats more slowly, blood pressure drops, the respiratory rate diminishes, blood sugar drops, and there is a fall in body temperature. Electroencephalograms indicate that there are cycles in sleep, a rhythmic rise and fall in the level of excitation which changes the depth of sleep. If the process of sleep is undisturbed, a person awakens with a feeling of having been refreshed, an eagerness to start the day's activities, and, normally, a desire for food. Rising from a good night's sleep, one feels a distinct sensation of pleasure, as if the body were somehow aware of its harmonious functioning. Similarly, going to sleep when one is tired but relaxed is a most delightful sensation.

The simple pleasure of sleep escapes many people, if we can judge by the demand for sleep-inducing pills. These people complain of being tired, and their need for sleep is evident, yet they do not easily fall asleep when they go to bed. In such cases something is obviously wrong with the normal self-regulating processes of the body. The inability to fall asleep is a form of falling anxiety; a fear of letting go, an anxiety about the loss of consciousness. For a young child the transition from a state of consciousness to unconsciousness can be a frightening experience. The immature ego of the child experiences the surrender of consciousness as a return to darkness, and this raises the fear of death, the great unknown.

Nursing babies fall asleep on the breast, feeling secure in this contact with the mother. And even after nursing ends, the child wants someone near him or in the same room as he passes through the shadowy land between consciousness and unconsciousness. Since sleep is a surrender to the unconscious, the Great Mother, one needs some assurance that "she" will be warm, accepting and supportive. The nightmares so many children experience suggest that this assurance is missing. It is an assurance that the real mother gives her child by her warm acceptance and support. The anxieties which a child has about its mother are covered up during the day but break through during sleep in dreams. Other anxieties may disturb a child's sleep, such as a hostile father, but these anxieties will be minimal if the child feels secure in its relation to his mother.

The inability to fall asleep easily reflects the persistence of a state of excitation in the conscious layers of the personality. Sometimes this excitation is an undischarged sexual tension, but more often it is due to unresolved conflicts that are not fully repressed. Despite the best efforts of the individual to distract his mind, it returns again and again to the problem, unable to succeed but unwilling to accept defeat. When conflicts are repressed, a focus of excitation develops in the unconscious mind and in the body which subsequently surfaces in dreams. Freud pointed out that dreams have the function of guarding the state of slumber by releasing this excitation. However, the excitation may be so strong that the person is awakened by the dream, or the restfulness of his sleep is disturbed by the intensity of the dream. The person who knows the pleasure of undisturbed and restful sleep is blessed.

Rhythms of Movement

The third big root of pleasure lies in our relationship to the external world. This includes all our contacts with people, the work we do, and the environmental conditions under which we live. In this relationship we are usually conscious actors, receiving stimuli and responding with movement. The part of the body that is most involved in these activities is the outer tube of the organism. This consists of the skin, the subjacent tissues, and the striated, or voluntary, musculature. These structures form a sheath about the body and constitute a veritable tube. The mammalian organism is built on the principle of the worm; it is a tube within a tube.

The outer tube is directly concerned with the perception of and response to environmental stimuli. For these functions it is richly supplied with nerve endings. We are therefore more conscious of sensations, particularly sensations of pleasure or pain, in this part of the body than in any other.

Every stimulus that impinges on the body surface and is perceived by the organism is either pleasurable or painful. There is no indifferent stimulus, for a stimulus that failed to evoke a sensation would not be perceived. What quality in the stimulus, we may ask, determines whether the response will be pleasurable or painful? Why, for example, are certain sounds delightful to the ear, while others are cacophonous and even painful? A cursory knowledge of human nature tells us that such questions cannot be answered objectively. People react differently to identical stimuli. One man's pleasure may be another's pain. So much depends on the mood and manner of the individual receiving the sense impression. There is a big difference between a caress and a slap, yet not everyone finds a caress pleasurable or a slap painful. Children object to being caressed when they are active, and a slap on the back may be received as an expression of appreciation.

Broadly speaking, we find sensory pleasure in stimuli that harmonize with the rhythms and tones of our bodies. Dance music is enjoyable when we wish to dance, but it can be disturbing when we are trying to think. Even a favorite symphony can be distracting when one is engaged in serious conversation. The same thing is true of all the senses. A well-prepared meal is a delight to a hungry person, but not to the person who has no appetite. A charming country scene is pleasurable to behold when one is quiet and contented, but not if one is restless and impatient. Pleasurable sensory impressions not only heighten our mood but increase the rhythmic activity of our bodies. They are, to put it simply, exciting.

Sensory pleasure, it would appear, can be had by everyone in one form or another. But consider the person who is "out of sorts" and finds no pleasure in the sights and sounds about him. He is, as we say, at sixes and sevens with himself. He is out of sorts because he does not have at the moment a condition of internal harmony. Lacking a consistent tone or pattern of rhythmic activity, he is unable to respond expansively to any stimulus from the environment. The depressed or withdrawn person is in a similar situation. Sensory pleasure or sensual pleasure is unavailable to him, because he cannot reach out or respond to the stimulus. Now, what is depressed in the withdrawn person is the rhythmic activity of his body. Without rhythm there is no pleasure.

The relation of rhythm to pleasure is most clearly seen in the motor function of the outer tube, that is, in the voluntary movements of the body. Any motor activity that is performed rhythmically is pleasurable. If it is performed mechanically, without a feeling of rhythm, it has a painful quality. The best example is walking. When one walks rhythmically, the walking is enjoyable. When one walks to get to a destination as quickly as possible, the physical activity becomes a chore. Even such tedious jobs as raking leaves or sweeping a floor can be pleasurable activities when the movements are rhythmical. One can gauge the pleasure or lack of pleasure in people's lives by the way they move. The rapid, jerky, and compulsive movements of most people in our culture betray the absence of joy in their lives. A saunter along any of the main thoroughfares in New York City can be a shocking experience. One is jostled, shoved, and stepped on by people who are grimly rushing to get somewhere, almost oblivious of their surroundings and the people about them. The person who lives pleasurably moves rhythmically, effortlessly, and gracefully.

Whether a person feels pleasure because his movements are rhythmical or whether his movements are rhythmical because he is in a state of pleasure is immaterial. Pleasure is rhythm and rhythm is pleasure. The reason for this identity is that pleasure is the perception of the rhythmical flow of excitation in the

ody. It is the natural and healthy mode of functioning of the
ody. If one is identified with the body and with its striving
or pleasure, one's movements become rhythmical, like the
movements of an animal. All the movements of an animal have
his lovely rhythmical quality.

Dancing is, of course, the classic example of pleasure in rhythmic movement. The music sets the beat going in our bodies,
nd this is then translated into the rhythmic pattern of the
ance step. It is painful to find oneself out of step with the
music, and it is disturbing to find that the music is out of harmony with one's internal beat. Marching music does for walk-
ng what dance music does for dancing. The music, by accentu-
ting the beat and focusing our attention upon the rhythm,
ncreases our pleasure in moving.

It is important to realize that the music does not create the
rhythm. The music is, in fact, an expression of the rhythm in
he composer's body, which finds an echo in the body of the lis-
ener. It would be correct to say that music evokes the rhythms
hat are within us. All bodily activity is inherently rhythmical;
he voluntary movements are no exception, although they are
under conscious control. But because they are under the control
of the ego, we can move unrhythmically if the ego ignores the
ody's feeling for pleasure and imposes an overriding goal.

Voluntary movements, in contrast to those that are involun-
ary, require a high degree of coordination before they become
rhythmical. The infant, whose sucking movements are coordinated at birth, performs this activity rhythmically and pleasur-
bly. It will take him considerable practice to develop the coordination to perform such activities as walking, running, talking,
nd handling tools rhythmically. As he gains increasing coordination in his body movements, these too become rhythmical
nd a source of pleasure to him. Watch a young child jumping
on a bed or an older girl skipping rope and you will gain some
idea of the pleasure these simple rhythmic activities afford the
young. One should remember that in the acquisition of these
nd other skills the ego is important, for it sets the goals and
ustains the effort.

Adults, who have more coordination, seek more complex
rhythms to excite their bodies. They find these rhythms in

sports. No matter what sport a person prefers, it is the rhythmical quality of his movements in that sport that provides his pleasure. Skiing and swimming, two sports I like, are good examples. Both of these sports require considerable coordination. When that is achieved and the skiing or swimming takes on rhythmical quality, the pleasure is great. The moment rhythm is lost, the activity becomes a painful struggle.

Sports play such a big role in people's lives because their daily activities have lost their rhythmic quality. People walk mechanically, they work compulsively, and they talk monotonously, without rhythm and sometimes without rhyme or reason. It may be that the lack of rhythm is due to an absence of pleasure in these activities. It is equally true that the lack of pleasure is due to the loss of rhythm.

We have divided our world into the things we do seriously, for a purpose or for gain, and the things we do for fun or for pleasure. In the serious affairs of life spontaneous rhythmic activity seems to have no place. We seek the cool efficiency of the machine. We then try, hopefully, to recover our rhythm and warmth in sports, games, and other forms of recreation. But here too we are too often frustrated by the ego's compulsive drive for success or for perfection.

Man is fascinated by the productive efficiency of the machine which can perform any single operation better than he can. The machine gains its efficiency by being limited to a single rhythmic pattern. Of course, a series of machines can perform more complex operations, with each unit performing only its single operation. In contrast, man has an almost unlimited number of rhythmic patterns to correspond to his different moods and desires. He is capable of changing rhythms as his excitement varies. He is capable of weaving complex rhythmic patterns to increase his pleasure and joy. He is, in other words, biologically structured for pleasure, not efficiency. Man is a creative being, not a productive one. Yet out of his pleasures have come great achievements. Unfortunately, out of his achievements he has found little joy, because productivity has become more important than pleasure.

The Rhythm of Love

To speak of love as a root of pleasure is poetic but illogical. In the hierarchy of personality functions, love as an emotion arises from pleasure. Yet as everyone knows, pleasure and joy stem from loving and being loved. To this point I have described the roots of pleasure in terms of one's relationship to the universe, to the mother as a representative of the earth, and to the world about one. If we look for the root of pleasure within ourselves, we shall find it in the phenomenon of love.

In this chapter so far I have divided the rhythmic activities of the body into three categories and have described them separately. This division does not imply the independence of one category from another. The functions of the inner tube, digestion and respiration, are intimately connected with the movements of the outer tube, or voluntary muscles. And both tubes are dependent on the rhythmic activities of the organs and tissues that maintain the internal integrity of the organism. In most situations of life, however, our attention focuses on one or the other category. We do not generally associate the operation of the vital organs with pleasure. We are for the most part unaware of their rhythmic activity. Let the heart skip a beat or suddenly increase its rhythm, and we are immediately alarmed. We are content, therefore, if nothing occurs to arouse our awareness. Yet these organs, especially the heart, play an important role in the experience of pleasure and joy. The heart is directly involved in the phenomenon of love. The relation of the heart to love was fully explored in my book *Love and Orgasm*. Here I would like to discuss love as a rhythm which begins with an excitation in the heart that extends to and embraces the whole body. This is the rhythm of love.

In its rhythmic activity the heart is unique among the organs of the body. I have previously mentioned that a strip of heart muscle suspended in a physiological salt solution will show spontaneous rhythmic contractions. An isolated frog heart, if perfused with oxygenated blood, will continue to beat without nervous stimulation. This means that the rhythm of the heart is inherent in its tissue, the cardiac muscle. Cardiac muscle is unique in that it is a cross between the voluntary and the involuntary type of muscle. It possesses striations like the voluntary musculature, but it is innervated by the autonomic nervous system, which otherwise activates only the smooth muscles of the body. Further, cardiac muscle forms a syncitium, that is, the cells merge with one another, which allows impulses to pass freely through the whole body of the heart. It has, therefore, a degree of motility possessed by no other organ of the body.

Love and joy are feelings that belong to the heart. The joy of love and the love of joy are bodily responses to an excitation that reaches and opens the heart. The connection between these two feelings and the heart is expressed in Beethoven's Ninth Symphony, which is also called the Choral Symphony because it ends with a choral rendition of Schiller's poem *Ode to Joy*. The chorus, as in a Greek tragedy, is intended, I believe, to represent the audience. Beethoven wanted each listener to experience the feeling of joy in nature and in the brotherhood of man. To do this he had to reach the hearts of his audience with his music. He had to make each listener feel the rhythmic beat of his own heart as it throbbed in common with the hearts of others.

Beethoven accomplished this objective in the first three movements of the symphony. The first movement expresses, as I feel it, the appeal of the individual for love and the response of the universe, "Be joyful." It is so powerful that one of my friends remarked, "It rips and tears open my chest wall, exposing my heart." The second movement is punctuated from time to time by two loud beats of the tympani. These sounds are so similar to the heart sounds that the meaning of this movement is clear. One can feel the rhythm of the heart, beating quietly and gently in some passages, then excitedly and with anticipation in others. All hearts are exposed; and as each instrument takes up the theme, we sense that no heart beats alone. The lyric third movement expresses, in my opinion, the emotional quality of the heart. It is the organ of love. Love resides in the heart. Once the heart is open and its love revealed, the audience can share the experience of joy, which is the theme of the final movement. The vocal rendition transforms the symphony from an objective presentation to a subjective expression and translates the experience from the dramatic to the personal level. In this symphony Beethoven, through his genius, opened our hearts to joy and so brought joy to our hearts.

Sexual love begins with an excitation that speeds the blood to the genital organs, producing an erection in the male and a lubrication of the vagina in the female. During coitus this excitation produces two rhythmic patterns of movement, one voluntary and the other involuntary. During the first phase of coitus the pelvic movements of both the man and the woman are consciously made and are under ego control. At this stage the bodily excitation is relatively superficial, although it deepens gradually through the frictional contact and the pelvic swings. Breathing is fairly quiet, though deep, and the heartbeat is only slightly accelerated.

When the excitation reaches its peak, it floods through the genital organs, ushering in the climax. In the man the seminal vesicles, the prostate, and the urethra begin a pulsation that culminates in ejaculatory spurts of the semen. In the woman the pulsation is manifested in the rhythmic contractions of the uterus and of the extended labia minora. If the excitation remains limited to the genital area, only a partial orgasm occurs. If it spreads upward and reaches the heart, the whole body goes into a convulsive type of reaction in which all voluntary control is surrendered to a primitive beat.

In the full orgasm the pelvic movements, which have been gradually increasing in frequency, become involuntary and faster. Their rhythm becomes coordinated with the rhythm of the genital pulsations. The breathing deepens and quickens to become part of this overall rhythm. The heart accelerates its beat, becomes conscious; and one feels the pulse of life in every cell of the body.

There are many ways to interpret what happens in the full orgasm. In this context it can be said that in the convulsive reaction of orgasm the whole body becomes one big heart. This is ecstasy.

The ecstasy of orgasm is a unique bodily response to a sexual excitation that begins in the heart and ends with the heart so wide open that it embraces the world. Every feeling of love begins in the heart and irradiates the person. Any person who has known love has experienced its excitement in his heart. Love makes us feel lighthearted. Loss of love makes the heart feel heavy with grief. I do not believe these are empty metaphors. An excited heart is light. It leaps for joy. But it is not only the heart that leaps in joy. The lover skips and dances down the street. He cannot contain his heart's excitement. It pervades his whole being.

The beat of the heart is the rhythm of love.

11 · A Creative Approach to Life

What is Creativity?

This book has two themes, pleasure and creativity. The two are closely related, since pleasure provides the motivation and energy for the creative process, which in turn increases the pleasure and joy of living. With pleasure, life is a creative adventure; without pleasure, it is a struggle for survival. In the preceding chapters I analyzed the nature of pleasure and its role in determining behavior. I shall devote this chapter to a discussion of creativity in living.

A creative approach to life implies new and imaginative answers to the many situations that confront each person daily. New answers are urgently needed, because the values and social forms that governed relationships and regulated behavior in previous generations no longer provide a satisfactory format for modern living. This observation is inescapable, whether one looks at people's personal and family lives or at the broader social and political scene. The new answers we seek cannot be limited to the rejection of established concepts. Pure rebellion is not a creative attitude and only leads to a chaotic condition in which the search for pleasure and meaning most frequently ends in misery and despair.

The collapse of traditional codes and patterns offers a promise of greater pleasure and joy in living, but it also poses serious dangers. The promise lies in the fact that a wider area of life is open to a creative approach; the dangers are due to a lack of understanding of what creativity involves. In their confusion people tend to adopt every popular idea that promises a solution, naïvely assuming that the popularity of an idea is some measure of its validity. Since popularity is often determined by mass appeal and mass media, it is opposed to the concept of creativity, which implies an individual solution to a unique problem. No two artists will paint the same picture.

Another danger we face is the mistaken belief that experience is the only true value in life. Too many people, following this belief, expose themselves to situations that are destructive to their health and well-being. The use of drugs is often defended by the argument that one shouldn't limit one's experience. Indiscriminate and promiscuous sexual behavior is similarly justified. An experience in and of itself does not necessarily contribute to growth and development. For it to do so, it must be integrated into the personality. It must be creatively assimilated; that is, it must deepen one's self-understanding, broaden one's appreciation of pleasure, and, as in growth, expand one's total being. Experiences that are not creatively assimilated increase one's confusion and decrease one's sense of identity.

What does it mean to be creative? The creative person sees the world with a fresh vision. He doesn't attempt to solve new problems with old solutions. He starts from the proposition that he doesn't know the answers. Thus he approaches life with the open-eyed curiosity and wonder of a child, who is not yet structured in his way of thinking and being. The individual whose personality is not rigidly set is free to use his imagination in confronting the constantly changing circumstances of life.

To be creative is to be imaginative, but not every act of imagination is a creative activity. The daydreams, fantasies, and illusions that fill the minds and occupy the thinking of many people are not creative expressions. The Walter Mitty type of image is a mental compensation for a person's inability to resolve his inner conflicts. Such compensatory images bear little relation to reality, and since they cannot be fulfilled, they leave the person in a heightened state of tension. The creative imagination starts with an appreciation and acceptance of reality. It doesn't seek to transform reality, making it conform to one's illusion, but seeks instead to deepen the understanding of reality in order to enrich one's experience of it. The creative impulse begins with the imagination of the child but aims at the fulfillment of adult needs.

The fusion of adult realism and childlike imagination is the key to all creative action. It embodies the basic principle of creativity, namely that the creative act is a fusion of two seem-ingly contradictory views into a single vision. Arthur Koestler, in his book *The Act of Creation*, makes this theme the central point of his study and documents it with numerous examples. He says: "The creative act, by connecting previously unrelated dimensions of experience, enables him [man] to attain to a higher level of mental evolution. It is an act of liberation—the defeat of habit by originality." * The principle that creativity is a fusion and integration of opposite aspects is not limited to creative expression in art or science but applies to all forms of creative expression in life. I shall illustrate its applicability to a common situation in modern living.

Most parents today are plagued in their dealings with their children by the conflict between discipline and permissiveness. They cannot, with any assurance that it will work out well, ex-ercise the authority that parents formerly had. Despite the best intentions, the exercise of arbitrary authority only provokes feelings of rebellion and defiance in young people. Yet the ab-sence of authority and the resulting attitude of permissiveness seem to produce an equally desperate situation. Many young people today are more confused than liberated by an attitude of complete permissiveness, and the result is often a greater separation of the generations.

It is not and cannot be a question of authority versus permis-siveness. Neither is a creative answer to a relationship based on love. The parent who loves his child would like him to be happy; he wants the child to enjoy life. The child's good feel-ings and pleasure are his primary considerations. In furthering the child's desire for pleasure, he is being not permissive but loving. The child, in turn, will respect the parent who behaves in this fashion, and he will listen to his parent's counsel out of respect and not because of the parent's authority.

Yet the parent who is loving does have authority. It is not an arbitrary authority based on power and on the assumption that he knows best (nos best). It is an authority based on the respon-sibility a parent has for the welfare of his child, that is, for the well-being or pleasure of the child. This responsibility gives the

* Arthur Koestler, *The Act of Creation*. New York, The Macmillan Company, 1964, p. 96.

parent authority to set up rules for the orderly functioning of family life. These rules necessarily impose a certain discipline on the members of the family, but the discipline, like the authority, is not arbitrary. It is designed to further the enjoyment of each member of the family and loses its validity when it defeats this purpose. Thus a loving parent is a responsible parent who is neither disciplining nor permissive.

It is a creative act to raise a child so that he feels loved, respected, and secure. And because it is a creative act, it cannot be done by following a formula. The child's desire for pleasure and need for self-expression must be understood by his parents. They can only do this if they are free from personal guilt about pleasure and able to express their own feelings openly and honestly. When a parent feels guilty about pleasure, his permissiveness will be tainted with anxiety that will be sensed by the child. This anxiety undermines the child's pleasure and turns him into a restless and fretful being who cannot be calmed by further permissiveness or discipline.

To raise a child with love for his being and respect for his individuality requires a creative attitude on the part of the parents. They cannot follow the patterns of child raising used by their parents, because their style of living is different. Today's parents are more psychologically sophisticated, and many of them have become aware of the faults in their own upbringings. Yet psychology provides no answers, only warnings. Each parent is consequently faced with the necessity of developing a new form of parent-child relationship. This calls for sensitivity, imagination, self-awareness, and self-acceptance, qualities that characterize the healthy person and the creative individual.

The need for a creative attitude is no more pressing in the parent-child relationship than it is in other areas of living. We find the same confusion in the sexual sphere, where the alternatives seem to be the old-fashioned morality or no morality. The double standard that governed sexual attitudes and behavior for centuries has collapsed under the impact of psychoanalysis, antibiotics, the Pill, the automobile, and other forces. Its demise has not led to the sexual fulfillment hoped for but to sexual chaos and misery. This development was explained in my book *Love and Orgasm*. Neither the old moral code nor the new amoral code, the morality of fun, provides a meaningful answer to the problem of sexual behavior in today's world. Obviously there is no answer. Each individual has to develop a personal moral code based on a creative attitude to love and sex.

The big question is: How do we know if our attitude is creative or destructive? A creative attitude is one that integrates the opposing aspects and needs of the personality into a single expression, a unitary response. A destructive attitude is one that fragments the unity of the personality, setting one need against another. Consider, for example, the conflict between pleasure and achievement.

Despite my emphasis on pleasure, one cannot make the naked pursuit of pleasure the goal of life. It is the nature of pleasure that the more one seeks it, the more it eludes one's search. Pleasure is indissolubly tied to achievement, and a life in which there is no achievement is equally devoid of pleasure. We are all familiar, however, with people whose compulsive striving for achievement and success has robbed them of pleasure and made the enjoyment of life impossible. There is an antithesis between pleasure and achievement which arises from the fact that achievement requires self-discipline. The commitment to a goal or task necessarily involves the sacrifice of some immediate pleasures. If a person is unable to postpone the immediate gratification of his desires, he is like an infant, whose achievements are nil and whose pleasures are meaningful only to an infant.

The conflict between pleasure and achievement cannot be resolved by apportioning one's time between these two needs. Such an arrangement increases the conflict: One will resent the time spent at work, and consequently, one will not be able to fully enjoy the hours of leisure. If there is no pleasure in work and no possibility of creativity in pleasure, the result will be a feeling of frustration, not a sense of joy. Even the creative process requires a measure of travail or labor to yield the joy it promises.

All work should provide an opportunity for the use of a worker's creative imagination. There is no job that cannot be done better, more easily, or more pleasurably. It just requires a little creative imagination. But creativity flourishes only in an atmosphere of freedom where pleasure is the motivating force. If productivity, in the form of either goods or wages, is the only consideration in a work process, the individuals connected with that process become transformed into human machines incapable of any creative imagination. Such a situation exists in our economy today, and what it shows is that neither the goods nor the wages that are produced further the joy of living.

Antithetical drives such as those mentioned above are polar phenomena. Within the framework of the total personality each drive complements its polar opposite. Thus, the more pleasure one has, the greater can be his achievement. The more one achieves, the greater will be his feeling of pleasure. Polar drives oppose each other only when they are dissociated from the total function of the person. The search for pleasure as an end in itself proves disappointing. No one has ever found pleasure by looking for it. Similarly, an achievement that bears no relation to a person's life is an empty gesture.

In a healthy person the need for security and the need for challenges complement each other. The individual who accepts the challenges inherent in any active exploration of life feels more secure than the individual who isolates himself against these challenges. The secure person moves out into the world and by this very action enhances his inner security, while the frightened person who isolates himself and erects defenses against his fears increases his sense of insecurity.

Polar drives and needs are biologically connected by a rhythmic or pulsatory movement of feeling between the two poles. The simplest illustration of this concept is the relationship between sleep and wakefulness. Each night there is a descent into sleep and each day an ascent to consciousness. The well-being of a person depends on this rhythimc oscillation. Without an adequate amount of sleep a person's consciousness is dulled and his activity reduced. Without an active and energetic daytime life sleep tends to become disturbed. Each polar drive furthers the movement toward the other. In a healthy individual these two polar needs are balanced and attuned to the person's life style. He enjoys sleeping as much as being awake.

The pulsation that unites polar forces and creates a movement of feeling between them is also evident in the relationship of love and sex. Both love and sex reflect the need for closeness and intimacy with another being. Love, however, occupies an antithetical position with respect to sex. The feeling of love flows upward in the body as one reaches out for contact. In sex the feeling flows downward, charging the genital organs. Love increases the tension of a relationship by raising the level of excitement. Sex decreases the tension by discharging the excitement. Love is inspiring; its pleasure is anticipatory. Sex is fulfilling; its pleasure is satisfying. Logically it may appear that the pleasure of sex terminates the feeling of love, but actually the contrary is true. Just as heightened love feelings increase the pleasure of sex, so the pleasure of the sexual discharge reinforces the love one feels for the sexual partner. Wilhelm Reich noted that a reversal of flow occurs in the orgasm, the energy and feeling that were concentrated in the genitals flooding the entire body. Thus, the biological pulsation between love and sex is a continuing process that insures the growth of a relationship.

Sex without love provides the minimal pleasure that can be obtained from a number of sexual partners. It is an experience that offers no possibility of creative development. Love that is not biologically fulfilled in sex or some other form of pleasurable contact is an illusion, a daydream, or a fantasy. The mother who talks of love but fails to nurse her child, hold it affectionately, or care for it tenderly is a fraud. The lover who does not give some object to the loved person as an expression of his feeling is dishonest. And the husband who proclaims his love for his wife but has no sexual feelings for her is deceitful. Love is a promise that must be fulfilled in action. Sex is the fulfillment that renews the promise.

The dissociation of love from sex and sex from love is due to a disruption of the pulsatory movement that unites the different aspects of man's personality. The result is a division of man's unitary nature into opposing categories—flesh and spirit, nature and culture, intelligent mind and animal body. These distinctions exist, but only as rational concepts. When they become structured in bodily attitude and behavior, they produce a schizoid condition. In the schizoid personality the flow of feeling between the upper and the lower halves of the body is blocked by tensions in the diaphragmatic area. This problem is more fully explored in *The Betrayal of the Body*. Love and sex can oppose each other only at the cost of pleasure and joy.

United by the rhythmic flow of feeling in the body, love and sex form a creative potential. True sexual lovers are not content with the status quo; they are impelled to do things for one another, to beautify their surroundings, and to build a future together. Certainly part of this future is the creation of new life that will embody the joy they know with each other. This joy pervades their environment and enriches everyone who comes into it. In this atmosphere of love and sex children grow beautiful and strong, while the personality of each parent expands in wisdom and understanding.

Creativity and Self-Awareness

The creative fusion of the antithetical aspects of the personality cannot be the result of a conscious effort. Koestler emphasized that the act of creation is a function of the unconscious mind. I too would like to stress this fact. The conscious mind can only operate with images that are already present in it. By definition, the creative act is the formation of an image that did not previously exist in the mind. This is not to say that consciousness plays no role in the creative process. The problem is always consciously perceived, the solution never so. If one knows the answer to a given problem, one may be right, but the right answer is never a creative act.

A creative approach to life is possible only for the person whose roots extend into the unconscious layers of his personality. The creative thinker dips deep into the wellsprings of feeling for the solutions he seeks. He is able to do this because of a greater self-awareness than the average person possesses. There is a growing realization of the need for more self-awareness. The many books on psychology and the increasing recourse to psychotherapy reflect this realization. Yet too many people still believe that a formula will be found which will solve their difficulties without the necessity for the inner probing that self-awareness entails. I believe these people are headed for depression when their illusions collapse.

If we can accept the fact that no one knows the answers, then the path to joy is open. This path leads through self-awareness and the understanding of personality to a creative attitude toward life. It is the purpose of this book to provide some of this understanding, and it is the hope of the author that it will deepen the reader's self-awareness.

In the preceding chapters I attempted to show some of the interrelationships that exist among the different aspects of the personality. The opposition between power and pleasure led us into a discussion of the antithesis between the ego and the body. The ego is the representative of the conscious self, while the body is the representative of the unconscious self. These two aspects of the personality are not sharply divided from each other. Like a cork floating on the surface of the ocean, consciousness rises and falls with each wave of feeling that passes through the body. A self-awareness that is limited to one's conscious perceptions is very superficial. A deeper self-awareness informs us that these conscious perceptions are strongly influenced and even determined by unconscious processes. By extending our consciousness down into the body, we can at times become aware of what these processes are. A person's self-awareness is determined by how much he is in touch with his body.

Human beings have a dual nature. They are conscious actors and unconscious responders. They walk on two feet, and when they move, their attention shifts from one leg to the other. As they step forward, attention focuses momentarily on the leg that presses on the ground, then shifts to the leg that approaches the ground. This oscillation of attention underlies the feeling of surefootedness that characterizes the person whose walk is smooth and graceful. I can also illustrate this concept with the example of a public speaker. As he faces his audience he must be in contact with two realities, his audience and himself. If he focuses too intently on what he has to say or his manner of delivery, he will lose his audience. If he is too aware of his audience, he will lose a sense of himself and become confused. A good speaker is able to alternate his attention rapidly between these two realities so that while at any one instant his focus is only upon one, the overall effect is that he keeps in touch with both realities.

The concept of polarity applies to these situations as to all others. To say of a speaker that he is more aware of his audience than of himself is not true. When he becomes overconscious of his audience, he does not see it as it is. In his unconscious mind it has become an image of some terrifying and threatening force. Similarly, the speaker who is overly self-conscious is not fully in touch with himself. He has, in fact, lost his self-possession, and all he senses is either a deep anxiety or an overriding compulsion which has taken possession of him. The more self-possessed a speaker is, the more he holds and possesses his audience.

In the relation between the ego and the body, the conscious and unconscious aspects of the self, the same principle is operative. The ego is as strong as the body is alive. In a repressed body the ego is in a collapsed state. To put it another way, the person who allows his unconscious responses free expression is actually a more conscious individual than the person who is afraid of his unconscious responses. Thus, "letting go" to the unconscious strengthens consciousness and the ego functions. But this principle is a two-way street which goes only as far in one direction as it does in the other. Like a pendulum whose swing is equal in both directions, a person can "let go" only to the extent that he can also hold back consciously. This principle is overlooked by those who advocate a Dionysian life of abandonment to sensuality as a meaningful form of existence.

This emphasis on the body, pleasure, and "letting go" is not intended to deny the value of the ego, achievement, and self-restraint. Without a polarity, there is no movement. Without movement, life is flat and boring. If we negated the values associated with cerebration, discipline, and prestige, we would be committing the same fault as those who extol the superior virtues of the ego functions at the expense of the bodily or unconscious processes.

The next major polarity in the functioning of the personality, which we studied earlier, is the relation between thinking and feeling. I tried to show that the quality of a person's thinking is determined by his feelings. The specific aspect which most clearly illustrates this polarity is the connection between sub-jectivity and objectivity. I stressed the fact that true objectivity is impossible without a proper subjectivity. The person who doesn't know what he feels cannot be objective about himself, and it is extremely unlikely that he can be objective about an-other person. His lack of self-awareness necessarily limits his awareness of others. But this proposition operates in reverse, too. The person who is unaware of others cannot be fully aware of himself. His insensitivity dulls him to all aspects of reality.

To know oneself is as much a cognitive function as it is a sensory one. Sensations must be interpreted correctly if they are to have any meaning. If feeling is divorced from thinking, the personality is just as split as when thinking is divorced from feeling. A body without a head is no better off than a head without a body. The de-emphasis of cerebration is not to be taken as a denial of the value of cerebration. The ability to think clearly is as important to the personality as the ability to feel deeply. If one's feelings are confused, one's thinking is blurred, but it is just as true that confused thinking dulls one's feelings.

Whichever aspect of the personality we look at, we find the same principle of polarity manifest. On the emotional level it is expressed in the polarity of affection and hostility, anger and fear, gladness and sadness, and so on. And on the level of pri-mary sensation it is reflected in the pleasure-pain spectrum. What this means is that the person who suppresses his awareness of pain also suppresses his perception of pleasure. The explana-tion for this observation is simple. If one deadens the body to reduce the feeling of pain, one also reduces by the same maneu-ver the body's ability to experience pleasure.

Self-awareness, as opposed to awareness itself, requires a dual approach to all experiences. First, an experience must be per-ceived on the body level, where it represents the organism's unconscious response to a stimulus or a situation. These bodily experiences may be sensory or motor or, more commonly, both. The smell of food may make my mouth water. The sight of a baby may stir an impulse to touch it. Such reactions denote an awareness of one's environment. Self-awareness arises when an experience is polarized, that is, when it is related to and integrated with an experience of the opposite sign. Thus, the smell of food becomes an element of self-awareness when it evokes the feeling of hunger. The polarity of food and hunger makes one conscious of the self in relation to the outer world and therefore of the self and the outer world. The polarization of experience is the second element in the process of self-awareness. It is a function of the ego, which relates all experiences to the life history of the individual.

Let us go back to the relation between thinking and feeling for a better understanding of self-awareness. Just to be aware of one's thinking or of one's feeling is a limited kind of self-awareness. The individual who is fully self-aware is conscious of how his thinking relates to his feelings and how his feelings are conditioned by his thinking. His attention or perception oscillates between his mind and his body. He has, in effect, a double awareness of what is going on, although at any single instant the focus is on one or the other aspect of his experiencing. A contrasting picture is that of the absentminded professor whose compulsive focus on his intellectual activities leads him to ignore the reality of his body and its sensations.

The polarity of love and sex provides another good example of how the recognition of polar relationships increases one's self-awareness. Sex in its purely physiological aspects requires no awareness of the other person. It is doubtful, however, that the human sexual response is ever purely physiological. Image and fantasy cannot be eliminated from conscious behavior, and we must assume, therefore, that some degree of self-awareness is always present in this act. But when love is consciously experienced in relation to the sex act, the polarity is greatly intensified. Love makes one conscious of the other and forces the attention to oscillate between the self and the other, increasing the consciousness of the self in relation to the other. Thus, the lover who is more conscious of the other is at the same time more self-aware. His self-awareness heightens his excitement and greatly enhances the pleasure of its discharge.

Self-awareness contains the potential for creative expression. It is the state of being that makes possible the fusion of opposites within the self and between the self and the external world. Every creative action is a reflection of one's self-awareness, which itself is an expression of the creative force within the personality. Every creative person has self-awareness in the area of his creative talent. And every self-aware person has a creative potential in all areas of his awareness.

It would be tempting to say that man as the uniquely creative animal is the only one that possesses self-awareness. But I don't believe that this is so. It is more correct to say that both self-awareness and creativity are more highly developed in man than in other animals. It is logical to postulate a polar relationship between them. The more self-aware a person is, the more creative he will be, and vice versa.

The Loss of Integrity

The duality in man's nature, which is responsible for his self-awareness and creative potential, is also the predisposing cause of his self-denial and self-destructive attitudes. As the conscious actor and unconscious responder in the drama of life, man is subject to an internal strain when these two sides of his personality draw apart. How much strain a personality can tolerate before its unity is disrupted depends on its vital energy, which is the cohesive force of the organism. A personality whose energy level is low will split under a degree of tension that a more strongly charged personality can withstand. When a split occurs, one aspect of the personality turns against the other, producing self-destructive behavior.

The ego is the aspect of personality that functions as the conscious actor, while the body is that aspect of the personality which responds involuntarily to situations. Generally, these two different modes of behavior, acting and reacting, are harmoniously integrated. When a person is eating, for example, both modes of behavior are involved. His immediate response to the smell and taste of the food is purely involuntary. It will be pleasurable or unpleasurable. If it is pleasurable, he will consciously act to bring the food to his mouth. If it is unpleasant, he will push the food away. These latter actions are consciously made, that is, ego directed. Normally no conflict between them arises. But imagine that the person at the table is a child who doesn't like vegetables, and sitting opposite him is a parent who insists that he must eat them because they are good for him. The child in this situation faces a dilemma. If he doesn't eat the vegetables, he will be in conflict with his parent. If he does eat the food, he will be in conflict with his feelings. This simple example illustrates the kind of tension to which a person in our culture is often subjected. The difference between human behavior and animal behavior in a similar situation is portrayed by the aphorism that you can lead a horse to water, but you can't make him drink.

The civilizing process involves the imposition of conscious restraints on the body's involuntary responses. It is not, however, an unnatural phenomenon; every aspect of learning, whether it be a motor skill or an intellectual understanding, depends on it. In Chapter 6 I pointed out that much of our conscious thinking requires a preliminary inhibition of involuntary responsiveness ("stop to think"). There are, however, limits to the amount of strain or tension a personality can tolerate. When these limits are exceeded, the polar forces in the personality break their connection with each other and become independent functions. This produces a schizophrenic condition.

To understand this development, picture the ego (conscious actor) and the body (involuntary processes) as two forces pulling in opposite directions on a coiled spring. Ordinarily the amount of force exerted by the ego is not constant, and so the tension in the spring fluctuates. It may even be completely absent at moments, such as during a full orgasm, when the involuntary processes of the body take over the whole personality. The normal increase and decrease of tension in the spring correspond to the increase and decrease in the level of excitation. If the two forces are properly balanced, the rise and fall of tension produce feelings of pleasure.

Should the spring be stretched beyond its level of tolerance, it will lose its elasticity. This can happen when too great a strain is imposed on the spring or when a just-tolerable tension is maintained for too long a time. If the elasticity of the spring is gone, the vital connection between the ego and the body is broken. They no longer have a dynamic relationship to each other. This analogy would be incomplete if I did not point out that the elastic strength of the spring can be weakened, which would correspond in the human personality to a reduction of the cohesive force between the ego and the body.

The duality of man's nature has many facets. They can be grouped under the two headings "ego" and "body." A partial list follows.

Ego	Body
a. Conscious activity	a. Involuntary responsiveness
b. Achievement	b. Pleasure
c. Thinking	c. Feeling
d. Adult	d. Child
e. Individuality	e. Community
f. Culture	f. Nature

We have already studied the polar relationship that exists between b and c. In this section I shall discuss a, d, e, and f.

a. No person exists whose behavior is entirely consciously controlled. Yet there are some individuals in whom the body's involuntary responses are so suppressed that they look and act like automatons. The more extreme cases are found in mental institutions. Less seriously disturbed cases are described in my book *The Betrayal of the Body* as schizoid individuals. This disturbance is manifested by a lack of spontaneity, a dulling of the personality, and a diminished capacity for pleasure. Depression is quite common, and suicidal feelings are frequently present. These people commonly complain of an inner emptiness, which is quite understandable in view of the reduced motility of their bodies and the corresponding absence of feeling.

What is less understandable is the widespread view that such disturbances are purely mental, that the problem is purely psychological. When the personality is identified with the mind, or the ego, the body is reduced to a mechanism. Such an attitude destroys the integrity of the personality, since it disclaims the interrelationship of all personality functions. It renders impossible any significant therapeutic effort to change the personality structure. It is not a creative approach either to therapy or to living.

It is obviously equally disastrous when a person loses all conscious control of his behavior, that is, loses his self-possession, and is reduced to a quivering mass of protoplasm. I have seen this happen, and it is not a pleasant picture. It cannot be the therapeutic goal. What is wanted is an integration of. the conscious and the involuntary, and this can only happen when every conscious act is infused with feeling and every involuntary response is consciously perceived and understood. This is the meaning of the expression "being in touch with the body," and it is the way to self-possession.

d. The adult-child polarity is the key to the creative personality. With the adult we associate all the ego qualities: self-consciousness, achievement, rationality, individuality, and culture. The child is the symbol of the qualities associated with the body: spontaneity, pleasure, feeling, community, and nature. Deep within the personality of every adult is the child he was. His maturity is only a surface layer which too often rigidifies into a structured facade. When this happens, a person loses touch with the child within him. That the child is still alive is evidenced, however, by occasional relapses into childish behavior which occur when the facade gives way in the face of stress. These childish outbursts are destructive in nature and represent, poetically speaking, the anger of the child at being imprisoned by a frightened but dictatorial ego.

In the integrated personality adult and child are in constant communication, the child through feeling and the adult through intelligence. Each supports and strengthens the other, the child adding imagination to the realism of the adult, while the latter provides the knowledge that clarifies the child's intuitive responses. The statement that the creative person reaches deep into his unconscious for imaginative answers to problems can be interpreted to mean that he consults the child within him. And since the child is identified with the body, to be in communication with the child is the same as being in touch with the body.

It is significant that almost every patient in psychotherapy has very few memories of his childhood. Sometime in the course of growing up the experiences of childhood and the feelings associated with them are walled off. The experiences are repressed from memory. The feelings are suppressed from consciousness. The walling off occurs because the child was made to feel wrong about his feelings. He was born an animal innocent of any desires but to have pleasure and be joyful. But civilization in the form of his parents demanded that he develop control, become rational, and submit to authority. The struggle of wills that goes on in the bringing up of most children is too well known to need repeating. In this struggle the child always loses, and his submission is marked by the denial of his animal nature.

In the interest of survival a child has no alternative but to suppress his feelings and erect a façade of behavior that is acceptable. This façade becomes structured in his body and mind; in the former as a postural attitude, in the latter as an ego image. The ego becomes identified with this image and dissociated from the body. Masked by this image, the individual sees himself again as an innocent person, unaware that in his unconscious he harbors hostile and negative feelings associated with the traumatic experiences of his earlier life. The suppressed emotions show through and occasionally break through, necessitating a whole series of rationalizations and self-justifications to support the image. These constitute his ego defenses, while his muscular tensions represent what Wilhelm Reich called "body armoring."

Having accomplished the reversal from feeling wrong to feeling right, and entrenched behind the walls of its fortress, the ego sees itself as master of its domain, the conscious self. It has abandoned the body, the child, and the unconscious in its retreat. This image of mastery which the ego develops is a conceit. It is found in every emotionally disturbed person. In the paranoid schizophrenic it amounts to delusions of grandeur. In the schizoid personality it appears as arrogance. It is expressed as an exaggerated pride in the narcissistic individual and as self-righteousness in the masochist.

The conceited ego, seemingly secure in its imaginary fortress, dominates the personality like a tyrant. Like a tyrant, it strives to eliminate all the forces that could threaten its power. Yet the person senses his isolation, his alienation, and his loneliness. These feelings force him to submit to therapy. His submission, however, is conditional. His ego is not willing to expose its pretenses, surrender its defenses, and confront the underlying negativity. It seeks instead to master its weaknesses with the help of the therapist. In this effort it will fail. Only in failure will a person abandon an ego position that seemingly insured his survival.

When the personality is approached from the side of the body, the child is reached directly. When the body is mobilized through breathing, the first thing that occurs is an involuntary trembling that usually starts in the legs and extends through the body. The trembling often quite spontaneously turns into sobbing, and the patient begins to cry. He may not even know what he is crying about. The sound seems to erupt from within, surprising the patient. This crying will occur many times during the therapy until it becomes infantile in quality and the patient can sense the wail of the imprisoned child.

Each chronic muscular tension represents the inhibition of an impulse. The contraction is designed to prevent these impulses from being expressed. The inhibited impulse has a negative valance, which is why it was suppressed in the first place. Associated with every chronic muscular tension in the body are feelings of anger, fear, and sadness. The impules that are released in the course of body therapy are crying, screaming, yelling, hitting, kicking, biting, and so on. These are channelled toward the couch and not acted out on another person. What always emerges is a hurt and angry child who needs to express his negative feelings before he can honestly express his positive ones.

Chronic muscular spasticity is an unconscious limitation of motility and self-expression. It says, in effect, "I can't." By transforming this into a consciously expressed "I won't," the tension is released. Similarly, getting a patient to feel and express his hostility as "I hate you" makes it possible for him to say "I love you" with sincerity. As these feelings come to the surface, the repressed memories of childhood flood back. The body work must be accompanied, therefore, by a proper analysis to bridge the gap between the past and the present.

Working through on both levels simultaneously, the physical and the psychological, enables the patient to identify with, accept, and integrate the lost child with his adult understanding of life. It deepens his self-awareness and frees his creative potential.

e. The person who is in touch with the child within him is a true communal being. It is not fortuitous that primitive people, who have a strong sense of communal living, have a childlike quality about them. Children have a greater natural capacity for closeness and identification than adults. The sense of individuality is a function of the ego which aims to promote the uniqueness and separateness of the person. When the ego is dissociated from the body, the adult is divorced from the child he was. In this state individuality becomes transformed into isolation, uniqueness into alienation, and separateness into loneliness.

Social consciousness is the ego's substitution for the childlike quality of belonging and being part of a group or community. It is a compensation for modern man's alienation and isolation and no true replacement for the feeling of community that is so lacking today. The feeling of community has a personal element based on physical participation in a common effort. Pioneers, soldiers, and militant groups may have it, but it is a far different thing from an identification based on guilt and the giving of money.

f. Children are also more in tune with nature than adults. They are closer in spirit to natural phenomena, for they still feel themselves to be part of the natural world. The exploitation of nature to satisfy ego desires is not part of their way of life. When man loses his vital connection with the child in him, he also loses the regard and awe which the child has for natural life.

> Every nature lover is a child at heart.
> Every creative artist is a child in part.
> Every joyous person is a child in rapture.
> For joy and creativity are at the heart of nature.

A creative person has a warm feeling for children, since he recognizes the kinship of his spirit and theirs. He rejoices in children, his own and those of others, because every child is a new being, whose fresh enthusiasms add excitement to one's life. He shares his pleasures with children, for this increases his own pleasure. He wants every child to know the joy of life that flows unbidden when one feels free to follow one's natural impulses.

He has known this joy. He cannot see a child hurt without feeling its pain, for he too is a child at heart.

Self-Realization

No patient ever fully resolves all his conflicts or releases all his tensions in therapy. There are two reasons for this fact. The first is that the psychological and physical mechanisms of suppression are so deeply structured in the personality that they cannot be completely eliminated. I have on more than one occasion demonstrated to a patient that one cannot totally erase a pencil line from a paper. There is always some trace. Our experiences are similarly etched into our bodies. The second reason is that the traumatic experiences of an individual are part of his being and cannot be discarded or ignored. They can, however, be either repressed or accepted. If they are repressed, the person is in trouble. If they are accepted and understood, they can serve to broaden his outlook and deepen his sensitivity. And they can become the raw material for the creative process.

Fortunately, patients do not ask to be made new again. They seek a renewal of the feeling that life can be enjoyable. They had this feeling once, since their dreams of happiness are based on it. Even to think that it is possible presupposes that one knows what it is. I don't believe a human being would survive if he didn't have some moments of joy as a child. The memory of those experiences, however dim, sustains his spirit in his later torment. Every patient I have treated, no matter how desperate or disturbed, was able to recall such moments. He wants to feel that joy again, not as a memory but in terms of his present situation. He wants to understand what happened to make him lose that feeling and to know how to prevent a recurrence of the loss.

The difficulty of achieving these goals lies in the process of renewal. A patient has to relive his life in feeling and thought, if not in action. He goes over it again, but proceeding backward from the present to the past. This backward progression insures his foothold in reality. He has to know what he is now in order to find out how he became that way. The present can only be understood in terms of the past, but the past itself is meaningful only because it has determined the present. I make this point because the tendency of patients, and of most people, is either to ignore the past or to live in it. Both attitudes diminish the present and therefore the self. One has to accept what happened in the past and not confuse it with the present.

In the progression backward from adult to youth to child to infant, one will encounter the reversal that substituted the ego image for the true self. The sequence which changed the child's feeling of innocence to one of guilt began with its opposition to its parents. In this opposition the child first feels right. This feeling, however, gives way to a sense of being wrong when it fails to modify the parent's attitude. The sense of being wrong is intolerable; in submitting to parental authority the child gains righteousness, but loses rightness. The reversal (from feeling right to feeling wrong, from feeling innocent to feeling guilty) was not a conscious decision. It occurred gradually as negative and hostile feelings were repressed and then replaced with thoughts and attitudes more acceptable to the parents. It is not recalled, therefore, as a single event and must be reconstituted from the memory of past experiences. These memories, however, are tied to the suppressed feelings and cannot be evoked until these feelings are reactivated.

Reactivating suppressed feelings is the difficult part of therapy. The process is opposed by the ego defenses on the one hand and by the fear of these feelings on the other. The ego has established a relative degree of security in the personality by suppressing feeling, and it is not prepared to risk that security by evoking past conflicts. The ego is supported in this position by the patient's fear of intense feeling. The patient is afraid that his anger will get out of control and turn into a murderous rage or fury. He is afraid that his sorrow will overwhelm him and that he will drown in his despair. He is afraid that his fear will change into panic or terror and immobilize him. When these feelings are reactivated, they have an immediate reality that makes the fear of them seem valid.

The difficulty is further increased by the feeling of helplessness that also arises in this process, since it was part of the original situation that led to the suppression of feeling. The child had to abandon its opposition to its parents or risk being abandoned by them. Parents use the withdrawal of love or the threat of its withdrawal as a means of controlling a child. The feeling of helplessness raises the issue of survival again, an issue that is still unresolved in the unconscious mind of the patient. Since self-denial insured one's survival, self-assertion seems to pose a threat to survival. Yet some degree of self-assertion is necessary for survival in the world.

Releasing the suppressed feelings and getting through to the child in a patient requires consistent work on both the psychological and physical levels. The ego defenses that inhibit the acceptance of the natural emotional responses of a child to pleasure and pain must be analyzed. The chronic muscular tensions that block the full range of emotional expression must be released. This goal cannot be reached by an approach that is directed at one level alone. Psychotherapy, whether analytic or otherwise, that does not provide for the expression of suppressed feelings furthers control at the expense of spontaneity and strengthens the ego at the expense of the body. If the therapeutic work is limited to the expression of feeling, impulsiveness is encouraged at the expense of integration.

Creativity in therapy, as in life, results from the fusion of polar forces. The ability to express a feeling and the ability to control its expression are two sides of the same coin, namely, the mature individual. In the beginning of therapy this control is exercised by the therapist. The patient is encouraged to "let go," with the assurance that the therapist can handle the situation. The anger is directed at the couch and never becomes destructive. He can give in to his sadness, knowing that he is not alone and has a sympathetic listener. He can voice his fear by screaming, aware that support is available. He can afford to be helpless because he believes that his therapist is powerful. Gradually this control passes to the patient as he learns that by accepting and trusting his feelings they lose the character of being alien forces that threaten his ego. He gains the understanding that his negative and hostile feelings are a response to pain and that his affectionate feelings are a response to pleasure.

The steps from the defensive position of ego control to the exposed position of a creative attitude are taken as the patient develops a grounding in reality. The first step toward reality taken by a patient is his identification with his body. Through the therapy he comes to see himself in terms of his body, not in terms of an ego image that conflicts with his body. He becomes aware of his muscular tensions and senses their effect on his attitudes and behavior. And he learns how to reduce these tensions through appropriate physical movements. This identification with the body is also the first step toward self-realization.

The second step toward reality is recognition of the pleasure principle as the basis of one's conscious activities. The motivation for all our actions is the striving for pleasure and the avoidance of pain. We may follow different paths as we pursue this aim, but we are driven by one desire. The individual who does not recognize that his actions are motivated by the desire for pleasure or who is inhibited by the fear of pleasure (guilt) is out of touch with the reality of his animal nature.

The third step is an acceptance of one's feelings. Feelings are the spontaneous responses of an organism to its environment. One cannot alter one's feelings; they are not subject to the will or the mind. An individual can express a feeling or withhold its expression, depending on the situation. If he turns against his feelings, he turns against himself. If a person rejects his feelings, he rejects himself.

The fourth step is an understanding of the interdependence of all personality functions. The person who is grounded in reality has a subjective attitude. He knows that his thinking is related to his feelings and determined by his bodily responses. He can be objective because he is aware of his subjectivity. Even at its most abstract, his thinking is not dissociated from its connection with the human condition. He does not say "I am because I think." If he were to say anything, it would be "Because I am, I think."

The fifth step is humility. Humility is the realization of one's relative helplessness in the universe. It is the opposite of ego conceit. We are helpless in all the important matters of life. We cannot buy true love with all the money in the world. We cannot produce pleasure with all the power of our advanced technology. Human life flows unbidden from the belly of a woman and ends inexorably in the bowels of the earth. We do not make it, and we cannot preserve it eternally. Our conscious concern should be to live it fully.

Humility is the mark of a person who accepts himself. Such a person is neither humble nor arrogant. He is not an egotist, nor is he self-effacing. Though he recognizes that he is a unique individual, he is also aware that he is part of a larger order. And while he realizes that his existence and function are subject to forces that are outside his own personality, he senses that these forces, natural and social, are also within himself and are part of his being. He is therefore both subject and object, actor and "acted upon," in the workshop of life.

The condition of being human is a state of seeming contradictions which are spontaneously resolved in the creative process of living. Every human being is an animal and a culture bearer at the same time. When these two opposing forces fuse creatively in his personality, he becomes a cultured animal. His culture is a superstructure erected on the base of his animal nature and is designed to enhance and glorify that nature. This fusion does not occur when the cultural process, or the civilizing process, attempts to modify and control a person's animal nature. If it succeeds, the person becomes a domesticated animal whose creative potential has become subverted for productive ends. If it fails, it leaves the person with a tormented and infuriated animal nature that often breaks through the facade of cultural sophistication in rebellious and destructive behavior.

Actually, the attempt to modify an individual's animal nature is only partly successful. The domestication process can go just so deep. Behind an attitude of submission one always finds a layer of defiance and rebellion associated with suppressed negative and hostile feelings. And behind the overt rebellion and destructiveness of many young people today is a layer of submissiveness associated with suppressed feelings of fear and despair. In adults the submissive attitude is a defense against inner feelings of rebellion and hostility, while an outer rebelliousness is a reaction to the inner submissiveness. Neither is a creative attitude, and in neither case is there self-acceptance.

Therapy, to be successful, must reach through these layers to the heart of an individual. To open a person's heart to joy, it must restore his innocence. It must restore his faith in himself and in life. It must, in other words, return him to that state in which these qualities characterized his existence. That state is childhood.

The person who can accept the child within him has the capacity to enjoy life. He has the sense of wonder that opens him to new experiences. He has the excitability to respond with fresh enthusiasm. And he has the spontaneity necessary to self-expression. Little children are close to joy, because they still retain some of the innocence and faith with which they were endowed. This is why Jesus said of them, "They are the kingdom of Heaven."

The creative person is not a child. Adults who try to be children in their pursuit of fun are unrealistic and self-destructive. Their behavior is childish, their motivation is escape, and their attitude is sophisticated. The mature adult is close to wisdom, since he has lived and suffered. Despite this suffering and his knowledge of the world, he is in touch with the child he was and to some extent still is. Our feelings for life, love, and pleasure do not change as we grow older. Though our modes of expressing these feelings may change, at heart we are still little children. In a creative person there is no separation or barrier between the child and the adult, between the heart and the mind, between the ego and the body.

In one respect, every successful therapy ends in failure. One does not achieve his image of perfection. The patient realizes that he will always have some shortcomings. He knows, however, that his growth is not completed and that the creative process begun in therapy is now his personal responsibility. He does not walk away from therapy on a cloud. Those who do are headed for a fall. He feels that his feet are on the ground, he has gained an appreciation of reality, and he has developed a creative attitude toward the problems he will face. He has experienced joy, but also sorrow. He leaves with a feeling of self-realization that includes a respect for the wisdom of his body. He has regained his creative potential.

Some other books published by Penguin
are described on the following pages.

Alexander Lowen, M.D.

DEPRESSION AND THE BODY
The Biological Basis of Faith and Reality

This is a distinguished psychiatrist's revolutionary plan for conquering depression. According to Dr. Alexander Lowen, depression is caused by loss of touch with reality—and especially with one's own body. Drawing on his vast experience with depressed patients, Lowen advocates a return to the body—a reestablishment of communication with our one instrument of self-expression. He outlines a series of simple but remarkably effective exercises that can activate dormant life forces and awaken the depressed person to his own inherent energies. An unprecedented aid to understanding why we become depressed and how we can fortify ourselves against it, *Depression and the Body* is the first work exclusively devoted to exploring the causes, symptoms, and treatment of this alarmingly widespread problem.

Alexander Lowen, M.D.

BIOENERGETICS

Bioenergetics is the revolutionary new therapy that uses the language of the body to heal the problems of the mind. This exciting body-mind approach to personality has a liberating and positive effect on emotional, physical, and psychic distress. Dr. Alexander Lowen, founder and prime mover of this fast-growing therapy, writes that increased joy and pleasure are possible in everyday life through an understanding of how your body functions *energetically*: how it determines what you feel, think, and do. Dr. Lowen points out that lack of energy is the result of chronic muscular tensions, a condition caused by the suppression of feelings. These tensions can be dissolved through the direct body work in bioenergetic exercise, which restores the potential for living a rich, full life. Dr. Lowen analyzes common physical ailments like headaches and lower back pain and shows how they too can be overcome by releasing the muscular tensions that create them. Generously illustrated with line drawings of bioenergetic exercises, this book is sure to bring freedom, confidence, and pleasure to thousands of men and women.

Roberto Assagioli, M.D.

THE ACT OF WILL

This important book brings human will back
the center of psychology, education, and everyday
life. Dr. Roberto Assagioli discards the old concept
of will as cold, stern, and repressive. Instead, he
sees it not only as strong but also as skillful. In this
volume he shows how to train the will so that each
of us can act with a minimum of effort and a maximum of effectiveness, and he proposes specific exercises that the reader can practice at home. The
rewards of such work are peace of mind, satisfying
human relations, and a sense of harmony with the
evolution of man and with the cosmos itself. A
pioneer of Freudianism in Italy, Roberto Assagioli
developed a comprehensive psychology known as
psychosynthesis, which integrates various psychological techniques into an approach that is unique
for each individual.